Marx, Capital and the Madness of Economic Reason

Marx, Capital and the Madness of Economic Reason

DAVID HARVEY

OXFORD
UNIVERSITY PRESS

OXFORD
UNIVERSITY PRESS

Published in the United States of America by Oxford University Press
198 Madison Avenue, New York, NY 10016, United States of America

© Oxford University Press 2018

First published in Great Britain by Profile Books.

First issued as an Oxford University Press paperback, 2019

Library of Congress Cataloging-in-Publication Data

Names: Harvey, David, 1935– author.
Title: Marx, capital and the madness of economic reason / David Harvey.
Description: New York, NY : Oxford University Press, [2018] | Includes
  bibliographical references and index.
Identifiers: LCCN 2017032817| ISBN 9780190691486 (hardcover : alk. paper) |
ISBN 9780190050795 (paperback : alk. paper) | ISBN 9780190691509 (epub)
Subjects: LCSH: Marx, Karl, 1818–1883. Kapital. | Capital. |
  Marxian economics.
Classification: LCC HB501.M37 H3364 2018 | DDC 335.4/12–dc23
  LC record available at https://lccn.loc.gov/2017032817

Printed in Canada on acid-free paper

Contents

List of figures

Mad world! Mad kings! Mad composition! ...
That smooth-fac'd gentleman, tickling commodity,
Commodity, the bias of the world;
The world, who of itself is peised well
Made to run even upon even ground.
Till this advantage, this vile-drawing bias,
This sway of motion, this commodity,
Makes it take head from all indifferency,
From all direction, purpose, course, intent.
And this same bias, this commodity,
This bawd, this broker, this all-changing word ...
And why rail I on this commodity?
But for because he hath not woo'd me yet.
Not that I have the power to clutch my hand
When his fair angels would salute my palm;
But for my hand, as unattempted yet,
Like a poor beggar, raileth on the rich.
Well, whiles I am a beggar, I will rail
And say here is no sin, but to be rich;
And being rich, my virtue then shall be
To say there is no vice but beggary.
Since kings break faith upon commodity,
Gain, be my lord, for I will worship thee.

William Shakespeare, *King John*

Prologue

Throughout his life Marx made a prodigious effort to understand how capital worked. He was obsessed with trying to figure out how what he called 'the laws of motion of capital' affected daily life of the common people. He relentlessly exposed the conditions of inequality and exploitation that lay buried in the morass of self-congratulatory theories propounded by the ruling classes. He was particularly interested in why capitalism seemed to be so crisis prone. Were these crises, like those he experienced firsthand in 1848 and 1857, due to external shocks, such as wars, natural scarcities and bad harvests, or was there something about the way capital itself worked that made such destructive crashes inevitable? This question still bedevils economic enquiry. Given the sad state and confusing trajectory of global capitalism since the crash of 2007–8 – and its deleterious impacts on the daily lives of millions of people – it seems a good moment to review what Marx managed to figure out. Maybe there are some useful insights here to help clarify the nature of the problems we are now facing.

It is not, alas, easy to summarise Marx's findings, and follow his intricate arguments and his detailed reconstructions. This is partly due to the fact that most of his work was incomplete. Only a small fraction of it ever saw the light of day in a form that Marx thought fit for publication. The rest exists as an intriguing and voluminous mass of notes and drafts, comments of self-clarification, thought experiments of the 'what if it worked like this' variety, and a host of rebuttals of real and imagined objections and criticisms. To the degree that Marx himself relied a great deal on a critical interrogation of how classical political economy answered these kinds of questions (where figures like Adam Smith, David Ricardo, Thomas

Malthus, James Steuart, John Stuart Mill, Bentham and a host of other thinkers and researchers held sway), so our reading of his findings often demands a working knowledge of those he is criticising. The same is true with respect to Marx's reliance upon classical German philosophy for his critical method, where the imposing figure of Hegel dominates backed up by Spinoza, Kant and a host of other thinkers stretching way back to the Greeks (Marx did his doctorate on the Greek philosophers Democritus and Epicurus). Add the French socialist thinkers, such as Saint-Simon, Fourier, Proudhon and Cabet into the mix, and the huge canvas upon which Marx sought to construct his oeuvre becomes intimidatingly apparent.

Marx was, moreover, a restless analyst rather than a static thinker. The more he learned from his voluminous reading (not only of the political economists, anthropologists and philosophers but of the business and financial press, Parliamentary debates and Official Reports), the more he evolved his views (or some would say changed his mind). He was a voracious reader of classical literature – Shakespeare, Cervantes, Goethe, Balzac, Dante, Shelley and on and on. He not only spiced up his writing (particularly in the first volume of *Capital*, which is a literary masterpiece) with lots of references to their thinking but he genuinely valued their insights into how the world worked and drew much inspiration from their method of presentation. And if that did not suffice there was a voluminous correspondence with fellow travellers in multiple languages along with lectures and talks to British trade unionists or communications in and around the International Working Men's Association formed in 1864 with its pan-European working-class aspirations. Marx was an activist and polemicist as well as a theorist, scholar and thinker of the first rank. The closest he ever came to getting a steady income was as a regular correspondent to the *New York Tribune*, which was one of the largest circulation newspapers in the United States at that time. While his columns asserted his distinctive views, they also entailed up-to-date analysis of current events.

In recent times there has been a flurry of comprehensive studies of Marx in relation to the personal, political, intellectual and economic milieu in which he was writing. The major works of Jonathan Sperber and Gareth Stedman Jones are invaluable, at least in certain respects.[1] Unfortunately, they also seem aimed at burying Marx's thinking and massive oeuvre along with Marx himself in Highgate Cemetery as a dated and defective product of nineteenth-century thought. Marx was an interesting historical figure for them but his conceptual apparatus has little relevance today, if it ever did. Both of them forget that the object of Marx's study in *Capital* was capital and not nineteenth-century life (about which he certainly had many opinions). And capital is still with us, alive and well in some respects while plainly ailing if not spiralling out of control, drunk on its own success and excess, in others. Marx considered the concept of capital foundational for modern economics as well as for the critical understanding of bourgeois society. Yet one can read to the end of the Stedman Jones and Sperber volumes without having the foggiest clue as to what Marx's concept of capital was all about let alone how it might be put to good use today. Marx's analyses, though obviously dated in some ways, are, I find, even more relevant now than they were at their time of writing. What, in Marx's day, was a dominant economic system in only a small corner of the world now blankets the earth with astonishing implications and results. In Marx's time, political economy was a far more open terrain of debate than it is now. Since then, a supposedly scientific, highly mathematised and data driven field of study called economics has achieved the status of an orthodoxy, a closed body of supposedly rational knowledge – a true science – to which no one else is admitted except on state and corporate business. It is now supplemented by a growing belief in the powers of computer capacity (doubling every two years) to construct, dissect and analyse enormous data sets on almost everything. For some influential analysts, sponsored by the big corporations, this supposedly opens the way to a techno-utopia of rational management (e.g. of smart cities) where artificial intelligence rules. This fantasy rests on the assumption that if something cannot be measured and condensed into data points then it is either irrelevant or does not exist. Make no mistake, large data sets can be extremely useful but they do not exhaust the terrain of what needs to be known. They do not help solve problems of alienation or of deteriorating social relations.

Marx's prescient commentaries on capital's laws of motion and their internal contradictions, its fundamental and underlying irrationalities, turn out to be far more incisive and penetrating than the one-dimensional macroeconomic theories of contemporary economics that were found so wanting when confronted with the crash of 2007–8 and its long-drawn-out aftermath. Marx's analyses along with his distinctive method of enquiry and his mode of theorising are invaluable for our intellectual struggles to understand the capitalism of our times. His insights deserve to be taken up and studied critically with all due seriousness.

So what, then, are we to make of Marx's concept of capital and of its purported laws of motion? How might this help us understand our current predicaments? These are the questions I shall explore here.

1

The Visualisation of Capital as Value in Motion

The transformation of a sum of money into means of production and labour-power is the first phase of the movement undergone by the quantum of value which is going to function as capital. It takes place in the market, within the sphere of circulation. The second phase of the movement, the process of production, is complete as soon as the means of production have been converted into commodities whose value exceeds that of their component parts, and therefore contains the capital originally advanced plus a surplus value. The commodities must then be thrown back into the sphere of circulation. They must be sold, their value must be realized in money, this money must be transformed once again into capital, and so on, again and again. This cycle, in which the same phases are continually gone through in succession, forms the circulation of capital.

Capital, Volume 1, p. 709

I need to find some way to systematise Marx's voluminous writings on political economy, such as the three volumes of *Capital*, another three volumes of *Theories of Surplus Value*, the earlier published works such as *A Contribution to the Critique of Political Economy* and the recently edited and published notebooks such as the *Grundrisse* along with the notebooks from which Engels painstakingly reconstructed (not without criticism or controversy) the posthumously published versions of the second and third volumes

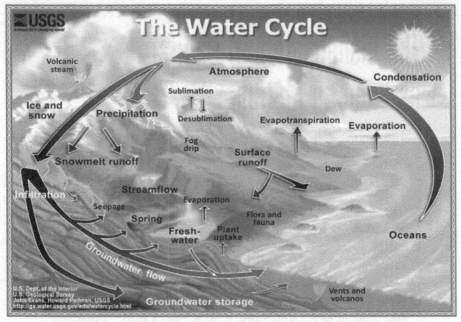

Figure 1 *The hydrological cycle as depicted by the US Geological Survey*

of *Capital*. I then need to find a comprehensible way to represent Marx's basic findings.

In the natural sciences we find many simplified representations of complex processes, which help visualise what is going on in some field of enquiry. One such representation I find particularly interesting and which I shall use as a template for depicting how capital works, is that of the hydrological cycle (Figure 1). What I find particularly interesting is that the cyclical movement of H_2O entails transformations of form. Liquid in the oceans evaporates under the glare of the sun and moves as a vapour upwards until it condenses out as the water droplets that form clouds. If the droplets form at a high enough altitude they crystallise out as ice particles, which form the high-flying cirrus clouds that give us beautiful sunsets. At some point the droplets or ice particles merge and as they become heavier so they drop from the clouds under the force of gravity as precipitation, which occurs in a variety of forms (rain, fog, dew, snow, ice, hail, freezing rain). Once returned to the surface of the earth some of the water falls directly back into the oceans, some of it gets stuck on high ground or cold regions as ice that moves extremely slowly if at all, while the rest flows downwards across the land as streams and rivers (with some water evaporating back into the atmosphere) or under the land as ground water back into the oceans. En route it is used by plants and animals that transpire and perspire to return some water directly to the atmosphere through evapo-transpiration. There are also large amounts of water stored in ice fields or underground aquifers. Not everything is in motion at the same pace. Glaciers move at the proverbial glacial pace, torrents rush downhill, groundwater sometimes takes many years to travel a few miles.

What I like about this model is that it depicts H_2O passing through different forms and states at different rates before returning to the oceans to start all over again. This is very similar to how capital moves. It begins as money capital before taking on commodity form passing through production systems and emerging as new commodities to be sold (monetised) in the market and distributed in different forms to different factions of claimants (in the forms of wages, interest, rent, taxes, profits) before returning to the role of money capital once more. There is, however, one very significant difference between the hydrological cycle and the circulation of capital. The driving force in the hydrological cycle is incoming energy from the sun and that is fairly constant (though it oscillates a bit). Its conversion into heat has in the past changed a great deal (plunging the earth into ice ages or phases of tropical heat). In recent times the heat retained has been increasing significantly due to entrapment by greenhouse gases (arising out of fossil fuel use). The total volume of water equivalent circulating remains fairly constant or changes slowly (measured in historical as opposed to geological time) as ice caps melt and underground aquifers get drained dry by human uses. In the case of capital, the sources of energy, as we shall see, are more varied and the volume of capital in motion is constantly expanding at a compound rate because of a growth requirement. The hydrological cycle is closer to a genuine cycle (though there are signs of speed-up due to global warming), whereas the circulation of capital is, for reasons we will soon explain, a spiral in constant expansion.

Value in motion

So what, then, would a flow model of capital in motion look like and how can this help visualise what Marx's capital is all about?

I start with Marx's favoured definition of capital as 'value in motion'. I plan here to use Marx's own terms, offering definitions as we go along. Some of his terms are unusual and on the surface may sound confusing, even mysteriously technocratic. In fact, they are not too hard to understand when explained and the only way to be true to my mission is to tell the story of capital in Marx's own language.

So what is meant by the 'value' that is in motion? Marx's meaning is very special so this is the first of his terms that requires some elaboration.[1] I will try to unfold its full meaning as we go along. But its initial definition is *the social labour we do for others as organised through commodity exchanges in competitive price-fixing markets*. This is a bit of a mouthful but not really too hard to digest. I have shoes but I make shoes to sell to others and I use the money I get to buy the shirts that I need from others. In such an exchange, I in effect exchange my labour time making shoes for the labour time someone else spends making shirts. In a competitive economy with many people making shirts and shoes it would make sense to think that if more labour time on average is taken up in shoe-making as opposed to shirt-making, then shoes should end up costing more than shirts. The price of shoes would converge around some average and the price of shirts should also converge on some average. Value underlines the difference between these averages. It might show, for example, that one pair of shoes is equivalent to two shirts. But notice it is the average labour time that counts. If I spend an inordinate amount of labour time on the shoes I make I will not get the equivalent back in exchange. That would reward inefficiency. I will receive only the average labour time equivalent.

Marx defines value as *socially necessary labour time*. The labour time I spend on making goods for others to buy and use is a social relation. As such it is, like gravity, an immaterial but objective force. I cannot dissect a shirt and find atoms of value in it any more than I can dissect a stone and find atoms of gravity. Both are immaterial relations that have objective material consequences. I cannot over-emphasise the importance of this conception. Physical materialism, particularly in its empiricist garb, tends not to recognise things or processes that cannot be physically documented and directly measured. But we use concepts like 'value' all of the time. If I say 'political power is highly decentralised in China', most people will understand what I mean even though we cannot go into the streets and measure it directly. Historical materialism recognises the importance of immaterial but objective powers of this sort. We typically appeal to them to account for the collapse of the Berlin Wall, the election of Donald Trump, feelings of national identity or the desire of indigenous populations to live according to their own cultural norms. We describe features such as power, influence, belief, status, loyalty and social solidarity in immaterial terms. Value, for Marx, is exactly such a concept. 'Material elements do not make capital into capital,' writes Marx. Instead, 'they recall that capital is also in another respect a value, that is, something immaterial, something indifferent to its material consistency'.[2]

Given this condition, a crying need arises for some sort of material representation – something we can touch and hold and measure – of what value is about. This need is satisfied by the existence of money as an expression or representation of value. Value is the social relation and all social relations escape direct material investigation. Money is the material representation and expression of this social relation.[3]

If capital is value in motion then how, where and why does it move and take on the different forms that it does? To answer this I have constructed a diagram of the general flow of capital as Marx

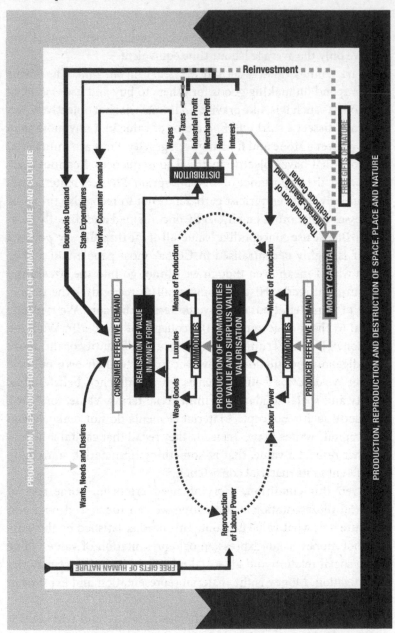

Figure 2 *The paths of value in motion as derived from the study of Marx's writings on political economy*

depicts it (Figure 2). The diagram is a bit intricate at first sight but no more difficult to understand than the standard visualisation of the hydrological cycle.

Capital in money form

The capitalist appropriates a certain amount of money to be used as capital. This presumes there is a well-developed monetary system already in place. The money floating around in society in general can be and is used in all sorts of ways. It is out of this vast ocean of money already in use that a part is syphoned off to become money capital. Not all money is capital. Capital is a portion of the total money used in a certain way. This distinction is foundational for Marx. He does not support (though he does sometimes cite it as a common understanding) the more familiar definition of capital as money being used to make more money. Marx prefers his definition of 'value in motion' for reasons that will later become apparent. It allows him, for example, to develop a critical perspective on what money is about.

Armed with money as capital, the capitalist goes into the market place and buys two kinds of commodities – labour power and means of production. This presumes that wage labour already exists and that labour power is waiting there to be bought. It also presumes that the class of wage labourers has been successfully deprived of access to the means of production and must, therefore, sell its labour power in order to live. The value of this labour power is set by its costs of repro-duction at a given standard of living. It is equivalent to the value of the market basket of commodities the labourer needs to survive and reproduce. But note that the capitalist does not buy the labourer (that would be slavery) but buys the use of the labourer's labour power for a fixed period of time (for an eight hour day, for example).

The means of production are commodities that come in a variety of forms: raw materials taken directly as free gifts from nature, par-tially finished products like auto parts or silicon chips, machines and the energy to power them, factories and the use of surround-ing physical infrastructures (roads, sewers, water supplies, etc., which may be given free by the state or paid for collectively by many capitalists as well as other users). While some of them may be used in common, most of these commodities must be bought in the market at prices which represent their values. So not only must there already be a monetary system and a labour market in existence, there must also be a sophisticated commodity exchange system and adequate physical infrastructures for capital to use. It is for this reason that Marx insists that capital can originate only within an already established system of circulation of money, commodities and wage labour.[4]

Value at this point in the circulation process undergoes a metamorphosis (much as liquid water becomes water vapour in the hydrological cycle). Capital initially had the form of money. Now the money has disappeared and value appears in the guise of commodities: of labour power waiting to be deployed and the means of production assembled together ready for use in production. Keeping the value concept as central permits Marx to enquire into the nature of the metamorphosis that converts value from the money form into the commodity form. Could this moment of metamorphosis become problematic? Marx invites us to think about this question. He sees in it the possibility – but only the possibility – of crises.

Production of commodities and production of surplus value

Once the labour power and the means of production are successfully brought together under the supervision of the capitalist, they are put to work in a labour process to produce a commodity for sale. It is here that value is produced by labour in the form of a new commodity. Value is produced and sustained by a movement that runs from things (commodities) to processes (the activities of labouring that congeal value in commodities) to things (new commodities).

The labour process entails the adoption of a certain technology, the character of which determines the quantitative amounts of labour power, raw materials, energy and machinery which the capitalist earlier purchased in the market. Plainly, as the technology changes so do the ratios of the inputs into the production process. Plainly, also, the productivity of the labour power deployed in production depends on the sophistication of the technology. A few labourers working with sophisticated technology can produce far more widgets than hundreds of labourers working with primitive tools. The value per widget is far lower under the former technology compared to the latter.

For Marx the question of technology looms large as it does in almost all forms of economic analysis. Marx's definition is broad and all-encompassing. Technology does not only refer to the machines and tools and energy systems put in motion (the hardware as it were). It also includes organisational forms (divisions of labour, structures of cooperation, corporate forms, etc.) and the software of control systems, time and motion studies, just-in-time production systems, artificial intelligence and the like. In a competitively organised economy the struggle between firms for technological advantage produces a pattern of leap-frogging innovations in technological and organisational forms. For this reason (and others that we will later study in more detail) capital becomes a permanently revolutionary force in world history. The technological basis of productive activity is constantly changing.

There is, however, an important contradiction here that Marx makes much of. The more sophisticated the technology the less labour is congealed in the individual commodity produced. Even more troubling, less total value may be created if the total output of commodities does not increase enough to compensate for the decreased value of the individual items. If the productivity doubles then I have to produce and sell twice the volume of commodities to keep the total value available constant.

But there is something else that happens during the process of material commodity production. To understand this we have to go back to the value theory of labour. The value of labour power, we said, was equivalent to the costs of the commodities needed to reproduce the labourer at a certain standard of living. This value may vary from place to place and over time, but in a given contractual period it is known. At a certain point in the production process the labourer has created the value equivalent of the value of labour power. At the same time the labourer has also successfully transferred the values of the means of production into the new commodity. In Marx's notation, a point arrives in the working day when the labourer has produced the equivalent of V (the value of labour power which Marx calls 'variable capital') and transferred the value of C (the means of production which Marx calls 'constant capital') into the form of the new commodity.

The labourer does not at that point cease to labour. His or her contract says he or she should work for the capitalist for ten hours. If the value of labour power has been covered in the first six hours then the labourer ends up working for capital for free for four hours. Those four hours of free product create what Marx calls surplus value (which he designates as S). Surplus value lies at the root of money profit. The conundrum that had flummoxed classical political economy – where does profit come from? – is solved in an instant. The total value of the commodity is C + V + S. The capitalist's outlay is C + V.

Notice something important here. What has been produced is a material commodity. Value and surplus value lie congealed in commodity form. When we look for the value that is supposedly in motion then it simply exists as a pile of widgets on the factory floor. And no matter how hard I poke and prod the widgets I can see no sign of value in motion. The only motion that will count at this point is that of the capitalist hastening to take the widgets to market to convert their hidden value back into money form.

But before we follow 'Mr Moneybags', as Marx liked to call him, to market, we need to recognise something that happens in the hidden abode of production. What is produced there is not only a new material commodity, but a social relation of exploitation of labour power. Capitalist production has a dual character. It entails not only the production of material commodities for use, but also the production of surplus value for the benefit of the capitalist. At the end of the day, capitalists care only about the surplus value, which will be realised as monetary profit. They are indifferent as to the particular commodities they produce. If there is a market for poison gas then they will produce it. This moment in capital circulation encompasses not only the production of commodities but also the production and reproduction of the class relation between capital and labour in the form of surplus value. While the fiction of the individualistic exchange of equivalents in the market (where everything is transparent) is maintained (the labourer receives the fair value of labour power), an increment of surplus value has been produced for the capitalist class in a labour process which is not transparent and which the capitalist is at pains to keep hidden from view. From the outside it seems as if value has the magical capacity to increase itself. Production is the magical moment in which what Marx terms 'the valorisation' of capital occurs. Dead capital (C the constant capital) has been given a new lease of life while labour power (V), the only means by which value can be expanded, is put to work to produce what Marx calls 'absolute surplus value'. The technique is simple: extend the working day beyond that point where the value of labour power has been recuperated. The longer the working day the more surplus value is produced for capital.

That this is a key feature in capital's history is abundantly illustrated by the more than two hundred year struggle over the length of the working day, the length of the working week and year, and even the length of a working life. That struggle has been never-ending and goes back and forth depending on the balance of power in class forces. Over the last thirty years, as the power of organised labour has in so many places crumbled, more and more people are working eighty hour weeks (two jobs) in order to survive.

Each time capital passes through the process of production it generates a surplus, an increment in value. It is for this reason that capitalist production implies perpetual growth. This is what produces the spiral form to the motion of capital. No sensible person would go through all the trials and troubles of organising production of widgets in this way in order to end up with the same amount of money at the end of the day as they had in their pocket at the beginning. The incentive is the increment which will be represented by monetary profit. The means is the creation of surplus value in production.

The realisation of value in money form

The commodities are taken to market to be sold. In the course of a successful market transaction, value returns to its money form. In order for this to happen, there must be a want, need or desire for the use value of the commodity backed by the ability to pay (an effective demand). These conditions do not come about naturally. There is a long and intricate history of the creation of wants, needs and desires under capitalism. Furthermore, the effective demand is not independent of the facts of monetary distribution which we will take up shortly. Marx calls this key transition in the value form 'the realisation of value'. But the metamorphosis that occurs when value is transformed from commodity to the money form may not go smoothly. If, for example, nobody wants, needs or desires a particular commodity then it has no value no matter how much labour time was expended in its production. Marx thus refers to the 'contradictory unity' that must prevail between production and realisation if the flow of value is to be sustained. Hang on to this idea because it is very important in Marx's presentation. We will later return to look more closely at the possibilities for crises to occur at this moment of realisation.

Marx distinguishes between two forms of consumption involved at this moment of realisation. The first is what he calls 'productive consumption'. This concerns the production and sale of the use values that capital needs as means of production. All the partially finished commodities that capitalists need for their production have to be produced by other capitalists and these goods flow back directly into the production process. So part of the total effective demand in society is constituted by money capital buying means of production. The wants, needs and desires of capitalists for these commodities are perpetually changing in response to technological and organisational innovation. The commodity inputs required to make a plough are very different from those needed to make a tractor and these are very different again to those required to make an airliner.

The second concerns final consumption, which includes both wage goods required by workers to reproduce themselves, luxury goods mainly if not entirely consumed by class factions within the bourgeoisie and the goods needed to sustain the state apparatus. With final consumption the commodities disappear from circulation entirely which is not the case with the production of means of production. The last chapters of Volume 2 of *Capital* are devoted to a detailed study of the proportionalities that must be achieved in production of wage goods, luxuries and means of production if the flow of value is to continue unscathed. If those proportionalities are not observed, then some value will have to be destroyed to keep the economy on an equilibrium growth path. It is in the context of realisation and transformation into the money form that Marx builds his theory of the role of effective demand in maintaining and in some instances even impelling the overall circulation of value as capital.

The distribution of value in money form

Once values are transformed from commodity to the money form through a sale on the market, then the money is distributed among a whole series of participants who, for one reason or another, can make a claim upon a share of it.

Wage labour

Labour will claim its value in the form of money wages. The state of class struggle is one of the factors that determine the value of labour power. Labour may improve its wages and living conditions through class struggles. Conversely, counter-attacks by an organised capitalist class may reduce the value of labour power. But if wage goods (the goods labourers require to survive and reproduce) are getting cheaper (e.g. through cheap imports and technological changes) then a declining value share can be compatible with a rising material standard of living. This has been a key feature of recent capitalist history. Workers in general get a declining share in total national income but now have mobile phones and tablets. Meanwhile, the top 1 per cent take an ever increasing share of total value output. This is not, as Marx is at pains to point out, a law of nature but without any counterforce this is what capital does. While the value produced is broadly divided between capital and labour depending upon the organised (or disorganised) power of each in relation to each other, individual groups in the work force are differentially rewarded according to skill, status and position while there are also differentials due to gender, race, ethnicity, religion and sexual preference. It needs also to be said, however, that capital appropriates the skills, capacities and powers of human beings as free goods wherever and whenever it can. The knowledge, learning, experience and skills stored within the working class are important attributes of the labour force upon which capital often relies.

The money that flows to labour in the form of wages returns to the overall circulation of capital in the form of an effective demand for those commodities produced in the form of wage goods. The strength of this effective demand depends upon the wage level and the size of the wage labour force. In its return to circulation, however, the labourer takes on the persona of buyer rather than worker while the capitalist becomes the seller. There is, therefore, some degree of consumer choice at work in the way the effective demand emanating from the workers is expressed. If workers have a customary taste for tobacco, says Marx, then tobacco is a wage good! There is here considerable scope for cultural expression and the exercise of socially cultivated preferences within the population to which capital will find it advantageous and profitable to respond.

The wage goods support social reproduction. The rise of capitalism accomplished a separation between the production of value and surplus value in the form of commodities on the one hand and the activities of social reproduction on the other. In effect capital relies upon the workers and their families to take care of their own processes of reproduction (with perhaps some assistance from the state). Marx follows capital and likewise treats of social reproduction as a separate and autonomous sphere of activity providing in effect a free gift to capital in the persona of the labourer who returns to the workplace as fit and ready for work as possible. The social relations within this sphere of social reproduction and the forms of social struggle occurring within it are quite different from those involved in valorisation (where the class relation dominates) or in realisation (where buyers and sellers confront each other). Questions of gender, patriarchy, kinship and family, sexuality and the like become more salient. Social relations in reproduction also extend to the politics of daily life as orchestrated through a whole host of institutional arrangements such as Church, politics, education and various forms of collective organisation in neighbourhoods and communities. While wage labour is hired for domestic and care purposes, some of the work done here is voluntary and unpaid.[5]

Taxes and tithes

A certain portion of the value and surplus value is appropriated by the state in the form of taxes and taken by other institutions in civil society in the form of tithes (e.g. to the Church) or charitable contributions to support key institutions (e.g. hospitals, schools and the like). Marx does not provide any detailed analysis of any of these, which in the case of taxes is rather surprising since one of the main focuses of his critique of political economy was David Ricardo's *Principles of Political Economy and Taxation*. I suspect the reason for this neglect is that Marx intended (according to the plans laid out in the *Grundrisse*) to write a separate book on the capitalist state and civil society. It would be characteristic of his method to delay any systematic consideration of a topic such as taxation until that work was done. Since Marx never even began upon such a work it remains an empty box in his theorising. At various points in his writings, however, the state is invoked as an active agent and element in securing the further circulation of capital. It guarantees, for example, the legal and juridical basis of capitalist market institutions and governance and takes up regulatory functions with respect to labour policies (the length of the working day and the factory acts), money (coinage and fiat moneys) and the institutional framework of the financial system. This last problem preoccupied Marx no end, according to the notes that Engels fashioned into

Volume 3 of *Capital*. The state exercises considerable influence by way of the effective demand it commands in seeking to procure military equipment, all sorts of means of surveillance, management and bureaucratic administration. It also engages in productive activities particularly with respect to investments in public goods and collective physical infrastructures such as roads, ports and harbours, water and sewage provision. In advanced capitalist societies states take on all manner of functions such as subsidising research and development (in the primary instance mostly for military purposes) while also operating as a redistributive agent by subsidising the social wage through provision of education, health care, housing and the like to working people. So extensive can state activities become, particularly if it pursues a politics of nationalisation of the commanding heights of the economy, that some analysts prefer to write out a distinctive theory of state monopoly capitalism. This kind of capitalism works according to different rules than those derived from the perfect competition, which Marx, following Adam Smith, presumed in his explorations of the laws of motion of capital. The degree of state involvement and its associated levels of taxation depend to a large extent on the balance of class forces. It is also affected by the ideological fight over the benefits or disadvantages of state interventions in the circulation of capital as well as over its geopolitical power and position within the state system. In the wake of massive crises (such as that of the Great Depression of the 1930s) the clamour for more effective state intervention tends to increase. Under conditions of geopolitical threat (whether real or imagined) the demand for an increased military presence with associated expenditures also tends to surge. The power of the military-industrial complex is not negligible and the circulation of capital is clearly affected by the exercise of that power.

Whatever is taken out of distribution by taxes supports state expenditures that affect demand for commodities. This contributes to the realisation of values in the market. Strategies of state intervention to prop up effective demand (as envisaged in Keynesian theory) then become a real possibility particularly when the circulation of capital appears to be encountering difficulties or is lacking in vigour. A typical response to a situation in which profit rates are too low to encourage private investment in valorisation is to construct a 'stimulus package' by injecting stronger effective demand into the economy by a variety of usually state-orchestrated measures. In order to do this the state typically borrows from bankers and financiers (and through them, from the general public).

In other instances, however, these funds flow towards reinvestment in capitalist forms of production directly, albeit under state ownership. In Britain, France, Japan, etc. in the 1960s, major sectors were in state ownership as continues to be the case in China today. While these entities are nominally independent and autonomous relative to the politics of state power, their orientation as public utilities organised for the public good rather than as profit-seeking corporations changes the way they relate to the circulation of capital. A significant part of capital circulation passes through the state apparatus and no account of capital in motion would be complete without incorporating some consideration of this fact. Alas, Marx makes no attempt to integrate this into his overall theory. He sticks instead to a perfect competition model of how capital works and for the most part lays state interventions to one side.

Distribution among the various factions of capital

That portion of the value and surplus value that remains after labour and the state have taken whatever their share might be, is divided among various factions of capital. Individual capitalists receive, for reasons we will later consider, a share of the total value and surplus value according to the capital they advance rather than according to the surplus value they generate. Some of the surplus value is sucked up by property owners in the form of land and property rents or as licences and royalties to intellectual property rights. Hence the importance of rent-seeking in contemporary capitalism. Merchant capitalists likewise take their share as do bankers and financiers who form the core of a class of money capitalists who play a critical role in both facilitating and promoting the conversion of money back into money capital. Capital thus completes the circle and flows back into the processes of valorisation. Each of these named agents claims a share of the surplus value in the form of profit on industrial capital, profit on merchant's capital, rents on land and other forms of property right and interest on money capital.

Each of these forms of distribution have ancient roots that precede the rise of the form of capital circulation we are here describing. Marx in his historical chapters clearly recognises the past importance of what he calls these 'antediluvian' forms of capital. His approach to understanding these categories and claims is rather special. He asks, in effect, how is it that 'industrial capitalists', the producers of value and surplus value in commodity form, are willing to share some of the value and surplus value they generate once it is monetised with these other claimants? What, in short, is the indispensable function of the merchants, the landlords and the bankers within a mature capitalism? This ultimately has to give way to another question. In what ways do these other claimants organise themselves politically and economically to shamelessly appropriate as much surplus value as they can from the industrial capitalists way beyond what would be justified by the performance of their indispensable function? Factional struggles within the capitalist class are everywhere in evidence and Marx begins to acknowledge this in his preliminary presentations on banking and finance. But his most solid contribution comes in the way he answers the first question, leaving us to deal with the conjunctural conditions and power balances that are typically involved in giving any answer to the second question.

There is, however, a tendency to look upon distribution as the passive end-product of surplus value production. But Marx's presentation shows that this is not so. Finance and banking are not merely passive recipients of their aliquot share of the produced surplus value in money form. They are active intermediaries and agents for the circulation of money back into surplus value production through the circulation of interest-bearing capital. The banking system, with the central bank at its apex, is a crucible for money creation without regard for value creation in production. For this reason financiers and bankers are as much drivers of the further circulation of value as they are beneficiaries of past surplus value production. The circulation of interest-bearing capital which demands a return based upon the property right of ownership introduces a duality into what has so far been conceptualised as a single stream of value in motion. Industrial capitalists internalise this dual role: as the organisers of the production of surplus value they engage in one set of practices, while as the owners of capital in money form they reward themselves through payment of interest on the money they themselves advance. Either that or they borrow the money to start their business and pay the interest to someone else.

This introduces into capital circulation an increasingly important distinction between ownership and management. Stock holders demand a return on their investment of money capital whereas management demands its share through the active organisation of surplus value production in commodity form. Once the circulation of interest-bearing money capital acquires an autonomous status within the concept of capital, then the dynamics of capital as value in motion become disaggregated. A whole class of stock holders and investors (money capitalists) arises seeking monetary gains from investing the money capital at their disposal. This class hastens and tightens the conversion of mere money into money capital. Without this movement there can be no valorisation of capital in production, no growth and no return on money capital. At the same time it also entails a pure monetary orientation on the part of a powerful and influential segment of capital that can just as easily seek a return on their money by means other than valorisation in production. If the rate of monetary gain is to be had from speculation in land, property and natural resource markets, or from merchant capitalist operations, then they will invest there. If the purchase of government debts yields more than that obtained from production then money capital will tend to flow to these other sectors at the expense of the flow into valorisation.

Marx recognises such possibilities. But he tends to dismiss them on the grounds that if everyone invests in land rents or merchant capitalist activities and no one invests in value production, then the rate of return on the latter will soar until capital returns to what Marx considers its rightful vital functions. At worst, Marx tends to concede (at least in the cases of merchant capital and interest) that the rate of profit will tend over time to equalise between industrial capital and the other distributive forms. Even if this is so, it is still the case that capital as value in motion loses its simple singular structure and shatters into component streams that often move in an antagonistic relation to each other. This is rather like what happens in the hydrological cycle when precipitation occurs in many different forms. In recent times, for example, capital flow has tended to diminish with respect to value production while money capital seeks higher rates of monetary return elsewhere such as in land and property speculation. The effect is to exacerbate the long-run stagnation in value production that has characterised much of the global economy since the grand disruption of 2007–8.

The contradictory element of this is that the creation of indebtedness from within the financial system becomes a persistent driver of further accumulation. The frantic search for profit is supplemented by the frantic need to redeem debts. And some of that frantic search has to find ways to augment the valorisation of capital in production. Value does not return to the practices of valorisation that we began by analysing in the same form that it had when it began upon its journey. It evolves as it goes and expands as it evolves. But its expansion now encompasses not only the quest for surplus value but the added necessity to redeem the debts that are piling up within the distributive network that is required for capital circulation to function effectively.

The driving forces of value in motion

The visualisation of capital flow proposed here is, of course, a simplification. But it is not an unwarranted simplification. It depicts four fundamental processes within the overall circulation process of capital: that of valorisation where capital is produced in the form of surplus value in production; that of realisation when value is transformed back into the money form through the market exchange of commodities; that of distribution of value and surplus value among various claimants; and, finally, that of capturing some of the money that circulates among the claimants and converting it back into money capital from whence it continues on its way through valorisation. Each distinctive process is in some respects independent and autonomous. But all of them are integrally related within the circulation of value. These distinctions within the unity of value in motion, as we shall shortly see, have a key role to play in structuring *Capital* as a text. Volume 1 focuses on valorisation, Volume 2 on realisation and Volume 3 dissects the various forms of distribution.

It remains to offer a brief commentary on the driving force or forces at work, which keep this flow of capital in motion. The most obvious driving force rests on the fact that no rational money capitalist would undertake all the effort and suffer all the aggravations that attach to organising production of commodities and surplus value in the way they do unless they ended up with more money at the end of the process of valorisation than they had at the beginning. In short, it is the individual profit motive that drives them. We can, of course, attribute this to human greed but Marx for the most part refrains from viewing this as a moral defect. It is socially necessary if we are to produce the use values required to live. Since the origin of profit lies in surplus value production, then the process of valorisation has a built-in incentive to continue indefinitely on the basis of perpetual exploitation of living labour in production. The implication, however, is a perpetual expansion of surplus value production. The circle of reproduction of capital becomes a spiral of perpetual growth and expansion.

Marx by and large discounted the idea that a driving force might attach to the processes of realisation. There is, however, no inherent reason why not. This driving force could derive from public shifts in wants, needs and desires for different use values. While Marx was inclined to see the state of wants, needs and desires as 'rational consumption' as defined by capital, circumstances may arise in which this is not so. For example, when a significant segment of a population (whether workers or bourgeois does not matter) expresses a desire to achieve a different relation to nature, one in which the environmental degradations, habitat losses and climate changes deriving from actually existing capitalist practices might be rolled back, then the overall circulation process of capital may be pushed down alternative paths. To the degree that these wants, needs and desires are backed by an ability to pay (and here state incentives and subsidies can clearly make a difference) so environmental protections and renewable energies may begin to replace fossil fuels.

Marx did not consider questions of this sort, but the visualisation here constructed, based on his thinking, is easily adapted to take such questions into account. Furthermore, the state can become a driving force in accumulation to the degree that it exercises powerful influences over effective demand for military equipment, police and surveillance technologies and a variety of instruments of social control to say nothing of all the demands of routine administration and governance. So strong can this influence become that some analysts have preferred during certain historical periods to depict military Keynesianism as the main driver of accumulation. The state has also in practice played a very important role in fostering innovations and technological changes. Political and social struggles around questions of the realisation of values in fact abound but they have a rather different social structure and meaning to the classic struggles that occur around valorisation. This is because the basic social relation that prevails at the moment of realisation is that between buyers and sellers rather than between capital and labour as it is at the moment of valorisation.

It is likewise difficult to ignore the social and political struggles that occur within the general field of distribution. But to take these on board requires that we go much further than Marx who confined his analysis to the question of why these distributional forms could and should exist within a pure form of capitalism. A more dynamic perspective sees the rentiers, the merchants and the finance capitalists as distinctive power blocks acting in their own interest, seeking to appropriate as much value as they can get away with. The big question that then follows is what incentives exist for merchants, financiers and landlords to reinvest in valorisation when they are doing very well for themselves by just sitting back and living on their ill-gotten gains at the expense of those who take the trouble to engage in production? Why would anyone bother with production if they could live on land rents?

It is here that the distinctive form taken by the circulation of interest-bearing capital plays a critical role. Through the creation of indebtedness, which includes by the way the creation of money by the banks independent entirely of value production, the field of distribution internalises a tremendous incentive to perpetuate circulation through valorisation. It is not impossible to say that the incentive to redeem debts plays just as important a role in impelling future value production as the search for profit. Debts are claims upon future value production and, as such, foreclose upon the future of valorisation. Failure to redeem debts initiates the mother of all crises to the system of capital flow.

Looking then at the overall circulation process, there are multiple incentives to keep the system intact and in motion and no shortage of driving forces to keep value in motion. That there might also be multiple threats and difficulties in perpetuating value in motion is also very much in evidence. This is, however, a question we will take up later.

Capital, the book

The first condition of accumulation is that the capitalist must have contrived to sell his commodities, and to reconvert into capital the greater part of the money received from their sale. In the following pages (of Volume 1 of *Capital*), we shall assume that capital passes through its process of circulation in the normal way. The detailed analysis of this process will be found in Volume 2 ... The capitalist who produces surplus value ... is by no means its ultimate proprietor. He has to share it afterwards with capitalists who fulfil other functions in social reproduction taken as a whole, with the owner of the land, and with yet other people. Surplus value is therefore split up into various parts. Its fragments fall to various categories of person, and take on various mutually independent forms, such as profit, interest, gains made through trade, ground rent, etc. We shall be able to deal with these modified forms of surplus value only in Volume 3 ... On the one hand, then, we assume here that the capitalist sells the commodities he has produced at their value ... On the other hand we treat the capitalist producer as the owner of the entire surplus value or, perhaps, better, as the representative of all those who will share the booty with him ...

Capital, Volume 1, 709–10

If the map of the circulation of capital as a whole is a reasonable representation of how Marx conceives of the motion of capital as value, then where are the three volumes of *Capital* located on that map?

Volume 1

Once we get beyond the first three introductory chapters, Volume 1 focuses almost exclusively on the process of valorisation. It takes us from the moment when money becomes money capital up until the moment value is realised in its money form in the market. The flow of wages to buy the commodities needed to reproduce labour power along with the flow of profit to nourish reinvestment are the only links in the chain external to the movement from money to commodities, to production, to commodities and back to the money form again. Everything else within the overall circulation process is considered to operate in 'the normal way', by which I think Marx means in a trouble-free way. The assumption that all commodities exchange at their value means that there are no problems of realisation of value as money in the market place. The assumption that the split up of the surplus value into distributional shares does not matter (other than that between wages and profit in general) avoids all manner of complications. Perhaps the most far-reaching and significant of Marx's assumptions concerns the unchallenged power of private property rights in both production and exchange. It is in this context that he also assumes perfect competition in the market place.[1] He accepts Adam Smith's theory of 'the hidden hand' although he insists that the hidden hand is that of labour not that of capital. Monopoly power is assumed away. Why he adopted these assumptions is an interesting question. My guess is that Marx's primary intent in *Capital* is to deconstruct the utopian vision of free market capitalism that the political economists of the time were promoting. He wishes to show how market freedoms do not produce a result that is beneficial for all, as Smith and others supposed, but that it would produce a dystopia of misery for the masses and immense wealth for the propertied capitalist class.

Having cleared the decks by making these assumptions, Marx is free to examine valorisation in all of its intricacies and detail. He examines the forms of exploitation of living labour in production under conditions of equality in free market exchange. Capitalists pay labourers the value of their labour power and then use them to produce more value than they themselves receive from selling their labour power for a certain block of time. The basis of surplus value production and appropriation lies in the exploitation of living labour power in the process of production but not, please note, in the market. Marx then elaborates on the distinction between absolute and relative surplus value, the former resting upon the extension of the working day beyond that required to reproduce the equivalent value of labour power. The theory of relative surplus value explains the inherent technological and organisational dynamism of a capitalist mode of production organised on the basis of inter-capitalist competition. Increased productivity reduces the value of the commodities needed to reproduce the labourer. This means the value of labour power declines (assuming a constant material standard of living), leaving more surplus value for the capitalist.

Competition beween capitalists for market share transforms the circle of simple reproduction into the spiral form of perpetual accumulation for accumulation's sake. Finally, Marx builds two dynamic models of what he calls 'the general law of capitalist accumulation', the first based on the assumption of a constant technology while the second incorporates technological change. The consequences for labour are a major focus throughout. In the second model we see why capital cannot escape the imperative (already established in earlier chapters) to increasingly impoverish the labourer, both within and without the production process. This culminates in the production of an industrial reserve army of unemployed and underemployed labourers that anchors the disempowerment of the labourer. At the same time it confirms capital's capacity to maximise surplus value extraction through the increasing exploitation of living labour. The conclusion runs as follows:

> within the capitalist system all methods for raising the social productivity of labour are put into effect at the cost of the individual worker ... all means of the development of production undergo a dialectical inversion so that they become means of domination and exploitation of the producers; they distort the

worker into a fragment of a man, they degrade him to the level of an appendage of a machine, they destroy the actual content of his labour by turning it into torment; they alienate ... from him the intellectual potentialities of the labour process in the same proportion as science is incorporated in it as an independent power; they deform the conditions under which he works, subject him during the labour process to a despotism more hateful for its meanness; they transform his life-time into working-time and drag his wife and child beneath the wheels of the juggernaut of capital. But all methods for the production of surplus value are at the same time methods of accumulation, and every extension of accumulation becomes, conversely, a means for the development of these methods. It follows therefore that in proportion as capital accumulates, the situation of the worker, be his payment high or low, must grow worse. Finally the law which always holds the relative surplus population or industrial reserve army in equilibrium with the extent and energy of accumulation rivets the worker to capital more firmly than the wedges of Hephaestus held Prometheus to the rock. It makes the accumulation of misery a necessary condition, corresponding to the accumulation of wealth. Accumulation of wealth at one pole is, therefore, at the same time accumulation of misery, the torment of labour, slavery, ignorance, brutalisation and moral degradation at the opposite pole, i.e. on the side of the class that produces its own product as capital.[2]

Two things can be said about this conclusion. First, Marx here exposes the dystopian consequences of free market capitalism. There is no doubt that the history of capitalism and the working classes from its origins in industrialising Britain to the present day in, say, the contemporary factories of Bangladesh or Shenzhen, contains abundant evidence of the repeated recreation of the conditions that Marx describes, while the emphasis upon free market policies in the advanced capitalist countries over the last forty years has produced ever-greater levels of class inequality. But there is also abundant evidence to say that this is not the whole story, that there have also been redemptive elements at work within the dynamics of capital that point in a different direction. For example, life expectancy of workers has risen not fallen in many parts of the world. The lifestyle of the average worker in at least some parts of the world is not all doom and gloom. In some places it even seems to glow seductively in a world of compensatory consumerism.

Marx's conclusion to Volume 1 is entirely contingent upon the assumptions to which he appeals. As in any model-building exercise, change the assumptions and you change the results. Volume 1 offers a perspective on the totality from the standpoint of valorisation. As such it is invaluable. But it is partial.

Volume 2
Marx intended Volume 2 to be a study of capital circulation that occurs during and after capital enters the market. It takes up the story of value in motion where Volume 1 leaves off. The metamorphosis of value from commodity to money form is a crucial moment. It is so because the realisation of value and surplus value in money form is the moment when the actual achievement of value creation can be measured and recorded. Only here do we have tangible material proof that surplus value has been produced.

Volume 2 proposes a perspective on the overall circulation of capital from the standpoint of the realisation of value and its subsequent circulation. Marx pursues this aim under certain assumptions. First, he assumes a constant technology throughout. He ignores entirely the findings of his intensive investigations into technological change in Volume 1. 'We shall therefore assume here, both that commodities are sold at their values, and that the circumstances in which this takes place do not change. We shall also ignore any changes of value that may occur in the course of the cyclical process.'[3] To proceed as if changing value productivity does not matter seems unreasonably unrealistic. While he starts out saying he will assume this as a matter of convenience, he later asserts that 'as far as revolutions in value are concerned they change nothing',[4]

Secondly, he ignores the facts of distribution which, with the exception of wages and aggregate profits (as in Volume 1), are banished to Volume 3. This last assumption is particularly annoying since many times in Volume 2 he notes that problems of coordinating different turnover times and fixed capital investments have a ready solution by resort to the credit system. But he refuses to take up such solutions in Volume 2 because he has yet to develop his theory of interest and finance.[5] Oddest of all, given his interest in questions of realisation of value, is the assumption that all commodities trade at their value. This is what he assumed in Volume 1 so it is surprising to see this assumption resurrected here. In Volume 2, however, it plays a very different role. He starts from the assumption that everything is in equilibrium and works backwards from that to define what would have to happen for things to end up that way. His innovative models of the reproduction schemas at the end of Volume 2 are generally seen as precursors to the economic modelling that more than a half a century later became the foundation of macroeconomics. They show mathematically the proportionalities that would have to hold between the production of wage goods for the workers and of investment goods and luxuries for the capitalists if the equilibrium between demand and supply is to be sustained.

This significant and in some respects magnificent achievement should not, however, mask the limitations imposed by the assumptions upon which it rests. Interestingly, a modicum of technological change is introduced into these models but only that which would be necessary to achieve balanced growth. Subsequent investigations have shown that there is indeed a path of technological evolution that could ensure balanced growth within these reproduction schemas, but there is no way that the competitive processes underpinning the production of relative surplus value as identified in Volume 1 could be restricted to that path. Hence crises of disproportionality are likely if not inevitable.

The limiting assumptions are not the only problem to be confronted in reading Volume 2. Far more bothersome is the incompleteness of the analysis. The materials that Engels fashioned into

Volume 2 of *Capital* are diffuse and in many instances tentative thoughts rather than finished products. They do not constitute a definitive analysis of capital circulation organised from the perspective of realisation and transformation into the money form. It, therefore, becomes necessary to reconstruct some of Marx's ideas through a study of other relevant writings. The *Grundrisse*, for example, is full of tentative ideas that need to be collated with those in Volume 2. But tentative ideas plus tentative ideas do not necessarily produce a definitive account. At best we have to guess what might have been said had the volume been completed. It is easier to figure out what happens when we drop Marx's assumptions than it is to guess at what of substance is missing from his account.

Volume 2 begins with a disaggregation of capital circulation as a whole into three circuits of production, commodity and money capital, albeit unified within the circuit of what Marx calls 'industrial capital'. Individual industrial capitalists need to play the three sometimes conflictual roles of producer, merchant and money manager. This prefigures the fragmentation of capital into different factions (producers, merchants and financiers in particular) in Volume 3. The main thrust of Marx's analysis is to show that the conditions for the realisation of value in money form depend upon the successful passage of capital through the moments of valorisation and commodity production. The same is true for the reproduction of productive capital and the reproduction of commodity capital. They are all of them interdependent and interlinked, but also autonomous forms. The industrial capitalist has to take care of all three moments in the circulation process. While Marx does not say this, there are plenty of examples of capitalists who are geniuses at organising production but fail miserably when it comes to understanding the money or marketing side of things.

The first four chapters emphasise the necessity for continuous flow of capital through valorisation in production and realisation in the market followed by the reinvestment of money capital. The penchant of capital to make technological and organisational revolutions here becomes a disruptive force. This may be the reason

Marx put innovations to one side and assumed a constant technology. It would have been difficult if not impossible to study the conditions of continuity of production and circulation when technological changes are exercising such a powerful and unpredictable disruptive force on that continuity. The overall effect of Marx's analysis is to disaggregate the flow of capital into three different streams (analogous to the different forms of precipitation in the hydrological cycle) with rather different characteristics. For example, as a general rule money is more geographically mobile than commodities and both are much more geographically mobile than production. This has important implications for understanding the role of financialisation in globalisation. Marx refers to money as the 'butterfly' form of capital (it flits around with ease and lands wherever it wants). We can extend the metaphor to think of the commodity as the caterpillar form and production as the chrysalis.

The rest of Volume 2 is concerned with circulation and realisation in the market. It pays close attention to the problems that arise from differential turnover times and the circulation of fixed capital. In so doing it frequently invokes the necessity for a credit system but puts off any examination of it until Volume 3. We are here introduced to capital with different working periods (the time it takes to make a discrete commodity like a car versus a pair of shoes), different circulation times (the average time a product remains on the market before being sold) and an overall measure of average turnover time of the capital deployed. Inter-capitalist competition puts considerable emphasis upon speed-up and the acceleration of turnover times and a lot of innovation is directed towards this end. Overall profits are jacked up by faster turnover times. The penchant for speed-up spills over from the realms of production and marketing to fundamentally transforming the rhythms of daily life. Speed-up in production at some point requires speed-up in consumption (hence the importance of fashion and planned obsolescence). At the same time, greater reliance on fixed capital investments to promote rising productivity slows down the turnover time of some investments. This is particularly true for investments in the built environment. A part of the turnover time of capital slows down in fixed capital and infrastructure form in order to facilitate speed-up in the motion of the rest. Here too the release of the hoarded money needed to build, maintain and replace long-lived and large fixed capital investments by resort to the credit system becomes critical. Discussion of this is put off until Volume 3.

It is hard to identify any unifying conclusion to Volume 2. If there is one idea that dominates from the substantive investigations it would be that of the powerful incentive towards speed-up and perpetual acceleration in the circulation of capital. But there is also a notable contrast to the conclusion of Volume 1:

> Contradiction in the capitalist mode of production. The workers are important for the market as buyers of commodities. But as sellers of their commodity – labour power – capitalist society has the tendency to restrict them to their minimum price. Further contradiction: the periods in which capitalist production exerts all its forces regularly show themselves to be periods of over-production; because the limit to the application of the productive powers is not simply the production of value, but also its realization. However the sale of commodities, the realization of commodity capital, and thus of surplus-value as well, is restricted not by the consumer needs of society in general, but by the consumer needs of a society in which the great majority are always poor and must always remain poor.[6]

The effective demand of the working classes is here implicated in keeping the market in balance and that effective demand is perpetually under threat given the analysis of Volume 1. It is difficult to introduce this question into Marxist theorising because this was one of Keynes's concerns also and in talking about it one immediately risks the accusation of importing Keynesianism into Marxism when, of course, the influence is the other way round. But here we have an explanation of why the fate of the working classes is to get lost in compensatory consumerism because that is how capital keeps its market intact. But as in the case of Volume 1, this tentative conclusion is contingent on the assumptions. But however one parses it, the findings in Volume 2 on this matter contradict those of Volume 1. The pressure to reduce wages that animates Volume 1 undercuts the capacity of the workers' effective demand to stabilise the economy in Volume 2. This signals a point of contradiction and instability within the circulation of value in motion. The weakening of the relative power of workers' effective demand over the past forty years of neoliberalism has contributed to the secular stagnation now being experienced in many parts of the capitalist world.

Volume 3

The main focus of Volume 3 is distribution. Engels also inserted some other important materials, such as chapters on competition and on the critique of the so-called 'trinity formula' of land, labour and capital, because they were interesting in their own right. But most of the text is given over to an analysis of the different forms of distribution and their consequences. In so doing it assumes away the questions of valorisation and realisation analysed in the other two volumes. The dynamics of technological and organisational change that underpin relative surplus value and contribute to the formation of the industrial reserve army are put to one side. Marx's technique in this volume, as is the case with the two others, is to take one phase of the circulation of value and examine it in detail while holding all the other features of the circulation process constant. As the lead quote to this chapter shows, Marx was quite explicit about doing this. Bearing this in mind, let us consider the main forms in which value and surplus value are distributed among the various claimants, other than the wages and taxes that we have already considered.

a) The distribution of value among individual capitalists
Individual capitalists are compelled by market forces to compete to maximise their profit. As a result, the rate of profit tends to equalise. This produces a curious distributive effect. The total aggregate

surplus value created is distributed among individual capitalists not according to the surplus value they produce but according to the capital they advance. Marx amusedly refers to this as 'capitalist communism' since the redistribution of the surplus value among individual capitalists is based on the principle 'from each capitalist according to the labour they employ and to each capitalist according to the capital they advance'.[7] The technical reasons why this occurs are too complicated to detain us here. Significant consequences follow. The redistribution of surplus value favours capital-intensive industries which employ fewer labourers and penalises labour-intensive industries where much surplus value is produced. In the absence of any countervailing tendencies, the basis for surplus value production (the employment of labourers) tends to diminish.

If the rate of surplus value extraction per labourer and the total labour force remains constant, then the total amount of surplus value available for distribution falls. The profit rate tends to fall along with it. The result is a critical contradiction within the laws of motion of capital. Individual capitalists pursuing their own interests under conditions of perfect competition tend to produce a result that threatens the reproduction of the capitalist class. This happens not because individual capitalists are stupid, greedy or mad, but because they are driven by the hidden hand of the market to pursue the maximisation of profit rather than the maximisation of surplus value production. In other words, the laws of distribution of surplus value among individual capitalists are antagonistic to the laws of production of surplus value. A potential for crises rests on this antagonism.

Perhaps even more important for Marx is the way in which the equalisation of the rate of profit 'completely obscures and mystifies the real origin of surplus value'.[8] The 'inner core' of what capital is about becomes unrecognisable not only to the capitalists themselves but to the economists who seek to represent it. In competition, 'everything appears upside down. The finished configuration of economic relations, as these are visible on the surface, in their actual existence, and therefore in the notions with which the bearers and agents of these relations seek to gain an understanding of them, is very different from the configuration of their inner core, which is essential but concealed, and the concept corresponding to it.'[9] It is, of course, the hidden and mysterious 'inner core' that is the focus of Marx's attention.

b) Industrial capitalists as a class fraction

Those capitalists who hire labour for the express purpose of creating surplus value in commodity form should be in a privileged position to capture the surplus value they produce for themselves. But the equalisation of the rate of profit redistributes the surplus value unequally among them according to the capital they advance and the taxmen constantly hound them to get their pound of flesh. Such capitalists are also obliged to pass on some of the value and surplus value in the form of profit for merchants, rent for land and property owners and interest for the bankers and financiers. Far from being privileged appropriators of the surplus value, 'industrial capitalists' as Marx calls them often end up taking whatever is left over after everyone else's claim has been satisfied.

c) Merchant capitalists

Capital is lost and suffers devaluation if it is not continuously in motion. The time taken to get the product to market and achieve a sale is lost time and time is money. For this reason industrial capitalists often prefer to pass the commodity on immediately to merchants. The merchant capitalist organises sales in an efficient way and at a low cost (chronically exploiting labour power in the process). The creation of warehouses, department stores and delivery services (now increasingly online) produces economies of scale in marketing. Merchant capitalists are also adept at marketing strategies and techniques of persuasion (e.g. advertising) that affect the state of wants, needs and desires in a population. For all of these reasons industrial producers have a strong incentive to pass on their commodities to merchants at a discount of the full value prior to the moment of realisation. In Marx's scheme of things this discount is the source of merchant profit. Merchants by and large create no value (there are some important exceptions such as transport to market). They mainly appropriate a part of the value already produced by industrial capital in return for rendering the realisation and monetisation of value more efficient, faster and more secure.

d) Landlords and rent

Land is a primary means of production and the systematic exclusion of labour from access to the land by its enclosure and privatisation is vital for the reproduction of wage labour. Only then is it possible to be assured that workers have to be wage labourers in order to live. When the frontier in the United States was open, labour scarcities along the industrial East Coast forced wages up, except when the inflow of immigrants was sufficient to force them back down again. The implication is that uncultivated land becomes a commodity that can be traded at a price even though it has no value, since no labour has yet been applied to its production. This raises the question of how to understand and analyse the circulation of capital in land markets.

Competition between capitalist producers on the land encounters differential advantages due to superior fertility and/or superior location relative to other forms of economic activity. These differences (which Marx studies through detailed investigations of what he calls 'differential rents') may be attributed in the first instance to nature, but over time they are increasingly produced through investments in land and property improvements (culminating, of course, in city building). Just as important are revolutions in space relations through investment and innovations in transport and communications. Locational advantages are relative not absolute. Remote lands which were commercially worthless suddenly become valuable because of the construction of a railway or a highway system.

Land and property owners who extract rent from these differential advantages do a signal service to capital in general: they equalise the conditions for perfect competition between industrial (in this case agricultural) capitalists working in or on the land. If industrial producer X earned a much higher rate of profit on a permanent basis than producer Y by virtue of occupying a superior location or land of higher fertility, then the driving force of inter-capitalist competition would be permanently blunted and the laws of motion of capital permanently impaired. Capital in effect makes a side payment to landlords for excluding labour from the land and smoothing the path to perfect competition across the uneven spaces of a national and even the world market.

Marx is mainly interested in the distinctively capitalist form of landed property and rent. In his historical writings he fully recognises, however, that land ownership and rent are social forms representing social relations of quite different sorts in a variety of pre-capitalist situations. The eradication of, for example, feudal residuals is even now by no means complete even after many years of capitalist endeavour. In Britain, the Church, the Crown and a few aristocratic families still own vast amounts of land. What Marx has shown, however, is that capitalism cannot possibly function without its own distinctive form of land rent. What he did not anticipate was that new forms of capitalist rent might also evolve within the evolutionary structures of capitalism and that rent-seeking might go well beyond that which he found both necessary and functional as well as politically tolerable for a mature form of capitalist development. Rent-seeking through speculation in land markets and resource endowments (like oil wells) is bad enough. But what are we to make of rent-seeking through ownership of intellectual property rights? This is an example of an extension that Marx did not anticipate, but with which we contemporary analysts have to contend. In the same way that merchants as a factional power block frequently go well beyond the remit that Marx allowed them as necessary for the proper functioning of capital, so the rentiers have a penchant for doing the same in land, property and asset markets of all sorts.

e) Banking, financial institutions
This is by far the most complicated and problematic distributional category. How it gets represented is of great import for understanding

the overall circulation of capital. In recent times much attention has been paid to it because of the seemingly determinant influence of financialisation over capital flows. Marx wrote voluminously about it, without coming to a firm determination as to how to integrate many of the activities he encountered (like financial speculation and the circulation of interest-bearing capital) into the concept of capital as value in motion. What he did uncover poses some serious problems for his general theory. We will pay close attention to them as we proceed.

There are many reasons why industrial capitalists (and others) are beholden to banking and finance. Coordinating the inputs and outputs of a particular form of commodity production means negotiating between radically different turnover times in the production of inputs and outputs. The cotton industry needs a daily supply of cotton but the cotton crop comes in once a year (though the advantage of a world market with many suppliers in different locations with different harvest times helps modify that problem). Cotton producers get paid for their crop once a year but need cash not only to produce but also to live on a daily basis for the whole of the year. Without a bank to turn to, the cotton producer would have to hoard the cash from the sale and take it out from under the mattress on a daily basis until the next sale comes around. Meanwhile, someone has to hoard the cotton as a commodity to release to the mills for production on a daily basis. For Marx, all that hoarded value in money or commodity form is dead and devalued capital. It sits there unused and unproductive for most of the year.

This problem becomes even more significant when we consider the circulation of fixed capital. A machine costs a lot up-front but lasts for several years. The initial value of the machine can be recuperated through annual depreciation payments. But at the end of its lifetime, the machine needs to be replaced. The capitalist must have saved (hoarded) enough money each year to buy a replacement. The result is a vast trove of dead and devalued capital sitting idle in the safes of the capitalists. The security of these hoards poses a problem since robbers are everywhere. The capitalist banking and credit system addresses these problems. Capitalists can safely (they hope) place their hoarded surplus funds in a bank in return for interest and the bank can then lend them out at a (slightly) higher rate of interest to someone else. Either that or industrial capitalists can borrow the money up-front to buy the machine and pay off the loan out of annual depreciations. In either case, dead and devalued capital is resuscitated for active circulation. Plainly, as capital becomes more complicated with respect to intersecting value chains and divisions of labour and relies more on large quantities of fixed capital (to say nothing of increasing demands for infrastructural provision and city building), so the demand for a more sophisticated credit and financial system grows. Either that or the whole system of capital circulation would gum up with more and more capital hoarded to deal with these temporal problems.

In the same way that rent covers a diversity of problems in the geographical and spatial dimensions to capitalist activities, so the credit system deals with the multiple temporalities involved in the organisation of productive activities. The credit system takes a seemingly infinite variety of temporalities at work in the daily organisation of capitalist production and reduces them to one singular metric: the rate of interest over time. To be sure, that metric is variable depending on the conditions of supply and demand for money not only as capital but for anything else (including private consumption and loans to landlords). The credit system introduces into capitalism wholly new dimensions to capital flow. In the same way that land rent rests on the fiction that land is a commodity that can have a price but no value, so also the credit system rests on the fiction that money is a commodity that has a price. The effect is to suggest that money, the representative or expression of value, has a value, which is clearly ridiculous. But money does have a price which is interest.

Banking and finance play multiple roles. They suck up idle pockets of money wherever they may be and convert that money into money capital by lending it to anyone interested in pursuing profitable investment opportunities. As intermediaries, banks and financial institutions operate as 'the common capital of the capitalist class'.[10] They play a key role in accelerating the equalisation of the rate of profit, extracting funds from those working in low profit sectors of the economy and redirecting them to wherever the rate of profit is higher. They also hold in their hands a certain power of money creation independent of any increase in value output. The independence and autonomy of the financial system along with its inherent powers of money creation may be subsumed within the overall circulation process of capital as value in motion, but not without having some major impacts.

Banks and financial institutions work with money as a commodity and not with value production. They lend to wherever the money profit rate is higher and that is not necessarily in productive activity: if profits can be made from speculation in land then the banks will lend for land and property purchases (as they did wholesale from 2001 to 2007 in the United States). 'The fetish character of capital and the representation of this capital fetish is here complete.'[11] What Marx means by this is that the financial system necessarily responds to money and profit signals within the different fields of distribution that can divert capitalist activity away from value creation and into unproductive channels. Banks can lend to other banks, to land and property companies, to merchant capitalists as well as to consumers (whether working class or bourgeois does not matter) and as well as to the state (the national debt is huge).

The result is a world of what Marx calls 'fictitious capital' circulation.[12] Banks leverage their deposits to lend out a multiple of the assets they actually possess. Their loans can be three times or in periods of 'irrational exuberance' as much as thirty times the assets they have on deposit. This is money creation over and beyond that needed to cover current value production and realisation. This money creation takes the form of debt and debts are a claim on future value production. An accumulation of debts is either redeemed by future value production or devalued in the course of a crisis. All capitalist production is speculative, of course, but in the financial system that characteristic is heightened into a supreme fetish. The financier, says Marx, has the 'nicely mixed character of swindler and prophet'.[13] Fictitious capital may or may not be realised through valorisation and realisation at some later date. At the apex of the world's financial and monetary system sit the central banks armed with seemingly infinite powers of money creation no matter what the state of value production. How does this fit with the theory of capital circulation and accumulation and with the requirements of valorisation and realisation?

Credit and debt have innumerable pre-capitalist forms but Marx is interested, as he is with respect to both the merchants and the landlords, in the distinctive form that credit instruments take in the circulation of capital. The rise of capitalism revolutionised what debt and credit were about (a revolution that David Graeber fails to notice in his history of debt[14]). In Marx's day this distinctive form was both growing and changing rapidly. Joint stock companies and new instruments of credit were in the process of formation. In our own times, innovations in the field of banking and finance have taken matters to yet another level.

To view distribution as a passive end-point to the circulation process is, we earlier argued, an egregious error. Distribution in the money form constitutes a distinctive transitional phase in the motion of capital. But how does this relate to valorisation and realisation? It is hard to come to a firm answer to that question but one of Marx's findings does provide an important clue as to how we might proceed towards at least a tentative conclusion.

f) The circulation of interest-bearing capital

Volume 3 does in fact recognise a framework for understanding how money might be ploughed back into the circle of valorisation and realisation. The autonomous power of credit creation that lies within the banking and financial system (with the central banks at its apex) unleashes a flow of interest-bearing capital into circulation. There is no necessity that impels that interest-bearing capital to flow into valorisation. It has multiple other opportunities varying from consumer credit to loans to merchant capitalists, to landlords and property speculators, to the state to fight wars or even to foreign powers. The circulation of interest-bearing capital claims its share of the surplus value on the basis not of its contribution to active production but as a pure property right. This right is conferred by the ownership of money as a commodity, whose use value is that it can be used to make more money.

A new dimension is here introduced into the picture of circulation. This was prefigured in Volume 2 where Marx looks at the circulation of money capital as a distinctive form. When industrial capitalists realise value as money, they come into possession of a commodity which has interest as its price. Capitalists here have a choice. They can invest in further production of value or they can put the money on the money market to earn interest. To stay in business, industrial capitalists must earn more than the going rate of interest. Otherwise all the aggravation and effort that goes into organising production does not make economic sense. The flow of capital through the hands of industrial capitalists in effect divides into two paths: the capitalist as a money holder receives interest on the money deployed while as a producer the capitalist profits from the exploitation of labour in production. The capitalist 'has the choice between lending his capital out as interest-bearing capital or valorising it himself as productive capital'.[15] Industrial capitalists can borrow the money they need to start up and pay interest on it while looking to retain the rest of the profit for themselves. Marx, in an aside, regards this as a singular virtue of capitalist finance for sustaining the power and legitimacy of the bourgeois capitalist class. It offsets the power of inherited wealth and allows pushy entrepreneurs and upstarts the possibility of breaking open the class barriers that would otherwise stand in their way. The political and psychological strength of the capitalist class is reinforced by incorporating these new elements into the dominant classes.

This dual role produces, Marx goes on to note, a distinction between ownership and management. Stock holders demand a return on their investment of money capital whereas management claims its share through the active organisation of production. A class of stock holders and investors (money capitalists) seeks monetary gains from investing the money capital at their disposal. This class hastens and tightens the conversion of mere money into money capital. Even more active is the fictitious capital created within the banking system that is lent out as circulating interest-bearing capital.[16]

Capital here shatters into component streams that often move in an antagonistic relation to each other. In recent times, for example, capital flow has tended to diminish with respect to value production while money capital seeks high rates of monetary return elsewhere. The effect has been to exacerbate the long-run stagnation in value production that has characterised most of the global economy since the grand disruption of 2007–8.

Marx could not have anticipated the contemporary situation in which a few powerful banks judged too big to fail, invest irresponsibly under conditions of moral hazard created by a state that reassures them that taxpayers will cover their losses if they fail. The circulation of interest-bearing capital puts immense pressure on both valorisation and realisation. It suffuses and can in some instances corrupt the whole system of capital as in motion. There are, however, good reasons why Marx depicts the circulation of interest-bearing capital as representing the interests of the whole capitalist class. To begin with it reduces an immense variety of temporalities to a single yardstick of the rate of interest. It introduces a fluidity into valorisation and realisation that would otherwise be lacking. Lending to consumers props up effective demand that stimulates realisation. In housing markets, for example, financiers fund developers to produce housing while the same financiers lend to consumers to realise housing values in the market. The circulation of interest-bearing capital bridges the contradictory unity of valorisation and realisation to harmonise both. Marx clearly recognises this distinction. Loans to facilitate valorisation (to industrial capitalists to set up production) are quite different from loans concerned to facilitate realisation (such as the discounting of bills of exchange that was common in Marx's time) even though they are clearly related to each other.

But this carries with it a danger. The word foreclosure here takes on a convenient double meaning. If consumers cannot pay the mortgage then they lose their house to foreclosure but if they do pay it then their future is in many respects foreclosed upon because they are condemned to debt peonage for thirty years. Of course, they are free to sell out at any point. But if house prices decline then they may find themselves 'under water', owing more on the house than it is currently worth. And if they sell out to retire their debt then they still have to find a place to live.

This is, it seems to me, a fitting conclusion to this aspect of capital circulation through financial markets. There is obviously much more to say and much more research that is needed, but the critical point to accept is the active roles that the different forms of distribution play in promoting the further circulation of capital. In this, the financial aspect is of paramount importance because it deals directly in money capital, credit and the fictitious forms of capital created within the financial system. This becomes one of the most persistent drivers of further accumulation through the imperative it imposes to redeem the debt through expanded value production. The frantic search for profit is supplemented by the frantic need to redeem debts. Preferably valorisation will realise both goals simultaneously. The visualisation of capital as value in motion has to be adjusted and modified accordingly.

The totality of capital

On several occasions Marx mentions his ambition to depict capital as a totality. The map of capital flows we have here constructed provides a simplified way to visualise what this totality might look like. Each volume of *Capital* provides us with a definite perspective on the totality viewed from a particular standpoint. It is rather like taking videos of what is happening in a square (Tahrir or Taksim, for example) from three different windows. Each video will tell its own story and will be true to its own standpoint, but the totality of what is going on in the square is best captured by looking at all three videos taken together. In the reading of *Capital* there is a strong predilection for favouring the standpoint of valorisation as articulated in Volume 1 over those of realisation and distribution as analysed and described in the other two volumes. This biased emphasis leads, I claim, to serious error. The point of considering capital as a totality is precisely to recognise how the different phases presuppose and prefigure the others. While each phase is autonomous and independent all phases are subsumed within the movement of the totality. My language here is that which Marx uses explicitly in his characterisation of finance capital and the movement of its interest-bearing offshoot.

The different moments within the circulation process of capital are loosely coupled and correlated rather than tightly bound together in a functional embrace. 'This organic system itself, as a totality, has its presuppositions, and its development to its totality consists precisely in subordinating all elements of society to itself, or in creating out of it the organisms which it still lacks. This is historically how it becomes a totality. The process of becoming this totality forms a moment of its process, of its development.'[17] Or, as he puts it elsewhere:

> The conclusion we reach is not that production distribution, exchange and consumption are identical, but that they all form the members of a totality, distinctions within a unity. Production predominates not only of itself, in the antithetical definition of production, but over the other moments as well. The process always returns to production to begin anew. That exchange and consumption cannot predominate is self-evident. Likewise, distribution as distribution of products; while as distribution of the agents of production it is itself a moment of production. A definite production thus determines a definite consumption, distribution and exchange as well as definite relations between these different moments. Admittedly, however, in its one-sided form, production is determined by the other moments. For example, if the market, i.e. the sphere of exchange, expands, then production grows in quantity and the divisions between the different

branches become deeper. A change in distribution changes production, e.g. concentration of capital, different distributions of the population between town and country, etc. Finally, the needs of consumption determine production. Mutual interaction takes place between the different moments. This is the case with every organic whole.[18]

The totality here is not that of a single organism such as the human body. It is an ecosystemic totality with multiple competing or collaborative species of activity, with an evolutionary history open to invasions, new divisions of labour and new technologies, a system in which some species and sub-systems die out while others form and flourish, at the same time as the flows of energy create dynamic changes pointing to all manner of evolutionary possibilities. Marx was fond of scientific analogies and metaphors but the organic and evolutionary analogies take pride of place. As he notes in the Preface to the first edition of Volume 1 of *Capital*, his 'standpoint' is one 'from which the development of the economic formation of society is viewed as a process of natural history'.[19] A great admirer of Darwin, Marx seeks to do for the social and historical sciences what Darwin did in promoting his theory of evolution in the natural sciences.

To dissect this organic totality fully would require at the very minimum a fusion of the perspectives of the three volumes of *Capital* into a holistic theory. Marx never tried to do this. The various outlines for his research project sketched out in the *Grundrisse* indicate that other volumes on topics such as competition, the state (and presumably taxes), the world market and crises would also be needed to complete his project.[20] He came nowhere near realising that aim. He did, however, acknowledge the complicated ways in which intersecting and cross-cutting instabilities within the organic ecosystem that constitutes capital were likely to produce crises. 'The contradictions existing in bourgeois production,' he wrote, 'are reconciled by a process of adjustment, which, at the same time, however, manifests itself as crises, *violent fusion of disconnected factors operating independently of one another yet correlated.*'[21]

A note on political relevancy

I am bound to be asked at some point as to the political relevancy of this visualisation. My answer is that it helps situate issues and proposals in the context of an understanding of capital circulation and in so doing allows an evaluation of the likelihood of political proposals succeeding in their objectives. Let me give a simple example.

During the Democratic Primary campaign Bernie Sanders pushed very hard for a $15 minimum wage as a fundamental part of his political programme. In August 2016 the alliance that formed around Black Lives Matter published a document that put forward a basic income as a foundational political proposal (targeted in the first instance to the black population as part of a reparations package for the years of slavery). In both instances the idea was that the quality of life associated with the reproduction of labour power could be radically improved by increasing the effective demand of those employed (Sanders) or of everyone who had suffered historically from slavery whether employed or not (Black Lives Matter). Both proposals raised the equivalent of money wages. This increased effective demand should mean an increase in the goods and services received by the respective populations. But that impact presumes nothing happens at the point of realisation to reduce the possibility of that effect. But we know from the analysis of the circulation of capital that a great deal of appropriation of value through predation occurs at the point of realisation. Increasing the minimum wage or creating a basic income will amount to naught if hedge funds buy up foreclosed houses and pharmaceutical patents and raise prices (in some cases astronomically) to line their own pockets out of the increased effective demand exercised by the population. Increasing college tuitions, usurious interest rates on credit cards, all sorts of hidden charges on telephone bills and medical insurance could steal away all the benefits. A population might be better served by strict regulatory intervention to control these living expenses, to limit the vast amount of wealth appropriation occurring at the point of realisation. It is not surprising to find that there is strong sentiment among the venture capitalists of Silicon Valley to also support basic minimum income proposals. They know their technologies are putting people out of work by the millions and that those millions will not form a market for their products if they have no income. By locating such proposals in the visualisation here provided, we can see immediately what the barriers to implementation as well as the hidden motivations might be. The visualisation also provides a map of the potential barriers to the continuity of the circulation of capital as a whole. It locates points where blockages might trigger crises. Every point of metamorphosis of value, for example, is a potential site for crisis formation.

The visualisation also sheds an interesting light on the different forms of social struggle that might reverberate throughout the totality. Struggles at the point of valorisation inevitably have a class character (which is much theorised and well known). Those at the point of realisation focus on buyers and sellers and trigger fights against predatory practices and accumulation by dispossession in the market place (e.g. against gentrification and foreclosures). Such struggles are not well theorised. In the field of social reproduction issues of social hierarchy, gender, sexuality, kinship and family and the like become much more predominant and the primary political focus shifts to the qualities of daily life rather than the labour process. These struggles have often been ignored in the Marxist literature. Struggles over distribution call for an analysis of the often antagonistic relations between different factions of capital and the state apparatus. These, along with the capital–labour struggles over wage rates in the market place complete a tentative map of the different potential loci of political struggle in and around the circulation of capital as a whole. It then follows that social and political struggles against the power of capital within the totality of capital circulation take different forms and call for different kinds of strategic alliances if they are to succeed. Traditional 'left' movements have not always acknowledged the importance of such alliances and the compromises necessary to make them work. In addition, there are all of those struggles that occur in the contextual field in which capital circulation is embedded. The question of not only what human nature is, but what it might be, is of huge significance politically. The human nature on display among supporters of Donald Trump, Geert Wilders, Marine Le Pen, Recip Tayyip Erdogan, Narendra Modi, Viktor Orban and Vladimir Putin is very different from that of followers of Mahatma Gandhi, Bishop Desmond Tutu, Nelson Mandela and Evo Morales, which is very different again from Vladimir Lenin, Fidel Castro, Gamal Abdel Nasser, Hugo Chavez, Franz Fanon, Leopold Senghor and Amilcar Cabral. While it may be a banal cliché of politics, that the hearts and minds of the people have first to be engaged, shaped and captured to pursue any kind of political-economic project, it is nevertheless the case that political struggles over what might be called 'the nature' of human nature will quite rightly lie at the base of concerns arising from economic questions of capital circulation. But as I think the visualisation of capital in motion makes quite clear, the relations between the value that circulates as capital and the perpetual construction and reconstruction of broader political, cultural and aesthetic values is in itself a matter of great import. But those that prioritise thinking and active struggles about the latter have to recognise that they do so in the context of the circulation of capital that constrains as it facilitates certain forms of thought and action. To the degree that capital is perpetually and necessarily engaged with the construction and reconstruction of wants, needs and desires, this forms one vital bridge between what sometimes may seem like two distinctive domains of human action. Margaret Thatcher, after all, set out not only to change the economy but 'to change the soul' and in this she had some success. Many people came to accept her dictum that 'there is no alternative'. This same set of conflictive concerns extends to the vast field of political and cultural struggles over our existing and future relations to an ever-evolving 'nature' that is already reconstituted in many respects as a 'second nature' through a long history of environmental transformations. How we are currently producing nature is a hugely contested question which, again, cannot be addressed independently of an understanding of how the circulation and expansion of capital works.

I do not presume that these broader struggles are subsumed within those that attach to the perpetuation of value in motion. If anything, the subsumption is the other way round. But what a study of value in motion allows is a far better understanding of what it is that must be subsumed within this broader politics and much of it is pretty hard to digest.

3
Money as the Representation of Value

Most of Marx's theoretical arguments throughout *Capital* are expressed in value terms. The economic data of the world and most of Marx's actual examples are expressed in money terms. Are we to assume that money is an accurate and unproblematic representation of value? If not, why not: and with what consequences? Given the history of representational forms, is it possible that money is founded on systemic distortions of the value it is supposed to represent? Map projections are notorious for accurately representing some features of the earth's surface while distorting others. Should we not worry about the possibility of similar distortions in the case of money in relation to value?

Value is a social relation. As such, it is 'immaterial but objective.' The 'phantom-like objectivity' of value arises because 'not an atom of matter enters into the objectivity of commodities as values'. Their status as values contrasts with 'the coarsely sensuous objectivity of commodities as physical objects. We may twist and turn a single commodity as we wish; it remains impossible to grasp it as a thing possessing value.'[1] The value of commodities is, like many other features of social life – such as power, reputation, status, influence or charisma – an immaterial but objective social relation that craves a material expression. In the case of value, this need is met through what Marx calls the 'dazzling' form of money.

Marx is very careful with his language. He refers to money almost exclusively as the 'form of expression' or as the 'representation' of value. He scrupulously avoids the idea that money is value incarnate, or that it is an arbitrary symbol imposed by convention on exchange relations (which was a widespread view in the political economy of his time). Value cannot exist without money as its mode of expression.[2] Conversely, however autonomous it may seem, money cannot cut the umbilical cord that ties it to what it represents. We should think of money and value as autonomous and independent of each other but dialectically intertwined. This kind of relationship has a long history. Here is how Marx thinks of it:

> It has become apparent in the course of our presentation that value, which appeared as an abstraction, is possible only … as soon as money is posited; this circulation of money in turn leads to capital, hence can be fully developed only on the foundation of capital; just as, generally, only on this foundation can circulation seize hold of all moments of production. This development, therefore, not only makes visible the historic character of forms, such as capital, which belong to a specific epoch of history; but also (in its course), categories such as value, which appear as purely abstract, show the historic foundation from which they are abstracted, and on whose basis alone they can appear … and categories which belong to more or less all epochs, such as e.g. money, show the historic modifications which they undergo. [3]

For Marx, all the major categories in *Capital*, taken together, are abstractions grounded in the historical experience and practices of capitalism. 'The economic concept of value does not occur in antiquity … The concept of value is entirely peculiar to the most modern economy, since it is the most abstract expression of capital itself and the production resting on it.' Categories that have a longer history, such as rent, interest and profit on merchant's capital, become adapted over time to the requirements of a capitalist mode of production. This is the case with money. The problem is how to distinguish between those characteristics of money that are unique to capitalism and the various money forms (like cowrie shells or wampum beads) that pre-existed it. This question becomes doubly important when it comes to analysing credit.

The constant continuity of the process (of circulation), the unob-
structed and fluid transition of value from one form into the
other, or from one phase of the process into the next, appears
as a fundamental condition for production based on capital to
a much greater degree than for all earlier forms of production
... It thus appears as a matter of chance for production based
on capital whether or not (this) essential condition ... is actually brought about. The suspension of this chance element by
capital itself is credit ... Which is why credit in any developed
form appears in no earlier mode of production. There was borrowing and lending in earlier situations as well, and usury is even
the oldest of the antediluvian forms of capital. But borrowing
and lending no more constitute credit than working constitutes
industrial labour or free wage labour. And credit as an essential, developed relation of production appears historically only
in circulation based on capital or on wage labour. (Money itself
is a form for suspending the unevenness of the times required
in different branches of production, to the extent this obstructs
exchange.)[4]

The distinctive qualities of both money and credit within a capitalist mode of production are to ensure the continuity of movement
of capital as value in motion. Conversely, the necessity to ensure
continuity brings together the categories of money, credit and value
into a specific historical configuration.

The first chapter of *Capital* is an object lesson in how to study
matters of this sort. Marx notes how the classical political economists drew upon a fictional past, that of the Robinson Crusoe myth,
to 'naturalise' their categories as if they arose out of a state of nature
(and were for that reason immutable, unchanging and unchange-
able). Marx prefers to examine pre-capitalist societies instead, to
emphasise how categories are embedded in actual histories rather
than derived from fictional stories. 'Let us now transport our-
selves from Robinson's island, bathed in light, to medieval Europe,
shrouded in darkness ...,' he writes. He briefly examines the social

relations and categories typical of feudal corvée labour and of the 'patriarchal rural industry of a peasant family'. But he then triangulates, as it were, on the specificities of capital today by imagining what the categories might look like after capitalism is transcended. He uses the pre-capitalist past and the *futur antérieur* of communism as standpoints to understand the particular nature of capital (as well as the qualities of money and credit) now. The *futur antérieur* is not a utopian imaginary of what might happen, but a specification of what must happen if we are to get to communism. 'Let us imagine, for a change, an association of free men, working with the means of production held in common, and expending their many different forms of labor power in full self-awareness as one single social labour force …' Under such unalienated conditions, 'the social relations of the individual producers, towards their labour and the products of their labour, are here transparent in their simplicity, in production as well as in distribution'.[5] In this world there is no hidden hand of the market or laws of motion going on behind everyone's backs that limit our freedoms and certainly no state dictation. It is from these perspectives of before and after that Marx gets behind 'the veil' of what he calls the 'fetishisms' that suffuse not only the writings of the political economists, but also corrupt common sense representations of commodity exchange in price-fixing markets. Money is the supreme example of such fetishism. We believe that money possesses social power over us as well as over others and, of course, to some degree it does (which is the whole point of Marx's theory of fetishism: it is real but wrong-headed).

So how, then, are we to understand the dialectical relation between value and its representation as money? This was a deeply contested political question in Marx's time. In the late 1840s, long before he had worked out many of the central ideas of *Capital*, Marx found himself at odds politically not only with Ricardian socialists in Britain but far more importantly with the imposing figure of Proudhon who had many followers among the French artisans. Proudhon and his followers posed the following perfectly reasonable question: why are capitalists so rich and the working classes so impoverished when all the leading political economists of the time – most notably David Ricardo – insisted that economic value was produced exclusively by labour?

Proudhon concluded that the fault lay in the way that labour value was being represented in the market. The irrationality of money and of market exchange was the crux of the problem. What was needed, he suggested, was an alternative way of measuring labour value and setting prices, a way which rested directly on the actual time workers spent making a product. Workers should be paid in labour time-chits, labour hours, or even coins designating the hours of labour actually worked. The Proudhonist movement looked to restructure the money system, organise the supply of free credit, reform central banking and create mutual credit institutions so as to solve the problem of social inequality and restore the rights of labour.

Marx vehemently objected to these ideas in *The Poverty of Philosophy* (published in 1847). The first part of the *Grundrisse*, the unpublished notebooks from 1857, is a lengthy rebuttal of the monetary ideas of Alfred Darimon, a follower of Proudhon.[6] The problem Marx had with Proudhon and his followers was their failure to grapple with the social relations that defined value. Under capitalism it is socially necessary labour time and not actual labour time that counts. The 'socially necessary' implies the existence of some 'hidden hand' or 'law of motion' to which both the capitalist and the labourer are subservient. As early as the *Economic and Philosophic Manuscripts of 1844*, Marx had concluded that value under capitalism was alienated labour exploited by capital in production, secured by private property and commodity exchange in price-fixing markets. These were the conditions that produced the social inequalities and degradations to which labourers were subjected even as they were engaged upon the valorisation of capital. The objective of socialist revolution was the radical transformation of the social relations under which workers laboured. Without such a transformation it would be impossible to create a world in which associated labourers made the decisions and in which actual labour times rather than socially necessary labour times might become the measure of value.

Alienated labour dominated by alien class power was the core of the problem. Money, in Marx's view, represented (alienated) labour values. It followed that 'to leave production relations intact while attempting to eliminate the irrationality of price formation on the market is inherently self-defeating since it assumes away the very irrationality of value production of which it is the expression.'[7] This was what was wrong with Proudhon's position.

To seek a better mode of representation (like time-chits) of alienated labour without offering a critique of the social relations upon which the capitalist law of value is founded, was simply to double down on the alienation. This is what Marx believed Proudhon and his followers along with many Ricardian socialists were unwittingly doing. This is why Marx's depiction of the *futur antérieur* of communism in Volume 1 of *Capital* is so important. It depicts associated labourers (a concept that Proudhon abhorred) with means of production held in common making conscious and, therefore, unalienated decisions in utter transparency without the social necessities dictated by capital–labour relations of domination or the interventions of any external power (such as the state or the market).

The manufacturing world from which Proudhon drew his categories was that of the Parisian workshops of the 1840s.[8] These were typically small-scale enterprises run by artisans controlling their own labour process with a workshop at the back and a store at the front. The main form of capital encountered was that of merchants who would buy from the workshops and then consolidate selling in their dry goods stores (precursors of the department stores that came in the 1850s). The artisans did not complain about their labour processes because they controlled them. From their standpoint their labour was not alienated at the point of production. Their main complaints were the low prices on offer from the merchants and the increasing domination by the latter through a putting out system in which the merchants placed orders and dictated specifications as to the nature of the finished product and in some instances provided the raw materials and even advanced credit (often at usurious rates). In this situation the demand for full recognition of the labour hours performed as opposed to the paltry monetary rewards offered by the merchants was understandable. The value of their labour was being expropriated (alienated) in the market. Proudhon's arguments about money and markets made some intuitive sense to this audience. Small wonder he was seen as a champion of workers' rights.

Marx was writing in the context of the factory system where capitalists controlled the labour process and alienated labour dominated at the point of production. It is difficult for us to imagine how huge this difference seemed at that historical time. Engels, who was familiar with artisanal labour systems in Germany, records his astonishment and horror at his first encounters with the factory system and capitalist industrialism in Britain. He was one of the very first commentators to depict its qualities in the *Condition of the Working Class in England* in 1844. There was a world of difference in labour processes between these two industrial systems. Marx was mightily impressed with Engels's account of factory labour. He tended to see the factory system teleologically as capital's future. It is to that future that Volume 1 of *Capital* is dedicated and from that world that Marx derived his categories.[9]

The differences that separate Proudhon and Marx reflect the different labour systems they addressed. It follows that we might also need to re-evaluate our own categories to reflect contemporary labour practices. The factory labour that Marx assumed was the future of capitalism has been, for example, much diminished in advanced capitalist countries and the teleology Marx broadly assumed has not unfolded in the way he imagined. Capital is currently constituted by an amazing mix of quite different labour systems in different places and times. Factory labour still dominates in some parts of the world (e.g. East Asia) but in North America and Europe it is much diminished and replaced by various other labour systems (digital labour and the like).

There is a great deal of current interest in Proudhonian-type monetary interventions with local currencies, time sharing and labour time moneys being used as an alternative to conventional modes of exchange of goods and services.[10] This has been associated in some political movements with attempts to revive small-scale and decentralised production systems (preferably under worker control). The latter became possible given the new technologies and organisational forms of flexible specialisation and small-batch production that emerged in the 1980s. At that time, Piore and Sable in their influential book *The Second Industrial Divide* read this as an opening for the left to realise Proudhon's dream of workshop mutualism. The small-batch self-organised production systems that emerged in Tuscany became a model for a socialist future in the 1980s. Unfortunately, this labour system turned out to be a neoliberal trap, dismantling the organised power of labour and expanding rates of exploitation in labour systems founded on decentralised precarity and insecurity. Flexible specialisation became flexible accumulation for capitalist corporations.[11] On the other hand the mass factory system is alive and well in East and Southeast Asia while employment patterns of digital labour and microfinance are highly decentralised though increasingly organised into configurations of self-exploitation that are every bit as oppressive as traditional industrial labour.[12]

It would be a huge error to assume that the social relations expressed in the labour theory of value could be reconstructed by reforms of the monetary system. 'The evil of bourgeois society is not to be remedied by "transforming" the banks or by founding a rational "money system" ...'[13]

> Just as it is impossible to suspend the complications and contradictions which arise from the existence of money alongside the particular commodities merely by altering the form of money (although difficulties characteristic of a lower form of money may be avoided by moving to a higher form), so also is it impossible to abolish money itself as long as exchange value remains the social form of products. It is necessary to see this clearly in order to avoid setting impossible tasks, and in order to know the limits

within which monetary reforms and transformations of circulation are able to give a new shape to the relations of production and to the social relations that rest on the latter.'[14]

The only ultimate solution as far as Marx is concerned is the total abolition of exchange value which, of course, also implies the abolition of value as socially necessary labour time leaving the organised exchange of use values as the only remnant of the categories Marx derived from capitalism.[15]

Marx in composing his critique of Darimon posed two basic questions. 'Can the existing relations of production and the relations of distribution which correspond to them, be revolutionised by a change in the instrument of circulation, in the organisation of circulation?' Marx's answer to this question is a resounding 'no!'. 'Further question: Can such a transformation of circulation be undertaken without touching the existing relations of production and the social relations which correspond to them?' Marx equivocates. 'It would be part of this general question whether the different civilised forms of money – metallic, paper, credit money, labour money (the last named as the socialist form) – can accomplish what is demanded of them without suspending the very relation of production which is expressed in the very category of money, and whether it is not a self-contradictory demand to wish to get around essential determinants of a relation by means of formal modifications?' But, he goes on to say, 'various forms of money may correspond better to social production in various stages; one form may remedy evils against which another is powerless; but none of them, as long as they remain forms of money, and as long as money remains an essential relation of production, is capable of overcoming the contradictions inherent in the money relation, and can instead only hope to reproduce those contradictions in one or another form'. In the same way that 'one form of wage labour may correct the abuses of another, but no form of wage labour can correct the abuse of wage labour itself', so one form of money may 'be handier, more fitting, may entail fewer inconveniences than another. But the inconveniences which arise from the existence of every specific instrument of exchange, of any specific but general equivalent, must necessarily reproduce themselves in every form, however differently.'[16]

The rise and adaptation of the credit system is an obvious example of what Marx is talking about here. Initially, long-standing practices were adapted to deal with the problem of excessive hoarding associated with widely differing turnover times of capital, fixed capital formation and long-term investments in collective means of consumption. More recently, interest-bearing capital has become a powerful independent driving force of accumulation on its own account. The result has not been human emancipation from want and need but increasing efficiency of circulation and surplus value production, had at the price of increasing debt peonage and increasing alienation across the politics of daily life.

The technologies of money forms and uses have been revolutionised several times over throughout capital's history. This does pose interpretive problems. What are we to make, for example, of the labour theory of value when central banks are engaging in quantitative easing or when credit creation within the banking system seems to be so out of control? Where is the discipline supposedly imposed by values upon money forms in an insanely speculative economy? Technologies of electronic banking and block chain technologies (pioneered by Bitcoin but now actively being developed by the banks) suggest that revolutions in the monetary form may be in motion and while such revolutions may not challenge the underlying value relations they must be closely monitored for their implications for social relations.[17] Marx recognised the existence of such problems. For answers, he goes back to the very foundations of his investigations.

When commodity exchange becomes a normal social act, then one or two commodities crystallise out to play the role of the general equivalent. In the capitalist era gold and silver became the preferred form of expression of value. But this leads immediately to certain contradictions. The use value of gold (a sensuous commodity) 'becomes the form of appearance of its opposite, value'.[18] The concrete physical labour embodied in gold production becomes the mode of expression of 'its opposite, abstract human labour'.[19] The 'private labour' involved in gold production 'takes the form of its opposite, namely labour in its directly social form'.[20] Finally, and perhaps most significant of all, 'money itself becomes a commodity, an external object capable of becoming the private property of any individual. Thus the social power that derives from social labour becomes the private power of private persons.'[21]

The distortions set up here are systemic and major rather than accidental and minor. Money becomes a measure of individual wealth and power, a supreme object of desire. It forms a singular basis for class power and class rule. Even more importantly, it becomes a vital means of production for valorisation to proceed. This social power is, however, systemically limited all the time the precious metals lie at the base of the monetary system. With the proliferation and increasing complexity of the social division of labour and of exchange relations, 'so grows the power of *money*', such that 'the exchange relation establishes itself as a power external to and independent of the producers. What originally appeared as a means to promote production becomes a relation alien to the producers. As the producers become more dependent on exchange, exchange appears to become more independent of them.'[22] Money is introduced as the servant of exchange but soon becomes its despotic master. Adam Smith's 'hidden hand' begins to take over. Producers become price takers rather than price makers. 'The gap between the product as product and the product as exchange value appears to widen. Money does not create these antitheses and contradictions,' Marx explains, 'it is rather the development of these contradictions and antitheses which creates the seemingly transcendental power of money.'[23] It is this transcendental power that now surrounds us at every turn.

These contradictions echo across all of Marx's writings. His account of capital's labour theory of value is inextricably entangled with them. The topic becomes even more complicated as Marx delves deeper into the multiple functions of money. It can be a measure of value, a mode of saving, a standard of price, a means of circulation, or it can function as money of account, as credit money, and last but not least as a means of production to produce capital.[24]

Several of these functions are incompatible. While gold is excellent as a measure of value, as a standard of price and as a vehicle for saving (because it is a metal that does not oxidise), it is hopeless as a means of circulation. The latter is better served by symbols of money like coins, fiat moneys issued by the state and ultimately electronic moneys. These forms of money cannot exist without guarantees as to their qualities initially in relation to the metallic base. 'The business of coining like the establishing of a standard measure of prices is an attribute proper to the state. The different national uniforms worn at home by gold and silver as coins' are 'taken off again when they appear on the world market', indicating a 'separation between the internal or national spheres of commodity circulation and its universal sphere, the world market'.[25]

The question then arises as to the interrelations between these radically different forms of expression of value (e.g. gold versus coins versus central bank money and national versus international monetary instruments). In this the parallel with map projections is useful. Some projections preserve accuracy of direction but distort everything else while others accurately represent areas, or shapes or distances at the expense of all the other features. And so it is with the different forms of money. Different representations serve different purposes. The hope is that things do not work at cross-purposes but, of course, they regularly do. Money used in one way (such as a means of saving) can suddenly switch into the role of being a means of circulation and vice versa. As Marx amusedly notes, if we are interested solely in money as a means to circulate commodities then counterfeit coins and notes do the job just as well as fiat moneys guaranteed by the state.[26]

The irony is that the need to find a physical material representation for social values led to the adoption of an unimpeachable metallic base (gold and silver) for money that was so dysfunctional for daily use that it required symbolic representations of itself (paper

and electronic moneys) to be effective. The symbolic moneys gradu-
ally became more dominant as trading expanded. Cutting out the
metallic base in the early 1970s produced two symbolic systems –
value and money – side by side in an awkward dialectical embrace.

Part of the awkwardness arises out of what Marx calls a 'quantitative incongruity between money price and magnitude of value'
which is 'inherent in the price-form itself'. Prices proposed and
realised in the market (no matter whether stated in gold, fiat or even
labour time moneys) can yo-yo all over the place but this is precisely
'what makes this form the adequate one for a mode of production
whose laws can only assert themselves as blindly operating averages
between constant irregularities'.[27] Only in this way can demand and
supply come into equilibrium and it is the equilibrium price that
comes closest to approximating value.

Even more troubling is that the money form 'may also harbour
a qualitative contradiction', such that 'price ceases altogether to
express value … Things which in and for themselves are not commodities, things such as conscience and honour, etc. can be offered
for sale by their holders, and thus acquire the form of commodities
through their price. Hence a thing can, formally speaking, have a
price without having a value.' In some instances these prices may
'conceal a real value-relation or one derived from it, for instance
the price of uncultivated land, which is without value because no
human labour is objectified in it'.[28]

On the surface this is particularly troubling for the labour theory
of value because, as the neoclassical economists early on com-
plained, if so much goes on in the price realm outside of the purview
of value, then why not analyse market prices and their movements
directly and forget about values entirely? The disadvantage of so
doing is obvious: if we erase the dialectical relation between prices
and values then there is no standpoint from which to mount a
critique of the monetary representations of the social labour that
labourers are called upon to do for others in the course of perform-
ing wage labour for capital. We will be powerless to explain where
the monetary aspects of crises might come from and why crises in

general are inevitably expressed in monetary form. Marx is at pains to explain this in Volume 1 of *Capital*.

'In a crisis, the antithesis between commodities and their value form, money, is raised to the level of an absolute contradiction.' So whence this contradiction? It is 'immanent' says Marx,

> in the function of money as a means of payment. When the payments balance each other, money functions only nominally as money of account, as a measure of value. But when actual payments have to be made, money does not come onto the scene as a circulating medium ... but as the individual incarnation of social labour ... This contradiction bursts forth in that aspect of an industrial and commercial crisis, which is known as a monetary crisis. Such a crisis occurs only where the ongoing chain of payments has been fully developed, along with an artificial system for settling them. Whenever there is a general disturbance of the mechanism, no matter what its cause, money suddenly and immediately changes over from its merely nominal shape, money of account, into hard cash. Profane commodities can no longer replace it. The use-value of commodities becomes value-less, and their value vanishes in the face of their own form of value. The bourgeois, drunk with prosperity and arrogantly certain of himself, has just declared that money is a purely imaginary creation. 'Commodities alone are money,' he said. But now the opposite cry resounds across the markets of the world: only money is a commodity. As the hart pants after fresh water, so pants his soul after money, the only wealth.[29]

This is the kind of analysis that is rendered possible by recognising the dialectical and fluid movement of money in relation to values. But the power of this dialectic has also to acknowledge that value itself does not remain untouched by the movements we have just described. If value arises through the proliferation of market exchange mediated by money then the qualities of money and of what it measures must have implications for the social qualities of value. The qualitative incongruity between prices and values cannot be ignored.[30]

Prior to abandoning the metallic base, Marx detected the existence not only of different moneys for different purposes but also an interesting hierarchy within the monetary system. The metallic base was quite literally the gold standard of value precisely because of its material qualities that remained constant over time along with quantities that could be increased only very slowly relative to the global stock of gold already above ground. This tightly constrained form of money contrasted dramatically with the effervescence of the credit system. Marx speaks of it this way: 'The monetary system is essentially Catholic, the credit system essentially Protestant. As paper, the monetary existence of commodities has a purely social existence. It is *faith* that brings salvation. Faith in money value as the immanent spirit of commodities, faith in the mode of production and its predestined disposition, faith in the individual agents of production as personifications of self-valorising capital. But the credit system is no more emancipated from the monetary system as its basis than Protestantism is from the foundations of Catholicism.'[31] When times are good, credit, 'a social form of wealth, displaces money and usurps its position' so that 'the money form of products appears as something merely evanescent and ideal, as a mere notion. But as soon as credit is shaken ... all real wealth is supposed to be actually and suddenly transformed into money – into gold and silver – a crazy demand but one that necessarily grows out of the system itself. And the gold and silver that is supposed to satisfy these immense claims amounts in all to a few millions in the vaults of the bank.'[32] The value of commodities must then be 'sacrificed to ensure the fantastic and autonomous existence of this value in money.' This sacrifice 'is unavoidable in capitalist production, and forms one of its particular charms'.[33]

'A certain quantity of metal that is insignificant in comparison with production as a whole is the acknowledged pivot of this system.' The structure is as follows: 'the central bank is the pivot of the credit system. And the metal reserve is in turn the pivot of the bank. It is inevitable that the credit system should collapse into the monetary system' in times of difficulty. As a result, the metallic base constituted 'both a material and imaginary barrier to wealth and its movement'. It was inevitable that capitalist production would 'constantly strive to overcome this metallic barrier' while 'time and time again, breaking its head on it'. Marx was of the opinion that this barrier could never be overcome. But he was wrong. Now that the metallic base has been abandoned and capital no longer has to 'break its head on it',[34] the only barrier is constituted by the policies and politics of the central banks and the states. This puts the question of the quality and quantity (as well as the form) of money into social hands as opposed to relying upon the fixed and immutable physical qualities and quantities of the gold supply as an external constraint.

The abandonment of the metallic base to the monetary system in the early 1970s allowed the circulation of interest-bearing capital to take over as the principle and unrestrained driver of endless capital accumulation. The analysis of this phenomenon requires a closer look at the position of banking and finance within the field of distribution more generally.

Let it first be said that there are some immensely complicated interactions that take place within the field of distribution as a whole. Financiers may channel money and investments towards land and property speculation, thus supporting the activities of the land and property-owning classes at the expense of everything else. Landowners use their land as security for taking out loans. In Britain many aristocratic landowners became bankers as a result. Merchant capitalists frequently extend and depend upon credit. In many parts of the world workers' incomes are augmented by the use of credit cards. Workers may be integrated into the circulation of interest-bearing capital by taking out a mortgage in the hope of becoming a homeowner. This, the World Bank assures us, confers social stability or, as the old adage has it: debt-encumbered homeowners do not go on strike. Workers are also sometimes required to put their money in pension funds that have to invest somewhere to exploit other workers to get a rate of return. Financiers lend to governments while governments in turn use taxes to guarantee and insure the activities of credit institutions. Meanwhile, banks in surplus lend to banks with deficits and both draw upon the reserves of the central banks when necessary. The various roles are porous and sometimes internally contradictory. Automobile companies support selling apparatuses that extend credit to consumers to buy their cars and it is often not clear whether the profits of the company come from valorisation, realisation or distributional activities. Financiers lend to developers to build houses and to workers to buy them thus internalising demand and supply within a single operation under their command. Workers press hard for wage increases that may depress the prices of the stocks in which their pension funds are invested. Unions may be compelled to invest in the debt of the companies that employ them. When Enron went bust the pensions of its workforce were gone. In the New York fiscal crisis of the 1970s, municipal unions were forced to invest their pension funds in municipal debt with predictable consequences. Governments set up systems of profit sharing for employees so that the latter then have an interest in repressing their own wage demands.

The flows and cross-flows within what might be called the 'distributional field' (the terrain of Volume 3 of *Capital*) have, as the above examples illustrate, become increasingly complex and voluminous over time even as the categories and roles become more porous and overlapping with respect to each other. In some parts of the world the volume of transactions and the associated turnover of capital within and across the distributional field outstrip valorisation activities by a very significant margin. The foreign exchange transactions market is huge compared to reinvestment in manufacturing. What is less easy to discern is how much of this activity is merely speculative froth or transactional noise having nothing to do with value creation.

Marx clearly sees that the centralisation of surplus funds in money form within the financial system meant that the disbursal of those funds must necessarily play a key role in guiding the dynamics of the reinvestment of money as capital. This is an issue to which we will return by way of conclusion. The financial system in effect forms a vast pool of liquid assets such that banking and finance came to enclose and represent the common capital of the capitalist class. This common capital is augmented sometimes by leveraging – lending out fictitious capital. This amounts to money creation within the banking system. At times this money creation can become excessive (when banks lend out, say, thirty times the amount of money they have on deposit). The financial system also functions as a clearing house for all manner of transactions. It becomes in effect the central nervous system of capital in general, orchestrating the flows of money capital into and across a wide range of activities, wherever the profit rate might actually or potentially be higher.

Behind all of this there emerges an investor class – individuals, institutions, organisations and corporations – desperately seeking a rate of return on their money capital.[35] This is a distinctive class of property owners – a 'financial aristocracy' – that impels the circulation of interest-bearing capital to get a rate of return without doing anything.[36] Pension funds want a return on their capital (indeed they have a fiduciary duty to do so) as do endowments of non-profit institutions (like private universities) and wealthy individuals with strong investment portfolios.

We also know from Marx's brilliant disaggregation of the circulation of capital into commodity, money and production forms in Volume 2 of *Capital*, that from the standpoint of the circulation of money capital, processes of valorisation and realisation are mere inconveniences on the way to profit making. If interest-bearing capital could find a way to augment itself without passing through valorisation and realisation then it would do so. This is precisely what all the churning that goes on within the distributive field allows. Banks lend to other banks and what could be easier pickings than to borrow from the US Federal Reserve at 0.5 per cent and buy ten-year treasury notes that yield 2 per cent? The incentives for money capital to skip investing in valorisation, particularly when the profit rate is low or labour relations troublesome, are multiple.

The hope is that failure to invest will create enough scarcity to raise prices and profit rates so as to encourage money capital to flow back into valorisation. But in the midst of all this churning there arise hedge funds and private equity companies that gain profits directly from betting on market movements of any sort both up and down and long and short. The rationale given for their activities is that they supposedly help markets clear more efficiently but when successful (which they usually are) they do so by sucking out vast monetary gains from the overall circulation of capital. Marx's penchant for deploying vampire images seems as appropriate here as it does in production.

Marx, in fact, had some choice things to say about the circulation of interest-bearing capital even in his day. With interest-bearing capital, he wrote, 'capital appears as a mysterious and self-creating source ... of its own increase'. It is here that the capital relationship is 'elaborated into its pure form, self-valorising value, money-breeding money'. 'The fetish character of capital and the representation of this capital fetish is now complete.' This is 'capital mystification in the most flagrant form'.[37] This is the great betrayal of value by way of its monetisation. This is the height of the distortion that money inflicts upon the value form, which it is supposed to represent.

The effects are far deeper than just surface froth of speculative activity in unstable markets. Marx did not know what to make of some of the institutional shifts that accompanied the increasing centralisation of capital flows within the financial system. The emergence of joint stock companies and relatively large-scale banking institutions in the 1860s suggested a break between ownership and management of corporations. Admiring as he was of the associationist ideas of Henri de Saint-Simon he looked in vain for some progressive consequences of the association of capitals, at one point suggesting this might mean 'the abolition of the capitalist mode of production within the capitalist mode of production itself'. It was, therefore, 'a mere point of transition to a new form of production'.[38] But in the light of the counter-revolutionary mobilisation of Saint-Simonian ideas in Second Empire Paris, incorporating the construction of new credit institutions and state financing of capitalist mega projects, Marx soon changed his opinions. The credit system 'gives rise to monopoly in certain spheres and hence provokes state intervention. It reproduces a new financial aristocracy, a new kind of parasite in the guise of company promoters, speculators and merely nominal directors, an entire system of swindling and cheating with respect to the promotion of companies, issues of shares and share dealings. It is private production unchecked by private ownership.'[39]

Not only did capital get redefined as 'command over other people's money', it also created a space totally out of control of value relations. 'All standards of measurement, all explanatory reasons that were more or less justified within the capitalist mode of production, now vanish. What the speculating trader risks is social property, not his own. Equally absurd now is saying that the origin of capital is saving since what this speculator demands is precisely that others should save for him.'[40] Hence the perpetual pressure to turn the pay-as-you-go Social Security System in the United States into stock market pension funds!! The effects of this were certainly not benign even in Marx's day.

> Conceptions that still had a certain meaning at a less-developed state of capitalist production, now become completely meaningless. Success and failure lead in both cases to the centralisation of capitals and hence to expropriation on the most enormous scale. Expropriation now extends from the immediate producers to the small and medium capitalists themselves. Expropriation is the starting point of the capitalist mode of production ... Within the capitalist system itself, this expropriation takes the antithetical form of the appropriation of social property by the few, and credit gives these few ever more the character of simple adventurers.[41]

The economics of expropriation and accumulation by dispossession enters into the picture in disruptive ways, orchestrated through the debt and credit system, only to be heightened as the difficulties of conventional paths to capital accumulation mount, as they have since the 1970s. Marx clearly sensed that of all the future dangers that the reproduction of capital faced, this was the one that might ultimately prove fatal. The irony being that the central contradiction in this case is not that between capital and labour; it lies in the antagonistic relation between different factions of capital.

4
Anti-Value: The Theory of Devaluation

The closing sentences of the first section of the first chapter of Volume 1 of *Capital* read: 'Nothing can be a value without being an object of utility. If the thing is useless, so is the labour contained in it; the labour does not count as labour, and therefore creates no value.'[1] With this one incisive thrust, Marx introduces us to the idea that the circulation of capital is vulnerable, that it can come to an abrupt halt; that the threat of devaluation, of loss of value, always hovers over it as it circulates. Moreover, the value of the means of production incorporated in the commodity is also lost along with that of the value added by labour. The transition from the commodity form to the money representation of value is a passage fraught with danger.

Throughout Volume 1 as we have seen, Marx for the most part lays aside questions of realisation in order to concentrate on the process of production of material commodities and surplus value. He knows full well, of course, that 'while living labour *creates value*, the circulation of capital *realises value*'. The unity that necessarily prevails between production and realisation is, however, a 'contradictory unity'.[2] Hence the warning shot at the outset of Volume 1. Commodities may be in love with money but 'the course of true love never did run smooth'.[3]

It would be very unlike Marx to formulate a key concept such as value without incorporating within it the possibility for its negation. In certain readings of Marx, much is made of the influence of Hegel's 'negation of the negation' on his thinking. He was certainly not averse to 'coquetting' (as he put it) with Hegelian formulations. The bourgeois mind, then as now, considered dialectics a 'scandal' and an 'abomination', he wrote, because dialectics 'includes in its positive understanding of what exists a simultaneous recognition of its negation; its inevitable destruction; because it regards every historically developed form as being in a fluid state, in motion, and therefore grasps its transient aspect as well'.[4]

Value in Marx exists only in relation to anti-value. While this may sound a strange formulation, physicists these days rely upon the relation between matter and anti-matter to interpret foundational physical processes. Marx often cited parallels between his conceptual frameworks and those to be found in the natural sciences. Had this analogy been available to him, he probably would have used it. The evolutionary laws of capital hinge upon the unfolding relation between value and anti-value in much the same way as the laws of physics rest on relations between matter and anti-matter. This opposition exists even in the act of exchange since a commodity has to be a use value for its buyer and a non-use value for its seller. Or, as Marx asserts more philosophically in the *Grundrisse*, 'since value forms the foundation of capital, and since it therefore necessarily exists only through exchange for counter-value, it thus necessarily repels itself from itself ... The reciprocal repulsion between capitals is already contained in capital as realised exchange value.'[5]

There is nothing mystical or obscure about the negation of value at the point of realisation. All capitalists know that the success of their enterprise is assured only when their commodity has been sold for a money value that is greater than that which they initially expended on wages and means of production. If they cannot do this then they are no longer capitalists. The value they imagined they would have after they put wage labourers to work making a commodity would not materialise. But the concept of anti-value has an even more omnipresent role than this. In Marx's world it is not an unfortunate accident, the result of a miscalculation, but a deep and abiding feature of what capital is. 'While capital is reproduced as value and use value in the production process, it is at the same time posited as not-value, as something which first has to be realized as value by means of exchange.'[6] Both the prospect and reality of anti-value are always there. Anti-value has to be overcome – redeemed as it were – if value production is to survive the travails of circulation.

Capital is value in motion and any pause or even slowdown in that motion for whatever reason means a loss of value, which may be resuscitated in part or *in toto* only when the motion of capital is resumed. 'When capital takes on a particular form – as a production process, as a product waiting to be sold, as a commodity circulating in the hands of merchant capitalists, as money waiting to be transferred or reinvested – then capital is 'virtually devalued'. Capital lying 'at rest' in any of these states is variously termed 'negated', 'fallow', 'dormant' or 'fixated'.[7] Or consider this: 'as long as capital remains frozen in the form of finished product, it cannot be active as capital, it is *negated* capital'. This 'virtual devaluation' is overcome or 'suspended' as soon as capital resumes its movement. It is clear from this collage of statements from Marx that he did not regard anti-value as 'hovering over' value in motion as an external threat but as a permanently disruptive force in the very gut of capital circulation itself.

The advantage of seeing devaluation as a necessary 'moment of the realisation process' is that it enables us to see immediately the possibility of a general devaluation of capital – a crisis. Any failure to maintain a certain velocity of circulation of capital through the various phases of production, realisation and distribution will produce difficulties and disruptions. We are forced to recognise the importance of maintaining the continuity and speed of circulation. Any slowdown of value in motion entails a loss of value. Conversely, accelerating the turnover time of capital is a vital feature for enhancing value production. This is one of the main implicit conclusions of Volume 2 of *Capital*. These features are, however, what the assumption of everything exchanging at its value in Volume 1 of *Capital* avoids. Crises will result if inventories build up, if money lies idle for longer than is strictly necessary, if more stocks are held for a longer period during production, and so forth. A 'crisis occurs not only because a commodity is unsaleable, but because it is not saleable within a particular period of time'.[8] This same principle applies with equal force to the labour time spent in production: if Korean factories can produce a car in half the time required in Detroit then the extra time spent in the latter place counts for nothing. 'As long as (capital) remains in the production process it is not capable of circulating; and it is virtually devalued. As long as it remains in circulation it is not capable of producing ... As long as it cannot be brought to market it is fixated as product. As long as it has to remain on the market it is fixated as commodity. As long as it cannot be exchanged for conditions of production, it is fixated as money.'[9]

Capitalists are, therefore, locked in a perpetual battle not only to produce values but to combat their potential negation. The passage from production to realisation is a key point in the overall circulation of capital where that battle is right royally fought out.

What circumstances might make it impossible for value to be realised in the market? To begin with, if no one wants, needs or desires a particular use value on offer in a particular place and time, then the product has no value.[10] It is not even worthy of being called a commodity. Potential buyers must also possess sufficient money to pay for the use value. If one or other of these two conditions is not met, then the result is no value. We will later investigate in some detail why these two conditions may not be fulfilled. But plainly the production and management of new wants, needs and desires has had a huge impact in the history of capitalism, turning what we like to call human nature into something necessarily changing and malleable rather than constant and given. Capital messes with our heads as well as with our desires.

But there is one feature at the moment of realisation of great significance. The foundational social relation involved in realisation is that between buyers and sellers. Even the lowest paid worker enters the market place endowed with the sacred right of consumer choice.[11] This is very different from the capital–labour relation that dominates in the process of valorisation. To be sure, the encounter between capital and labour in the market place is an encounter where the rules of market exchange formally apply (though capital has power over both demand and supply conditions of labour power through technological changes and the production of an industrial reserve army). But in the case of valorisation it is what happens in the hidden abode of production – the class relation between capital and labour as experienced in the labour process – that really matters. There is no equivalent for that in the process of realisation. In the latter case, the buyers of commodities (of no matter what class) exercise some degree of consumer choice (either individual or collective). While it is broadly true that the wants, needs and desires of the buyers have been manipulated over time by all sorts of direct and indirect means into patterns of 'rational consumption' as defined by capital, there have always been pockets and sometimes whole social movements of resistance to such manipulations. Collective consumer choices can be exercised in a variety of ways, including, for example, through state policies with regard to the social wage forced through by legislation at the behest of long-standing political movements. Resistances arise on moral, political, cultural, aesthetic, religious and even philosophical grounds. In some instances the resistance is to the very concept of commodification and market rationing of access to basic goods and services (such as education, health care and potable water). Many would regard such goods as basic human rights rather than as commodities to be bought and sold. The anti-value that arises from technical glitches and hold-ups in the circulation of capital morphs into the active anti-value of political resistance to commodification and privatisation.

Anti-value thereby defines an active field of anti-capitalist struggle. Consumer boycotts, though rarely successful, are one sign of this kind of politics but all movements against conspicuous or even compensatory consumerism constitute a political threat to realisation. Capitalists have to organise to counter this threat. But the existence of multiple ongoing struggles in and around the politics of realisation is undeniable. Organised struggles, resistances and agitations over daily life issues are commonplace no matter whether they are explicitly meant as anti-capitalist struggles or not. Marx did not investigate such questions. He merely notes them in passing.

But here the virtue of the overall framework that he constructs to represent the circulation of capital becomes more evident.

Realised value can remain capital only by circling back into production to be 'valorised' by the further application of labour in production. It is at the point of valorisation – when money returns to re-finance the labour process – that capital encounters its other most persistent threat of active negation, in the persona of the alienated and recalcitrant labourer. The working class (however defined) is the embodiment of anti-value. It is on the basis of this conception of alienated labour that Tronti, Negri and the Italian autonomistas build their theory of labour resistance and class struggle at the point of production.[12] The act of refusal to work is anti-value personified. This class struggle occurs in the hidden abode of production. It entails a quite different politics from that between buyers and sellers that dominates at the moment of realisation. In producing surplus value the labourer produces capital and reproduces the capitalist. The refusal to work is a refusal to do either.

In the same way that Marx invokes the idea of a contradictory unity between production and realisation from the standpoint of continuous capital accumulation, so there is a parallel need for anti-capitalist movements to recognise the contradictory unity of struggles over production and those waged around realisation. On the surface, the politics of realisation have a very different social structure and organisational form to that of valorisation. For this reason they are often treated on the left as entirely separate struggles with valorisation being prioritised as more important. Yet both sorts of struggles are subsumed within the overall logic and dynamism of capital circulation viewed as a totality. Why would their contradictory unity not be recognised and addressed by anti-capitalist movements?

The study of this contradictory unity reveals much about the contradictions that will play out in any post-capitalist order in which social labour – the labour we do for others – is almost certain to remain a central feature. Any anti-capitalist society will have to evolve out of the womb of contemporary capitalism, out of that world in which everything is, as Marx puts it, 'pregnant with its opposite'.[13] To the degree that 'all economy ultimately reduces itself' to 'economy of time' so 'even after the capitalist mode of production is abolished, though social production remains, the determination of value still prevails in the sense that the regulation of labour-time and the distribution of social labour among various production groups becomes more essential than ever, as well as the keeping of accounts on this'.[14] This would be so, for example, as associated labourers, in command of their own labour processes and means of production, set about coordinating their capacities with those of others, while satisfying their own wants, needs and desires with the help of those others. A perpetual jousting goes on in Marx's texts between what value currently is and what it might be in an anti-capitalist world.[15] The aim, it seems, is not to abolish value (though there are some who prefer to put it that way) but to transform its meaning and its content. And in this jousting, anti-value is constantly being invoked. In this sense, anti-value constitutes the subterranean soil in which anti-capitalism can flourish in both theory and practice.

While Marx is undoubtedly correct in seeing the struggle against capital in the hidden abode of production as different in kind and, therefore, of deeper political significance than struggles in the market place, we now clearly see production is not the only place where anti-value is of significance. Value and anti-value relate within the circulation of capital in a variety of ways. The role of anti-value is not always oppositional. It also has a key role in defining and securing capital's future. The struggle against anti-value keeps capital on its toes, as it were. The need to redeem anti-value is a compelling force over value production.

The debt economy

This brings us to study the role of debt as a crucial form of anti-value. The question Marx poses is why and how does debt arise and what its role might be within a perfectly functioning capitalist mode of production? Consider the case of long-term fixed capital investments. Capital is laid out to purchase a machine which has a relatively long life. The proportion of the value of the machine received back each year over the lifetime of the machine has to be hoarded (saved) in order to purchase a new machine when the old machine wears out. Hoarded money is, however, dead and devalued capital. Anti-value in the form of negated capital accumulates annually until enough money has been saved to purchase a new machine when the time is ripe.[16] The savings of consumers to buy big-ticket items like cars and houses are similarly structured. Vast amounts of dead capital (or fallow savings hidden under the mattress in the case of consumers) pile up. The accumulation of hoarded money savings increases with increasing mechanisation and increasing consumption of consumer durables. The credit system comes to the rescue. Money hoarded for whatever purpose can be placed in a bank to be lent out to other capitalists to earn interest. The industrial capitalist has in fact a choice: either borrow to buy the machine and pay back the debt in instalments over the lifetime of the machine or buy the machine outright and place the annual depreciation on the money market to earn interest until it is needed to replace the machine.

In either case, the money lent out – the debt incurred – becomes a form of anti-value that circulates within the credit system as interest-bearing capital. Trading in debt becomes an active element within the financial system. This creates greater liquidity and helps circumvent obstructions to continuous circulation posed by capitals with radically different turnover times. Money can continue to circulate smoothly even as commodity production itself is awkwardly lumpy and often discontinuous. This is what makes the credit system so special within a capitalist mode of production, differentiating it from all former constructions. 'The contradiction of production time and circulation time contains the entire doctrine of credit,' Marx notes. 'The anticipation of the future fruits of labour is … not an invention of the credit system. It has its roots in the specific mode of realization, mode of turnover, mode of reproduction of fixed capital.'[17] The credit system forms within the circulation of capital. It is not superimposed from without.

The immediate role of credit interventions is to resuscitate hoarded and, therefore, 'dead' money capital and put it back in motion. But the debt is a claim on future value production that can be redeemed only through value production. If future value production is insufficient to redeem the debt then there is a crisis. Collisions between value and anti-value spark periodic monetary and financial crises. In the long run, capital has to confront ever-escalating claims on future values to redeem the anti-value building up within the debt economy and credit system. Instead of an accumulation of values and of wealth, capital produces an accumulation of debts that have to be redeemed. The future of value production is foreclosed.

The anti-value of debt becomes one of the principal incentives and levers to ensure the further production of value and surplus value. The traditional and conventional view of where the energy propelling capital circulation comes from has always been the search for profit (the greed) of individual capitalists. Certainly, the figure of the small business owner and the enterprising entrepreneur hemmed in by government regulations frequently emerges as the hero of whatever it is that supposedly makes capitalism so dynamic. This evocation is probably more a rhetorical mask than a reality. But the search to maximise profit does not lead to the maximisation of surplus value production. Profit signals are misleading if not downright wrong. Following them, Marx shows, may lead to falling profits and crises. Two solutions then emerge: the centralisation of capital in large corporations to lessen the force of competition and/ or state interventions to incentivise accumulation through effective demand creation and the manipulation of the conditions of realisation. State and private debt-financing become an important means to sustain the continuity of value production. This was the case from 1945 to 1980 throughout much of the capitalist world. Competitive capitalism ceded ground to state monopoly capitalism while Keynesian state policies arranged market incentives along quite different lines focusing on debt-financed aggregate effective demand. This system faced two difficulties. First, significant segments of the working class were empowered whose anti-value and anti-capitalist sentiments became all too clear as the 1960s wore on. Secondly, the shift towards greater and greater reliance on debt-financing meant enhancing the power of anti-value via broader flows of interest-bearing capital into the circulation process of capital. The effect was to lock in value production way into the future and foreclose upon alternatives unless some massive disruption broke open a way to default on such obligations. Hence the debt crises that built up from the mid 1970s onwards (beginning with the technical default of New York City in 1975 proliferating through the developing world debt crises beginning with Mexico in 1982).

Valorisation, realisation and distribution have always been in play as independent but interrelated 'moments' (as Marx liked to call them) within the totality of capital circulation. But their relative importance has shifted with changing circumstances. The massive deployment of anti-value within the financial system to ensure future value production is relatively new. There have also been geographical shifts. Until very recently capital accumulation in China has been dominated by state investments in productive consumption (physical infrastructures) but there may be a dramatic shift underway towards the liberation of the financial system. Shifts of this sort pose problems for anti-capitalist opposition. It becomes harder and harder to put a face to the class enemy while the tentacles of indebtedness spread far and wide to implicate everyone who carries as much as a single credit card in their pocket.

Capital initially created debt as anti-value as a solution to specific problems, such as the dangers of excessive hoarding when dealing with different turnover times of capital in different industries. The power of anti-value was used to release all the dormant value and ensure continuity as far as possible. 'The boundless drive for enrichment' may 'be common to the capitalist and the miser; but while the miser is merely a capitalist gone mad, the capitalist is a rational miser. The ceaseless augmentation of value which the miser seeks to attain by saving his money from circulation, is achieved by the more acute capitalist by means of throwing his money again and again into circulation.'[18] And this he could only do if there was an active credit system and an open money market. Marx lightly touches upon this problem in Volume 1 of *Capital*. 'The role of creditor or of debtor results ... from the simple circulation of commodities.' This relation is implicit in market exchange. But Marx goes on to hint darkly at how this role is 'only a reflection of an antagonism which lay deeper, at the level of the economic conditions of existence'.[19] It is not clear from the text as to what this deeper antagonism is about. Is Marx referring here to the hidden dialectic of the value-anti-value relation? I like to think so.

Relations between debtors and creditors long preceded the rise of capital as a dominant mode of production. The issue for Marx and for us, as in the cases of rent and profit on merchant's capital, is how the debt-credit relation is perpetuated and transformed into a fundamental driving force of value in motion and with what consequences over the course of capital's history. The development of microfinance in India, for example, now has some 12 million individuals hooked into having to pay off loans by producing as much value as they possibly can. If they cannot do so or actively refuse as a matter of political will, then their assets (often land and property) are foreclosed upon (this is the famous trick of the sub-prime mortgage).[20] Piling up debt on vulnerable and marginalised populations is, in short, a way to discipline the borrowers into being productive labourers (productive defined as productive of value that can be appropriated by capital in the form of an exorbitant interest rate). More close to home, the future freedoms of debt-encumbered students and debt-encumbered homeowners are severely curtailed. It is no accident that this way of procuring value production has surged to the fore as capital finds it harder and harder to organise value production along conventional lines. We will return to this issue in the conclusion.

On the other side of the ledger, my pension fund is invested in debt in the belief that the debt will be redeemed.[21] But if that future does not materialise then the (fictitious) value of my pension fund disappears into the black hole of anti-value. Read about the state of pensions in the world today and you will see a crisis looming of unfunded liabilities stretching endlessly into the future. National debts appear even more intimidating. In the same way that individuals are controlled by their debts so states are weighed down by the anti-value wielded by their bondholders. The danger exists that the economic system will collapse under the dead weight of anti-value. What happened to Greece after 2011 is a small-scale example. When debt becomes so huge that there is no prospect for future value production to redeem it, then debt peonage, debt slavery rules. We celebrate Athens of the past as the cradle of democracy. The Athens of today is the epitome of undemocratic debt peonage.

The formation and circulation of interest-bearing capital is in effect the circulation of anti-value. It may seem strange to think of the main financial centres of today's global capitalism, such as the City of London, Wall Street, Frankfurt, Shanghai and the like as centres of anti-value formation but that is what all those debt-bottling plants that dominate the skylines in these global cities truly signify. The danger, which Marx hinted at in his writings on banking, finance and fictitious capital formation, is that capital will degenerate into one vast Ponzi scheme in which last year's debts are retired by borrowing even more money today. The central banks are currently creating sufficient new money to prop up stock exchange and asset values for the benefit of the oligarchy in the here and now. This then leaves the central bank with the problem of how to retire the debts they have accumulated on their balance sheets. The scenario of escalating social inequality that Marx depicted in his conclusion to Volume 1 of *Capital* will become even more emphatic, though achieved this time by different mechanisms of financial manipulation and exclusion. The rich grow richer through financial manipulations while the poor become poorer through the necessity to redeem their debts (both individual and collective as in state borrowings). Meanwhile, valorisation seems almost an afterthought, left to the poorest countries on planet earth to struggle with.

The concept of anti-value reaches it apogee in the massive devaluations that occur at times of major crises. In Volume 1 of *Capital* Marx provides us with a concrete example of how this works. He disputes Say's Law (accepted by Ricardo), which states that since every sale implies a purchase then sales and purchases must always be in equilibrium. Acceptance of this so-called 'law' implies that general crises are impossible.[22] This would be the case in a pure barter economy. In a monetised economy, however, simple circulation takes the form of commodity to money to commodity and back again. There is nothing that impels someone who has sold for money to immediately use that money to buy another commodity. If all economic agents decide, for some reason (e.g. a breakdown of faith in the system), to hold and save money, then circulation ceases and the economy crashes as value is negated. This is what Keynes later defined as the 'liquidity trap'. Anti-value prevails over value because value can remain value only through continuous motion. The cumulative loss (devaluation) of asset values in the United States in the crisis of 2007–8 was, for example, something of the order of $15 trillion (close to the market value of one year's total output of goods and services).

The importance of the pairing of value and anti-value in Marx's thinking is either ignored or given short shrift in presentations on the subject. But a dialectical formulation based upon the negation of value (a formulation that classical and neoclassical economics cannot possibly grasp given their positivist inclinations) is fundamental to understanding the crisis tendencies of capital. Whether Marx himself understood all the implications of this is an interesting question. His lengthy and often confusing investigation of the British financial system in Volume 3 shows he understood very well that 'an accumulation of money capital means for the most part nothing more than an accumulation of ... claims to production ...'[23] Banking and credit were becoming 'the most powerful means for driving capitalist production beyond its own barriers'. They were also becoming a 'most effective vehicle for crises and swindling'. An unchecked accumulation of fictitious capitals could mean that 'all connection with the actual process of capital's valorisation is lost, right down to the last trace'. The effect would be to confirm the illusion 'that capital is automatically valorised by its own powers'.[24] I put money in a savings account and it accrues interest at a compounding rate over time. It appears magical. I do nothing and it grows!! But now that seems to be the way in which the whole economy is supposed to grow. No wonder Marx thought of the financial system as the height of the fetish tendencies of capitalism.

The credit system is an 'immanent form of the capitalist mode of production' and one of the key powers that impels the endless accumulation of capital.

> The valorisation of capital founded on the antithetical character of capitalist production permits actual free development only up to a certain point, which is constantly broken through by the credit system. The credit system hence accelerates the material development of the productive forces and the creation of the world market ... At the same time, credit celebrates the violent outbreaks of this contradiction, crises, and with these the elements of dissolution of the old mode of production. The credit system has a dual character: on the one hand it develops the motive of capitalist production, enrichment by the exploitation of others' labour, into the purest and most colossal system of gambling and swindling, and restricts even more the already small number of the exploiters of social wealth; on the other hand however it constitutes the form of transition towards a new mode of production. It is this that gives the principal spokesmen for credit ... their nicely mixed character of swindler and prophet.[25]

Alas, today's 'masters of the universe', as the Wall Streeters are often called, have performed far better as swindlers, even as they cultivate the art of false prophecy to justify their swindling. Alas also, there are few signs that the evolution of the credit system and the clearly increasing power of the circulation of interest-bearing capital to dictate futures constitute a transitional stepping stone towards the emergence of some new mode of production. Indeed, the imaginary we are left with is of a horde of insatiably greedy investors possessed of deep enough pockets to buy off almost any serious opposition, force-feeding the rest of the world a diet of indigestible credit money.

Why would financiers celebrate the violent outbreaks of crises? At first blush this seems counter-intuitive. But when it comes to the circulation of anti-value then a crisis is indeed a moment of triumph for the forces of anti-value even as it visits despair upon all those engaged in the production and realisation of value. 'In a crisis,' said the banker Andrew Mellon way back in the 1920s, 'assets return to their rightful owners', i.e. him.[26] Crises typically leave in their wake a mass of devalued assets that can be picked up at fire-sale prices by those who have the cash (or privileged connections) to pay for them. This is what happened in 1997–8 in East and Southeast Asia. Perfectly viable firms went bankrupt for lack of liquidity, were bought out by foreign banks and then sold back a few years later at a huge profit.

In crises Marx typically evokes the possibility of (1) the physical *destruction* and degradation of use values, (2) the forced monetary *depreciation* of exchange values and (3) a concomitant *devaluation* of values as the only 'rational' way to overcome the irrationality of overaccumulation.[27] Notice the language here. Each of the forms involved – use value, exchange value and value – is subject to a specific form of negation and one form does not automatically imply the other. Devaluation and the depreciation of exchange values do not necessarily mean the physical destruction of the use values. The latter can become free goods for the revival of capitalist accumulation. This is one of the ways in which anti-value works to restore the conditions of value production. An underground system that went bankrupt (devaluing the underground and depreciating the investors' capital) left behind the use value of the tunnels that we still use when we travel the London Underground. The depreciation of housing values in the crisis of 2007–8 in the United States left behind a huge stock of housing use values that could be bought up by private equity companies and hedge funds for a song and put back into profitable use. Marx was fully aware of such possibilities. He notes how capital 'undertakes *investments* which do not pay and which pay only as soon as they have become in a certain degree *devalued* ... (and) the many undertakings where the first *investment* is sunk and lost, the first entrepreneurs go bankrupt – and begin to realize themselves only at second or third hand, where the investment capital has become smaller owing to *devaluation*'.[28] By the same token, a rapid appreciation of exchange values (e.g. in land and property markets) does not necessarily imply any increase in values and may not mean any substantial improvement in use values.

The dead weight of unproductive labour

The theory of anti-value has to embrace a whole range of activities which are not productive of value even though they are essential and necessary to the functioning of capital. This brings us to the fraught question of unproductive labour, which was discussed at great length by Adam Smith.

Marx agreed that workers employed in circulation (e.g. in marketing) do not produce value (otherwise he would have to concede that value could be produced by market exchange). They can, however, be a source of surplus value. They are like machines which cannot produce value but whose use can increase relative surplus value by lowering the costs of wage goods and so diminishing the value of labour power thereby producing more surplus value for the capitalist. Costs entailed in circulation and state administration, Marx argued, should be viewed as deductions out of value and surplus value production.[29] Costs of circulation in the market (other than those of transportation), no matter whether borne by the industrial or merchant capitalist, are considered as necessary deductions from potential value already produced. Economies in these circulation costs and reductions in circulation times amount, says Marx, to 'reducing the negation of created values'. But if less has to be deducted because of increasing the rate of exploitation of unproductive labour, then more surplus value is left over for the capitalist. Unproductive but socially necessary activities like bookkeeping, retailing and proper state regulation and law enforcement are not inherently anti-capitalist.

But if everyone tries to make a living by such means, while nobody engages in production, then capital would die out. Anti-value would prevail. The conclusion is obvious: excessive (as opposed to socially necessary) absorption of labour power in circulation (which does not produce value) along with hyper-bureaucratisation that produces no value (within corporations as well as in the state sector) is a threat to the reproduction of capital even without being explicitly anti-capitalist in form or intent. It is one of the accidental ways in which value in motion can gum up. Bloated costs and increasing inefficiencies of circulation, regulation and bureaucratic supports (including policing) can absorb vast amounts of value unproductively. If, as some conventional economists argue, far too much of the US economy is currently directed to 'busy but useless' activities then this acts as a drag upon value and surplus value production and circulation. Hence, some hypothesise, the 'great stagnation' of contemporary capitalism. It is standard fare in almost all right wing critiques of the state, that excessive regulation and bureaucratisation is the big enemy of market freedoms and hence of full-fledged capitalist development which supposedly benefits everyone. It was, of course, Marx's most signal accomplishment to show definitively in Volume 1 of *Capital* that totally unregulated free market capitalism would not benefit everyone but merely concentrate ever more wealth and power in the top 1 per cent. But the right wing critique has more than an element of truth in emphasising the deleterious effects upon value production and circulation of excessive resort to unproductive labour.

Economies and increasing efficiencies in the necessary costs of circulation are, therefore, crucial, Marx argued, if unproductive labour were not to become a major if unwitting locus of anti-value. One unsurprising result is that conditions of exploitation of living labour in these unproductive activities can be as vicious (and in some instances even more so) as in production.

The balance between socially necessary and excessive unproductive labour is hard to define. Much of the political debate about the regulatory environment is precisely caught up in trying to establish adequate norms. On this point Marx's discussion of the regulation of the length of the working day provides an interesting template.

Fierce inter-capitalist competition for absolute surplus value leads to such extensions of the working day and intensity of labour as to endanger the workers' life, health and ability to labour. It was, therefore, necessary, even from the standpoint of capital, to institute some collective forms of regulation, to put a floor under competition, as it were, so as to protect capital from the destructive effects on their labour force of ruinous competition. But if the organised power of labour in alliance with other interests became increasingly powerful so as to restrict the length of the working day even more dramatically, then this would constitute an anti-capitalist threat from the other direction. The adjudication between the rights of labour and the rights of capital over working hours depends on the balance of class forces: 'between equal rights, force decides'.[30] The balance between productive and unproductive labour in any capitalist social formation is likewise arrived at by the playing out of social and political processes and struggles.

The direct politics of anti-value

Anti-capitalist activities and politics, based in devising alternative ways of living outside of commodity production and exchange, are widespread, though often small scale. If, as Ollman insists, value *is* alienated labour, then the political quest for an unalienated existence entails the active and conscious negation of the capitalist law of value in individual and collective lives. There are various forms of anti-value politics. Solidarity economies and intentional communities, for example, may seek to ensure their own reproduction beyond the reach of value production.[31] Their exchange relations among themselves as well as with others will not necessarily be based on market mechanisms. Anarchist communes, religious-based communities and indigenous social orders constitute heterotopic spaces within the interstices of the capitalist system but outside of the rule of the law of value. There is always the danger that such non-value producing activities will either be appropriated by capital as a basis for value production (e.g. appropriated or taken as a free gift of human nature) or function as some kind of reserve for the reproduction of the industrial reserve army of increasingly redundant and disposable labourers.

Capital creates openings for oppositional politics as it circulates and expands. Through its mobilisation of the powers of art, science and technology, capital, despite itself, creates an opposition between the rule of value as socially necessary labour time on the one hand and disposable labour time or 'not labour time' on the other. It tends 'on the one side to create disposable time, on the other to convert it into surplus labour time. If it succeeds too well at the first, then it suffers from surplus production, and then necessary labour is interrupted, because no surplus labour can be realised by capital.'[32] The inability to realise value then becomes an insurmountable barrier. 'The more this contradiction develops, the more does it become evident that the growth of the forces of production can no longer be bound up with the appropriation of alien labour, but that the mass of the workers must themselves appropriate their own surplus labour.' This should allow 'the development of the power of social production such that ... disposable time will grow for all. For real wealth is the developed productive power of all individuals. The measure of wealth is then not any longer, in any way, labour time, but rather disposable time.'[33] The workers can recover that immeasurable sense of value that they lost in the original (fictional) wage labour contract with capital that condemned them to an alienated existence in which the valorisation of capital became their singular destiny.

Here we encounter some interesting political paradoxes. Much of the concern in recent critical commentaries has been to incorporate knowledge and science, unpaid household work and the 'free gifts' of nature into the value calculus. Are they not, after all, a source of value? Marx's answer is that they are analogous to the case of machines: they cannot be a source of value as capital defines it even as they are a source of relative surplus value for the capitalist class insofar as they contribute to the productivity of labour power. There currently is a widespread desire to incorporate the hitherto 'not valued' into the regime of capitalist value production and circulation. This strategy is understandable (partly because of the positive connotations that a term like value has and the understandable demand for recognition of what is all too often ignored). But it gets things entirely the wrong way round politically. It fails to understand the dialectical role of not- or anti-value (and of unalienated labour and disposable time) in oppositional politics. It is from the spaces of not-value and unalienated labour that a deep and widespread popular critique of the capitalist mode of production and its distinctive form of value and its alienations can be mounted. And it is from these sites too that the lineaments of a post-capitalist economy might best be identified. To be a producer of value and surplus value within a capitalist mode of production is, Marx noted, not a blessing but 'a misfortune'.[34]

Knowledge, information, cultural activities and the like can all be commodified and integrated into capitalism. At the same time their potential for unalienated and free activity forms a cutting edge for anti-capitalist politics. From this contradictory position cultural producers of all sorts form a significant potential block for radical political action. The search for an unalienated life among cultural producers in the face of the appropriation of their products by a parasitical rentier class is a growing point of tension. But for the most part their politics revolves around conditions of realisation even as their conditions of production are a contested terrain of capitalist control.

Likewise, the fact that household labour does not enter into the value calculus suggests this as another potential site for the articulation of an anti-capitalist politics (presuming that its own internal contradictions and alienations with respect to gender, patriarchy, sexuality and child-rearing practices and the like can be resolved). Even as more and more household labour activities become commodified and taken into the market (everything from take-out food to nails and hair cutting), labour time spent in the household increases in spite of (some would say because of) the advent of labour-saving household technologies (washing machines and robot vacuum cleaners). But the labour done for others within households and across the broader social solidarities configured around the production and protection of the commons, can become a powerful antidote to the dominance of capitalist commodity production and its associated social relations. Granting wages for housework (if it were realistic which fortunately it is not) simply reassures us that household labours can in principle be integrated into the capitalist mode of production (and accorded the status of alienated labour). The 'wages for housework' campaign launched by feminists in the 1970s was a brilliant intervention that focused attention on the gross neglect of gender questions in the Marxist tradition but was entirely wrong-headed (as some of its proponents later freely admitted) in the political remedies it proposed.[35] None of this would have occurred, I submit, had the relation between value and anti-value within a capitalist mode of production been more fully appreciated.

There have been parallel moves to integrate the free gifts of nature into the stream of value production by some arbitrary valuation devices (e.g. those proposed by environmental economists). This amounts to nothing more than a sophisticated green-washing and commodification of a space from which a fierce attack upon the hegemony of the capitalist mode of production and its (and our) alienated relation to nature through commodification can be mounted. These are all typical spaces from which an anti-capitalist critique can be fashioned. Yet the predominant political movement in recent times is for their integration into the value theory framework! If value under capitalism is about the production of alienated labour and the alienated labourer, then why on earth would anyone who is a progressive campaign to be subsumed within such a regime?

Devaluation, finally, can also hit the labourer as bearer of the commodity labour power. Wages are curtailed and the health and well-being of the labourer are threatened even as labourers retain their skills and labour capacities. During the effective nationalisation of General Motors in 2008, for example, a dual employment structure emerged in which the older workers maintained their wages and benefits while new workers were hired at much lower wages and with far weaker benefits. The devaluation of labour power and the depreciation of its values when prolonged or deepened can lead to physical destruction of the laboring population, even as capital usually falls far short of that for obvious reasons. But none of this passes by without eliciting some sort of political response from the labourers (both individual and collective).

The power of anti-value has to be confronted in relation to the value theory. If, as I suspect, this is 'the deeper antagonism' buried in the gut of capital circulating as value in motion, then making this contradiction legible is one important step towards confronting the debt peonage which increasingly seems enabled to dictate not only our contemporary social relations and well-being, but also our prospects for a future life. The fact that so many find it harder to envisage the end of capitalism than the end of the world has everything to do with the fact that the future of capital accumulation is foreclosed in a towering volume of debt as anti-value. For many, the only seeming hope is that some external intervention – an apocalyptic event of some sort – will save us. It will not. The only thing that can save us is an explicit winding down if not demolition of the tower of debt that dictates our future.

Anti-value signals the potential for breakdown in the continuity of capital circulation. It prefigures how capital's crisis tendencies can take different forms and move around from one moment (e.g. production) to another (e.g. realisation).[36] This insight is also crucial. Alas, it is often ignored. Crises do not, Marx tells us (contrary to much popular opinion), necessarily spell the end of capitalism but set the stage for its renewal. It is here that we see most clearly the dialectical role of anti-value in the reproduction of capital. 'Crises are never more than momentary, violent solutions for the existing contradictions, violent eruptions that re-establish the disturbed balance for the time being.'[37] But the reconstitution of capital is insecure and has limits. An accumulation of debts (claims on future value production) may outrun the capacity to produce and realise values and surplus values in the future. Even if the debts are successfully redeemed, the obligation to repay them forecloses on alternative futures. Debt peonage shackles the future for persons as well as for whole economies.[38] This is a theme to which we will return by way of conclusion.

5
Prices without Values

The qualitative incongruity between value and price is troubling and may be more significant than Marx allowed. The contradiction between them may have sharpened over time. If investors seek speculative gains in price-fixing markets for assets which have no value (such as art objects or currency and carbon futures) instead of investing in value and surplus value creation, then this indicates a pathway by which value can be leached out of the general circulation of capital to circulate as money in fictitious markets where no direct value production (as opposed to appropriation) occurs. When price signals betray the values they are supposed to represent then investors are bound to make erroneous decisions. If the money rate of profit is highest in property markets or other forms of asset speculation then a rational capitalist will place their money there rather than in the sphere of productive activity. The rational capitalist behaves irrationally from the standpoint of the reproduction process of capital as an evolving totality. The result could be a deepening tendency towards secular stagnation in the economy as a whole.

This may be counteracted by the fact that some use values enter into capitalist production as 'free gifts'. This occurs when the 'object of labour ... is something provided by nature free of charge, as in the case of metals, minerals, coal, stone, etc.'.[1] While capital rests materially on its metabolic relation with nature, this does not mean that nature in itself has value. It is a storehouse of free gifts that capital can use without paying anything. Such use values may, however, acquire a price if they are enclosed and become the private property of another. Their owner is then in a position to extract a money rent from these resources even though they have no value. The same applies to built environments, cleared and cultivated landscapes and cultural artefacts inherited from long ago. What is sometimes referred to as 'second nature' is also a treasure trove of free gifts to perform as use values in production.[2] Similar 'donations' of 'free goods' to capital can be extracted from the work of households, from the products of self-sufficient peasant and other non-commodity producing populations. 'While the maintenance and reproduction of the working class,' says Marx, 'remains a necessary condition for the reproduction of capital … the capitalist may safely leave this to the workers' drives for self-preservation and propagation.'[3] Even the self-learned skills of the labourers can be appropriated by capital free of charge. This is particularly the case with skills learned on the job and the storing of that knowledge in the brain of the worker. 'The socially productive power of labour develops as a free gift to capital whenever the workers are placed under certain conditions, and it is capital that places them under these conditions. Because this power costs capital nothing, while on the other hand it is not developed by the worker until his labour itself belongs to capital, it appears as a power which capital possesses by its nature …'[4] Experienced workers may, however, extract a monopoly rent for their skills if these skills are difficult to reproduce. Capital, as a result, wages a war against the reproduction of monopolisable skills in the labour force. The rapidly changing status of computer programmers in recent years – from skilled experts to routine workers – is a case in point.

These are not residual practices inherited from long ago. What workers learn by doing the job is an increasingly powerful feature of capital's political economy. But it is a power of labour that appears to be and is appropriated as a power of capital as a free good. Consider the sobering case of contemporary digital labour. Writes Michel Bauwens, founding member of the P2P Foundation: 'Under the regime of cognitive capitalism, use value creation expands exponentially, but exchange value only rises linearly, and is nearly exclusively realized by capital, giving rise to forms of hyper-exploitation … While in classic neoliberalism, labour income stagnates, in hyper-neoliberalism, society is deproletarianised, i.e. waged labour is increasingly replaced by isolated and mostly precarious freelancers; more use value escapes the labour form altogether' and 'the use value creators go totally unrewarded in terms of exchange value, which is solely realized by the proprietary platforms'.[5] The average hourly income of those actually doing the work 'does not exceed 2 dollars, which is way below the U.S. minimum wage'. The price form here conceals the 'hyper-exploitation' in what Bauwens considers to be a new 'neo-feudal' value regime that is even worse than traditional capitalism. This regime 'relies increasingly on unpaid "corvee" and creates widespread debt peonage'. This means a system of political economy based on the voluntary labour applied in commons-oriented peer production. What was initially conceived as a liberatory regime of collaborative production of an open access commons has been transformed into a regime of hyper-exploitation upon which capital freely feeds. The unrestrained pillage by big capital (like Amazon and Google) of the free goods produced by a self-skilled labour force has become a major feature of our times. This carries over into the so-called cultural industries. Inventive and creative work is mercilessly traded upon and plucked out by agents and cultural entrepreneurs and converted into profitable commerce. We need to look more closely at the position of this sort of labour in relation to value and surplus value creation and appropriation. This brings us to the question of the role of 'cognitive capitalism' in contemporary debates, which rests in turn on the question of the value productivity of creative activity and knowledge production.[6]

Consider how mental conceptions, knowledge and the imagination affect and relate to the circulation of capital. How do they relate to value and surplus value production? The theorists of cognitive capitalism make much of the idea that knowledge has become a form of value which circulates as capital. The economy used to be commodity-based and it is now knowledge-based, they say. Much of the knowledge produced these days certainly has a price given the rise of intellectual property rights as a crucial feature of contemporary capitalism. But the case for it as value that circulates is far-fetched and not established. Scientific and technical knowledge in particular is one of those items that can have a price but no value. It is built up bit by bit over many generations and should, according to Marx, be a free good, a gift of the cultural history of human nature, freely available to anyone who wants to use it. The fact that the knowledge commons is increasingly being enclosed, privatised and turned into a commodity tells us something about the contemporary trajectory of capitalism.

But the cognitive capitalists insist that this is the direction that Marx pointed to in the *Grundrisse*. In a much-cited passage he examines how products of 'the general intellect' affect the dynamics of accumulation. Marx focuses not on knowledge as a form of value but on how knowledge and mental capacities – the free gifts of human nature – get incorporated into the fixed capital of production of value so as to raise the productivity of labour to the point where labour, the agent of value production, becomes redundant (the turn to artificial intelligence in our own times is an example). This, Marx suggests, will render the labour theory of value redundant. The object of Marx's investigation is the fixed capital and not the knowledge *per se*.[7] All those knowledges that cannot be embedded in fixed capital are irrelevant. Marx is interested only in those forms of knowledge that can increase the productivity of labour. In this, management science is as important as genetic engineering and knowing how to build jet engines.

There is, however, a vital question as to how human imagination and creativity – free gifts of human nature – can be mobilised and appropriated to produce a technology or an organisational form as a commodity for sale in the market. 'What distinguishes the worst architect from the best of bees is this: that the architect builds the cell in his mind before he constructs it in wax.'[8] Ideas, knowledges and imagination, being free gifts of human nature, can perform as key use value inputs into the technologies of production. The positioning of human imagination in the labour process is significant. The human imagination, no matter how fertile or febrile, does not arise in a vacuum. The context of any new knowledge construction is always that of existing experiences and the diverse ways of understanding and interpreting that experience through language, concepts, narratives and pre-existing stories. The free gifts of human nature have a continuing vital role in defining what can be made and how it might be profitably produced. The long-standing critique of capital as a system in part focuses on the frustration of the creative potentialities of the mass of the population as capital takes control of not only what is being produced and how it shall be produced but goes on to appropriate the intellectual and cultural works of others as if they are its own. When the worst of architects is employed in a firm of architects selling plans and designs to capitalist developers or a research biologist works for Monsanto on isolating DNA sequences in plants that have been evolved over millennia in order to patent rights to cultivate those plants, then the human imagination is corralled and appropriated to the cause of surplus value production and appropriation. Marx extends this idea to the field of cultural production:

> Milton, who wrote *Paradise Lost*, was an unproductive worker. On the other hand, a writer who turns out work for his publisher in factory style is a productive worker. Milton produced *Paradise Lost* as a silkworm produces silk, as the activity of *his own* nature. He later sold his product for £5 and thus became a merchant. But the literary proletarian of Leipzig who produces books, such as compendia on political economy, at the behest of his publisher is pretty nearly a productive worker since his production is taken over by capital and only occurs in order to increase it. A singer who sings like a bird is an unproductive worker. If she sells her song for money, she is to that extent a wage labourer or merchant. But if the same singer is engaged by an entrepreneur who makes her sing to make money, then she becomes a productive worker, since she *produces* capital directly. A schoolmaster who instructs others is not a productive worker. But a schoolmaster who works for wages in an institution along with others, using his own labour to increase the money of the entrepreneur who owns the knowledge-mongering institution, is a productive worker.[9]

The definition of 'productive' here refers to the production of surplus value. Milton created no value when he wrote *Paradise Lost*. When he sold the exclusive right to someone else to use its content for £5 he expanded the sphere of monetary circulation without contributing to value production. The right to use the content has a price but no value. Such a commodity sale presupposes the existence of a legal system that enshrines exclusive intellectual property rights to content. Only when a publisher organised as a capitalist enterprise prints *Paradise Lost* in book commodity form does the possibility of value and surplus value production and realisation enter into the picture. The realisation of the value and surplus value congealed in the book as a commodity depends, however, on someone somewhere having the want, need and desire for such a book backed up by the ability to pay. But it is not any old book that is involved here, only a book with the unique and exclusive content of *Paradise Lost*. The uniqueness of this content can and often does allow for the possibility to charge a monopoly price and extract a monopoly rent, way above that warranted by the labour content of the book as a physical object. Furthermore, if the book is a first edition it may sell at an astronomical price as a collector's item.

It is this that often confuses the cognitive capitalists because it seems as if there is something about creative intellectual and cultural labour that makes its product exceptional and unique while the price seems to increase through the addition of something called 'reputational value', which has nothing to do with labour content.[10] On the other hand, no value or surplus value exists if the book lies gathering dust in a warehouse. Milton, therefore, created the condition of possibility for value production and the extraction of a monopoly rent when he wrote *Paradise Lost*, but it took several more steps before that condition of possibility could be realised through the circulation of capital.

The world is awash with writings awaiting a publisher. Putting a price upon them and circulating them in intellectual property markets would be potentially limitless. But this does not contribute to value and surplus value production. It merely heightens the contradiction between value and its monetary expression. In the process it further leaches value out of the circulation process of capital. The market for intellectual property rights and for collector's items can expand rapidly, with negative effects upon the production and accumulation of value. Cutting taxes on the ultra-rich may concentrate money power for investment. But if the rich prefer to invest in the art market (as is often the case) then this does nothing for value creation. Rising inequalities in income and wealth are in fact associated with secular stagnation in value production and ever-rising prices for Picassos.

Non-values (such as those generated in peer-to-peer computing) are converted gratis into use values for capital by a simple act of enclosure, commodification and appropriation. The degree to which value production rests on a basis of such free gifts varies, but is omnipresent in advanced capitalism.[11] It is not only the free gifts of nature that are involved. History, culture, knowledge, artistic constructions, skills and practices can all be enclosed, their content (like Milton's *Paradise Lost*) appropriated, commodified and traded at a price independently of any value they may ultimately engender. There is a lot of, for the most part, free and unalienated 'silkworm' labour that goes on in society, but as soon as the content is formed, then the enclosure, appropriation, monetisation and trading begins.

In the case of scientific and technical knowledge the free gifts of human creativity and of 'silkworm labour' enter into the circulation of capital in a different way. But Marx is only interested in the creations of what he called 'the general intellect' insofar as they affect the productivity of labour through the fixed capital formation.[12] His specific concern is with how technological and scientific knowledges become embedded in the fixed capital of production, so as to both displace and disempower labour through automation (and in our own times through robots and artificial intelligence). Scientific knowledge in itself Marx considers to be a free good.[13] If all else remains equal, then the displacement and disempowerment of labour from production through technological changes tends to shrink the contribution of labour, the active agent of value production. This invites us to consider what might happen when value and surplus value diminish or even disappear from circulation altogether even as the volume of physical commodities being cast into circulation rapidly increases because of rising productivity. The gap between the increasing physical production of commodities and their pricing and the decreasing social production of value and surplus value widens catastrophically, enunciating, in the view of many Marxists, the ineluctable path towards the final collapse of capitalism.

The German school of critical value theorists, inspired by the work of Robert Kurz, has been most vociferous in enunciating this view. But they do not argue that such a collapse is imminent.[14] Proponents of this theory (including Marx himself in some respects) see this contradiction as harbouring a long-run tendency towards stagnation, falling profits and the increasing constriction of value and surplus value production and realisation as a correlate of the persistent preference within capitalism towards labour-saving innovations.

One obvious antidote is to open up new lines of productive activity which are labour intensive to compensate for the loss of jobs in manufacturing and the more traditional sectors of value production. In recent times, for example, labour-intensive sectors such as logistics, transportation and food preparation (associated with a burgeoning tourist trade) have expanded significantly. Labour has increasingly been absorbed into everything from long-term infrastructural provisions to the staging of spectacles (that are almost instantaneously consumed so as to conform to the capitalist ideal of zero circulation time). Some of the labour released by the robotisation and automation of industrial jobs has been absorbed in these ways. The balance between job losses and job gains seems to be on a knife-edge although there is a rough consensus that the qualitative degradation of jobs underpins increasingly widespread alienation in workforces.

The other option is to increase the flow of free goods as inputs into capitalist production and to prevent the appropriation and extraction of monopoly rents from these flows. It is interesting that Marx thought a reduction in rents and taxes was one way to counteract falling profits.[15] It is also interesting that some of the most vigorous sectors of development in our times – like Google and Facebook and the rest of the digital labour sector – have grown very fast on the back of free labour. It is also significant that the so-called 'cultural industries', which draw heavily upon the unalienated and creative labour of the 'silkworm' sort, have expanded rapidly as fields of capitalist organisation and endeavour in recent years.

A lot of what goes on within capitalism is driven by activities in price-fixing markets that have nothing directly to do with value production except when use values are created which facilitate production of surplus value. This puts many activities and exchanges outside of the sphere of value production and circulation even as they are relevant to it as use value inputs. Tourism which trades upon free gifts of nature, of history, culture and natural spectacles as costless inputs which have no value is capitalistically organised and thereby produces value and surplus value. Some ambiguity arises because the preservation of and access to a commodified history, culture and even natural spectacle requires a labour of maintenance of qualities and of access. The mix of free gifts and of commodity values within a tourist package is intriguing. Such labour can also be capitalistically organised and hence contribute to value and surplus value production. This does not obviate the fact that many of the basic use value inputs into the production process of the tourist industry are free goods (e.g. sunny beaches or cultural heritage) which may acquire a money price even if they are of no value (unless they have been recently produced in the course of the invention of history, tradition and culture in the Disney mode). If historical and cultural artefacts do acquire a prior price then this is usually in the form of monopoly rent.[16] They can continue to be free goods only if they remain in the commons, unenclosed and not subject to appropriation as private property. Enclosure permits the prior appropriation of rent by owners before allowing access to the otherwise free goods of history, culture and nature. We experience the same thing when an entrance fee is required to enter a cathedral or view an ancient monument. While the fee may be justified as a cost of maintenance and access it can go way higher than that to furnish a basis for the extraction of a monopoly rent for the owner. In all of these sectors there are active and engaging struggles over what can remain in the commons and what might be enclosed to ensure the extraction of monopoly rents.

The treatment of the knowledge incorporated in production is in substance no different from that of the tourist industry's appropriation of history, culture and fantasy. Science and technological innovation can, as Marx recognised, become a business in its own right organised along capitalistic lines, even though scientific and technological knowledge in its own right, like history, culture and the land, is a part of the global commons, which in principle should be a free good. But in practice a price is exacted for access to much of it through patents, licences, intellectual property rights and the like.

The difference between formal and real subsumption of labour under capital is significant here.[17] Marx's purpose in introducing this distinction was to mark the transition between labour processes which remained under the control of the labourer versus labour processes designed and controlled by capital. Capitalism in the so-called manufacturing period typically made use of traditional artisanal skills and put them together through cooperation and divisions of labour into a production process such as building a coach. The main source of surplus value in such a system is absolute surplus value – the extension of labour time way beyond the socially necessary labour time required to reproduce labour power. Capital controls the product and its value but not the labour process. This contrasts with the factory system in which capital controls the labour process even to the point of subjecting the activities of the labourer to an external source of power under the command of capital. Relative surplus value, derived from rising productivity in the production of wage goods (the commodities required to reproduce labour power), here becomes dominant. While absolute surplus value remains the basis, relative surplus value production, which often rests on the privileged understandings derived from science and technology, becomes the driving force in the evolution of capital. But this is not always the case. In the case of digital labour, for example, labour practices have emerged that are uncannily similar to the putting out system of early textile manufacturing in Britain in the late eighteenth century. Putting out systems also characterised industrial structures in Paris throughout much of the nineteenth century. Zola's *L'Assomoir* provides a stunning example of such a labour system at work in nineteenth century Paris. For many years the success of the Japanese car industry rested on the basis of subcontracting to small workshops for the production of many of its parts. The formal–real distinction, like the absolute–relative distinction, is more dialectical than teleological in its application.

With such a yawning and ever increasing gap between value and its monetary form of representation, it is tempting to see the latter as the essence of what capital is about and to redefine capital as money in motion rather than value in motion. Such a redefinition facilitates concentration on the churning speculative market in property rights to culture, knowledge and entrepreneurial endeavours as well as to the widespread practices of speculation in asset markets as the distinctive form of contemporary capitalism. Hence the claim that we are entering a new phase of capitalism in which knowledge is pre-eminent and that a brilliant techno-utopia based on that knowledge and all its labour-saving innovations (such as automation and artificial intelligence) is just around the corner or, as someone like Paul Mason maintains, already here.[18] Such a redefinition may look about right from the perspective of Silicon Valley,[19] but it falls flat on its face in the collapsing factories of Bangladesh and the suicide-ridden employment zones of both industrial Shenzhen and rural India where microfinance has spread its net to foster the mother of all sub-prime lending crises. The churning and speculative profiteering that has characterised many asset markets in recent times (particularly with respect to housing, land and property) has undoubtedly redistributed values. But it does not in itself support any increase in value creation lest it be through the conversion of at least some of the monetary gains back into capital to seek valorisation or through the generation of effective demand sufficient to facilitate realisation.

We here encounter a second 'Great Contradiction' with which capital is confronted. The first arose out of the search for relative surplus value which concentrates on labour-saving technological changes which, if they succeed, diminish the labour force from which value and surplus value has to be extracted. The second is a potential tendency for capital in searching to maximise its monetary profit to be drawn to invest in areas that produce no value or surplus value at all. Taken to extremes, either of these tendencies could be fatal to the reproduction of capital. In combination, and the contemporary evidence is that both trends are discernible, they could be catastrophic.

The typical neoclassical response to all of this (as well as that of some working in the Marxist tradition) is to say that if it is the monetary aspects of all of this and pricing politics that are becoming hegemonic, then why bother with values at all (which is the neoclassical position) or why not evolve a monetary theory of value (as some Marxists currently propose) as the only feasible response to the theoretical dilemmas we are here encountering).[20] In so doing they cut off any possibility of explaining the secular stagnation that seems to be the prevailing condition of contemporary global capitalism and lose track of the importance of anti-value to value circulation. Such a move may permit both the revisionist Marxists and the neoclassical economists to take the reassuring and comforting position that all will be well with global capitalism once it has settled back into the equilibrium conditions dictated by perfectly functioning and properly regulated price-fixing markets. The same is true for those Marxists who either explicitly embrace a monetary theory of capital (such that capital is defined not as 'value in motion' but as 'money in motion' or, even more vulgarly, that capital is nothing more than money being used to make more money by whatever means possible). To ignore the money-value contradiction altogether is to cut off an important, though admittedly complicated avenue to understand the dilemmas of contemporary capital accumulation. It is only from the latter perspective that a critique can be offered to analyses which increasingly rely on sophisticated dissection of big data sets, failing to recognise that most of the empirical data are money measures which can and do diverge from if not betray the immaterial social relation they are supposed to represent. And this is so even without introducing the problems of how money is created and appropriated in the course of the movement of value through the fields of distribution. When the Federal Reserve and the European Central Bank engage in quantitative easing they create money in the absence of value. When that money circulates as interest-bearing capital it functions as the anti-value that must be and supposedly will be redeemed by future value and surplus value production. But when the money released circulates into asset markets like property, the stock market and the art market then the anti-value is not redeemed even as the ultra-rich get even wealthier from their speculations. A strong incentive then exists to create even more anti-value to redeem that issued earlier. The result is not only secular stagnation in value production but the creation of a Ponzi capitalism which is the dangerous path of endless monetary expansion we have recently been taking. If we accept a purely monetary theory of capital, then it becomes much harder to formulate the trenchant critiques of contemporary capitalism that Kurz and his colleagues have articulated. We lose the power to unravel the contradiction as to how the increasing concentration of monetary wealth necessarily occurs at the expense of the rest of humanity whose wants, needs and desires are not backed by an ability to pay. The wants, needs and desires of the mass of the population remain unfulfilled while the rich expand their taste for Picassos.

6

The Question of Technology

The question of technology is foundational for understanding the dynamics of capital in motion. Marx is one of the most incisive and prescient commentators on this topic. This is not to say his analyses are complete or can pass unchallenged. Technology in combination with science is a major focus throughout Volume 1 of *Capital* but is held constant in Volume 2. In Volume 3 he deals with some of the consequences of technological change for profits and rents along with occasional comments on certain technological and organisational features of financial intermediation and monetary circulation. Marx's main focus in *Capital* is on the role of technology and science in relation to the valorisation of capital and the production of commodities. In the *Grundrisse* he adopts a more expansive stance and provides intense, sometimes speculative and prescient commentaries on technological issues. But there is nothing substantial in his works about the technologies of realisation and circulation (apart from transport) or of social reproduction (including the reproduction of labour power) and the technologies of distribution are not systematically scrutinised either. The upshot is a rather one-sided view of technological and organisational change.

But Marx had good reason to take this position. Technical and organisational changes occur in the history of human societies all over the place and for all sorts of reasons affecting all sorts of activities. It sometimes seems that the technical and organisational ingenuity of human beings knows no bounds. Some of the new techniques and organisational forms last and some of them do not. Ancient China had a long history of remarkable technical and organisational innovations none of which were widely adopted or lasted. Only under capitalism do we find a systematic and powerful force for technological and organisational dynamism that is sustained and cumulative in its effects. This force, Marx believes, is concentrated at the moment of valorisation for very particular reasons. It is shaped by the perpetual search under capitalism for relative surplus value.[1]

Capitalists in competition with each other sell their commodities at a social average price. Those that have a superior technology or organisational form in production gain excess profits (relative surplus values) because they produce at a lower individual cost of production and sell at the social average. Conversely, those with inferior technology or organisational form attain lower profits or losses and are either driven out of business or are forced to adopt the new methods. The advantaged producers have an incentive to adopt even better methods to preserve their market share and their excess profits. The fiercer the competition the more leapfrogging innovations are likely to occur as one firm jumps ahead and others catch up or go even beyond the technological mix and the organisational form that reflect the social average. The forces shaping the labour process at the point of valorisation push incessantly towards raising the productivity of labour power. As the productivity of labour rises so the value of individual commodities falls. If wage goods become cheaper then the value of labour power (assuming a fixed physical standard of living) declines, leaving more surplus value for capital. All capitalists stand to gain higher profits (more relative surplus value) from rising labour productivity in the production of wage goods. Increasing relative surplus value sometimes goes hand in hand with a rising physical standard of living of labour. It all depends on the strength of productivity gains and how the benefits from increasing productivity are distributed between capital and labour. A small part of the relative surplus value is turned back to labour so they can acquire more use values, while most of it goes to capital. This depends on the state of class struggle (unions often negotiate productivity sharing clauses in contracts). The drive to produce relative surplus value underpins the incessant pressure towards technological and organisational changes in production.

For the capitalists, machines seem to be what they truly are: a source of extra surplus value. Capitalists infer from this that machines are a source of value. Marx argues that this cannot possibly be so. Machines are dead or constant capital and as such they cannot produce anything by themselves. Part of the value of the machine passes into the value of the commodity but it does so as constant capital (i.e. capital that does not change its value through use). Living labour (and not past labour) is the only source of surplus value. Machines merely assist to raise the productivity of labour power such that the total value remains the same while the value of individual commodities falls. The result is a paradox. Machines when combined with labour produce more surplus value for the capitalist even when the value produced remains constant. Most capitalists (in line with popular opinion) believe that machines produce value and they tend to act upon that belief. Marx considers this a fetish view. The fetishism of technology is widespread and this has important consequences. It leads, for example, to the widespread belief that there must be a technological solution to any social or economic problem.

The presumption in this argument is that competition is well established and fierce. But what happens if this is not the case? Capitalists, after all, prefer monopoly or oligopoly to what they often dub 'ruinous' competition. The driving force behind technological dynamism is attenuated by monopoly power. But it is displaced rather than destroyed. The social form of relative surplus value that derives from the reduction in the value of labour power via the reduction in the value of wage goods remains. This is sometimes accomplished by political means.

Marx provides an example of how this works. In the nineteenth century, British industrial interests saw wage levels tied to the price of bread. They campaigned (in alliance with workers) against the agricultural interests of the landed aristocracy to abolish the tariffs on imported wheat in order to bring down the price of bread. The industrialists' aim was not to raise the standard of living of labour (though they often claimed it was in order to get the workers' support) but to reduce wages and increase their relative surplus value (monetary profits). They preached the gospel of free trade as long as it was advantageous for them to do so.[2] The contemporary situation in the United States is similar. If the value of labour power is fixed by the price of, say, Nike shoes and Gap shirts, then free trade in these items is a convenient gospel to espouse for capital in general. Walmart's cheap prices on foreign imports allow for the reduction of the value of labour power and a rising rate of profit for all capitalists in the United States. The problem is that those manufacturing and working-class interests within the United States that want to make shirts and shoes lose out to all those other sectors of capital that relish cheap labour clothed, fed and entertained by cheap imports.

But there are other incentives to adopt new technologies apart from those deriving from ruinous competition. Many innovations are designed to disempower the labourer both in the market place as well as within the labour process. Technologies that displace skilled labour and the monopoly power that some skills confer with de-skilled job structures (of the sort that can be performed by women and children – or, as the time and motion study expert Frederick Taylor put it, by 'a trained gorilla') are a crucial weapon in the class struggle. 'But machinery does not just act as a superior competitor to the worker, always on the point of making him superfluous. It is a power inimical to him, and capital proclaims this fact loudly and deliberately, as well as making use of it. It is the most powerful weapon for suppressing strikes, those periodic revolts of the working class against the autocracy of capital.'[3] The creation of an industrial reserve army of unemployed labourers by way of technologically induced unemployment places an emphasis upon technological adaptations that are labour-saving. Innovations that improve efficiency and coordination, or accelerate turnover times in both production and circulation, yield more surplus values for capital. The necessity for the expansion of production to accommodate endless accumulation of capital creates a strong incentive to broaden the market for existing goods by reducing their price of production or the creation of wholly new product lines and industrial sectors (such as electronics over the last few decades). Product innovation and new technologies go hand in hand. These incentives exist even under conditions of monopoly and oligopoly. But they are all concentrated, for the most part, at the point of valorisation. The aggregate result is to assure the continuous and perpetually revolutionary dynamic of technological and organisational change under capitalism no matter what the balance is between competition and monopoly power. Whenever the attenuation of competition produces stagnation then the revitalisation of competition becomes a priority even as an objective of public policy. The problems of 'stagflation' in the core regions of capitalism in the 1970s were partially addressed by the opening up of world trade to a globalised structure of competition.

Marx's analysis of technological change may be narrowly concentrated on the forces affecting the productivity of labour power in the process of valorisation, but he takes a broad approach to the question of the means deployed. He recognises, for example, the importance of software and organisational form in addition to the hardware of machines. Computers and mobile phones need the programs and the apps to be effective as well as the communication networks. Find yourself somewhere with no signal and all the sophistication available to you on your mobile phone is for naught. The evolution of organisational forms (such as the modern capitalist corporation, communication networks and the research institutes and universities) has been just as important as the development of the hardware (the computer and the engineered assembly line) and the software (programmed design, facilitative apps, optimal scheduling and just-in-time management systems). While the hardware/software/organisational form distinctions are useful and important, we must learn to recognise each as an internal relation of the other. It is possible to write about the evolution of car design in itself, of course, but to do so as if Henry Ford's innovations with the assembly line played no role in the subsequent evolution of the industry is plainly to lose something vital to the story. It would be like the history of the computer without mention of Microsoft and the social and political consequences of the internet.

Circumscribed though it may be in focus, Marx's analysis of technology is interwoven with a broad approach to its role in capital's evolutionary trajectory. 'Technology,' Marx writes in a key footnote in *Capital*, 'discloses man's mode of dealing with Nature, and the process of production by which he sustains his life, and thereby also lays bare the mode of formation of his social relations, and of the mental conceptions that flow from them.'[4] 'Disclosing' and 'laying bare' do not denote 'determine.'

Marx was not a 'technological determinist'. The widespread view, common to many detractors and supporters of Marx alike, that he considered transformations in the productive forces as the prime motor of historical change, is incorrect. Certainly, the contradictory relations between technological dynamism and the social relations of capitalism have had an important and often destabilising role to play in capital's history but it has not been the only contradiction at work within that history.[5] Likewise, all history may be the history of class struggle but it is far from being only that. Many of Marx's one-liners on topics of this sort are misleading. They should always be checked against his substantive work to figure out if or how they might make sense. Why, for example, did he write Volume 2 of *Capital* under the assumption of zero technological change and make no mention whatsoever of class struggle? Surely the content of Volume 2 is relevant to capital's evolution? The grand contest as to whether the productive forces or social relations should be viewed as the prime mover of capitalist development misses the point. It fails to situate Marx's study of technology in the context of the totality of relations that constitute a capitalist social formation. It also assumes, for no good reason, that there must be a prime mover.

In Volume 1 of *Capital* Marx invites us to consider how all the different 'moments' listed above (to which I have added institutional arrangements of the sort described in the second chapter of Volume 1 of *Capital* for the sake of completeness) interact and relate. Our mental conceptions depend, for example, upon our ability to see, to measure, to calibrate and we now have telescopes and microscopes, X-rays and CAT scanners and the like to help us understand how the cosmos and the human body work. But then consider why it was that someone somewhere imagined something like a telescope or a microscope and who then found lens grinders and metal workers to make one as well as patrons to use them (often in the face of antagonism and opposition). The result has been the development of new ways of seeing, of new conceptions of the world of nature and of our place in it by way of these new instruments. As the poet William Blake once put it: 'What now is proved was once only imagin'd.'

All of the seven moments – technologies, the relation to nature, social relations, mode of material production, daily life, mental conceptions and institutional frameworks – relate within the totality of capitalism in a process of continuous evolution powered by the continuous circulation of capital that functions, as it were, as the engine of the totality. Developments across all seven moments, each of which is autonomous and independent but overlapping and relationally bound to the others, can move the totality in one direction or another. By the same token, recalcitrance or immovability around any one moment can stymie transformations in processes occurring elsewhere. Technological innovations in the money form lead nowhere, as we earlier saw, without at the very minimum parallel transformations in social relations, mental conceptions and institutional arrangements. New technologies (like the internet and social media) promise a utopian socialist future but get co-opted by capital into new forms and modes of exploitation and accumulation in the absence of other forms of action. But by the same token, autonomous changes on the part of one moment may impel dramatic changes everywhere else. The sudden emergence of new pathogens like HIV/AIDS, the Ebola virus or Zika requires rapid adaptation across all seven moments if they are to be controlled. The difficulty of organising to deal with climate change is that it will require drastic shifts across all seven moments. The fact that some people either deny the problem (mental conceptions) or naively believe that there is a single bullet technological solution (green capitalism) that can be implemented without changing anything else (like dominant social relations and daily life) dooms initiatives to failure.

Most work in the social sciences favours some 'single bullet' theory of social change. Institutionalists favour institutional innovations, economic determinists favour new technologies of production, socialists and anarchists favour class struggle, idealists highlight changing mental conceptions, cultural theorists focus on transformations in daily life, and so on. Marx cannot and must not be read as a single bullet theorist, even though there are many representations of his work that view him so. Volume 1 of *Capital* in particular cannot be parsed that way, even though there is tremendous emphasis in the text on the impacts of technological adaptations and dynamism. In Marx's substantive work, there is no prime mover, but a mess of often contradictory movements across and between the different moments that have to be uncovered and worked out.

This does not mean that in certain places and times one or other of these seven moments does not take a leading role in disrupting existing configurations or in stubbornly resisting change. So when we speak of technological revolutions, cultural revolutions, political revolutions, the information revolution or revolutions in mental conceptions, along with counter-revolutions in any or all of these fields, then we are acknowledging the contingent way that the history of capital as a whole typically unfolds across and through the different moments. Marx hoped, of course, for some kind of socialist or communist revolution (and at various points took a somewhat teleological view of the inevitable progression towards communism). But he was never able to specify what configuration of these seven moments might bring about such changes. The failure of Soviet communism can largely be attributed to the way the interaction between all seven moments was ignored in favour of a single bullet theory of the proper path to communism by way of revolutions in the productive forces.

In his more detailed historical studies as well as in *Capital*, Marx illustrates the contingency of it all. What constitutes a revolution is not a political movement or a disruptive event like the storming of the Winter Palace. Revolution is an ongoing process of movements across the different moments. Capital is innately revolutionary, according to Marx, because it is value in motion under conditions of continuous growth and technological innovation. Perpetual transformations in the technology of valorisation have reverberations everywhere else. But the neoliberal revolution was as much a revolution in popular mental conceptions as it was an institutional and technological revolution.[6] Conscious revolutionary change, by way of contrast, entails a redefinition and redirection of existing movements across all moments. People may change their mental conceptions, but this means nothing if they are not prepared to change their social relations, their daily lives, their relation to nature, their mode of production and their institutional structures.

But if organisational forms and modalities of operation are just as important as the hardware and software, and if the embedding of social relations and of knowledge, skills and *mentalités* in hardware forms is ineluctable, then the whole issue of the meaning and impact of technology upon social life and our relation to nature along with our social relations becomes much more complicated and diffuse. This, it seems to me, is the full import of Marx's commentary in the key footnote to chapter 15 of Volume 1. Ruling out the certitudes that attach to a narrow reductionism (technological in the hardware sense in this case) has the disadvantage, however, of confronting a world in which everything relates to everything else. Hence the longing, which must be resisted, to designate a prime mover. Hence, also, the tendency to fetishise technological change as not only a prime mover but also as an answer to every ill.

Since all of this is a somewhat different view of Marx's work than that which is commonly propagated by both Marxists and Marx critics alike, I need briefly to provide the evidence for it. This is best represented by the structure and argument of Volume 1 of *Capital*. Capital could not arise without certain pre-existing conditions already being in place. Commodity exchange, an appropriate monetary system, a working labour market, minimal institutional arrangements (such as juridical individuals, law and private property) and a consumer market to absorb the commodities produced were all minimal prior requirements (see Figure 2, page 6). So also was a certain level of productivity and skill of the labourer along with the availability of certain basic means of production (such as land, tools and other instruments of labour along with physical infrastructures such as transportation). Marx recognised that the initial productivity of labour depended on natural conditions (fertility and the free gifts of nature such as waterfalls, mineral resources, biological processes of growth and reproduction of plants and animals and the like) as well as upon cultural histories and achievements (the accumulation of skills, knowledges, mental conceptions, customary social relations, time discipline, etc.) of different peoples. The free gifts of nature and of the cultural history of human nature are the basis for capital accumulation to begin in earnest. Such free gifts continue to be of great importance even as capital increasingly seeks to enclose and privatise them and to extract rents from them (by imposing a price upon knowledge that has no value, for example).

Read Volume I of *Capital* carefully and you will see how frequently Marx reverts to reiterating all of these points. In Part 8 of Volume 1, Marx describes how many of these preconditions were constructed through processes of primitive accumulation. The key to capital itself lies, however, in the transformation from the making of products (some of which may be exchanged in a market) to the production of surplus value through the systematic production of commodities for market. The latter is the exclusive aim of the direct producers. Such producers are defined as capitalists.

Capital takes over existing conditions and processes as it finds them and turns them into something specially tailored to the requirements of a capitalist mode of production. And so it is with techniques. It takes over ancient capacities for cooperation (as exhibited in the construction of the Egyptian pyramids) and pulls them together in an organisational form suited to the reproduction of a capitalist class seeking to reap all the productivity gains from cooperation and increasing economies of scale for itself. In so doing it transforms the social relations between capital and labour (with foremen and administrators in between) within the labour process (see chapter 13 of Volume 1). It likewise takes over the divisions of labour that pre-exist and separates them into planned divisions of labour within the capitalist form and divisions of labour in society coordinated through market signals. It creates new hierarchies within the labour process and subjects both capital and labour to the discipline of capital in production and the indiscipline of anarchic market processes (see chapter 14 of Volume 1). It radicalises ancient techniques largely by transformations in the scale of production and the intricacy of the different trades brought together under the command of capital. It subdivides existing divisions of labour into ever finer-grained specialised divisions forming parts of a much larger whole. Finally, it arrives at a point where capital needs to control the labour process itself through the creation of the factory system. Marx characterises this as the move from a formal (coordinations through market mechanisms) to a real (under the direct supervision of capital) subsumption of labour under capital.[7] Technology is organised on a purely capitalist basis by locating an energy source outside and beyond that of the manual strength of the labourer. The highpoint comes with the production of machines by way of machines (an astonishing insight on Marx's part which is only now being fully worked out with the advent of artificial intelligence). Notice that the construction of productive forces suited to a capitalist mode of production comes at the end of this sequence so it is very hard to see how productive forces can be the driving force of historical transformation given the narrative that Marx constructs.[8] They are in fact the historical result. It would be typical of Marx to then argue that what is at one stage a result can at a later point become a primary driving agent (which is probably more true of technology and organisational form now than it was in the eighteenth century).

But in the process of studying these transitions Marx carefully depicts the other transformations that must occur for this revolutionary movement to be successfully completed. He argues, for example, that production which was once regarded as an art full of mysteries to be learned by apprenticeship must become a science which, when combined with capitalist control of the labour process, actually defines technology as a distinctive sphere of action specific to capital.[9] Pre-capitalist societies had techne, but capitalism has a technology that cannot abide mysteries, that scientifically dissects nature in order to exercise control. This required a change in mentalities not only towards production itself but also with respect to nature, which has to be construed as a dead object (rather than fecund and alive) open to human domination and manipulation (Marx cites Descartes on this point).[10] Meanwhile, the labourer becomes a 'fragment of a man' locked into a particular function within the division of labour under the domination of the machine rather than a whole person in command of his or her own labour process.[11] The organisational form of the factory and the factory system is a radical departure, as we have seen, from artisan production. The destruction of the latter and its transformation into factory labour changes the nature of social relations as does the employment of women and children and the reconfiguration of family life and labour within the working classes. A new and higher form of the family comes into being.[12] The flexibility and fluidity demanded of the labourer mandates that 'that monstrosity, the disposable working population held in reserve, in misery, for the changing requirements of capitalist exploitation, must be replaced by the individual man who is absolutely available for the different kind of labour required of him: the partially developed individual, who is merely the bearer of one specialised social function, must be replaced by the totally developed individual, for whom the different social functions are different modes of activity he takes up in turn'.[13] State regulation becomes important with respect to the working day and the factory acts, while the state also mandates compulsory education to ensure a workforce that is literate and readily adaptable to the changing needs of capital's evolving labour processes. All of these shifts are mentioned in chapter 15 of Volume 1.

Marx also notes how:

> the transformation of the mode of production in one sphere of industry necessitates a similar transformation in other spheres ... Thus machine spinning made machine weaving necessary, and both together made a mechanical and chemical revolution compulsory in bleaching, printing and dying. So too on the other hand, the revolution in cotton-spinning called forth the invention of the cotton gin ... it was only by means of this invention that the production of cotton became possible on the enormous scale at present required. But as well as this, the revolution in the modes of production of industry and agriculture made necessary a revolution in the general condition of the social process of production, i.e. in the means of communication and transport ... (which) gradually adapted themselves to the mode of production of large scale industry by means of a system of river steamers, railways, ocean steamers and telegraphs.[14]

At some point, however, large scale industry 'had to take over the machine itself, its own characteristic instrument of production, and to produce machines by way of machines. It was not till it did this that it could create for itself an adequate technical foundation, and stand on its own feet.'[15] This is the one point in *Capital* where Marx tracks externality effects by way of which what he called the 'industrial revolution' was secured and completed.

Finally, and perhaps most important of all, technology itself becomes a business.[16] With the invention of the steam engine an innovation came on line that had multiple applications within the fields of transportation, mining, ploughing, milling, to say nothing of factories with power looms. The analogy with computers which have innumerable applications in our own time is exact. Once technology becomes a business then it produces a commodity – new technologies or organisational forms – that need to find and even create a new market.

We no longer deal with the individual entrepreneur trying to figure out how to improve productivity by inventing and innovating on his or her own in a particular production establishment, but a vast sector of industry specialising in innovation and dedicated to selling innovations to everyone else (as both producers and consumers). The corner grocer or hardware store is cajoled, persuaded and eventually forced (by the tax authorities) to adopt some sophisticated business machine in order to manage inventory and keep track of sales, purchases and taxes. The cost burden of such a technology may drive small stores out of business in favour of the supermarkets and discount centres, thereby favouring the increasing centralisation of capital. The adoption of many of these innovations depends on their capacity to discipline and disempower labour, to raise the productivity of labour and to increase the efficiency and speed of turnover of capital in both production and circulation. Capitalism as a whole becomes, as a result, infatuated with technological change and the certainty of economic progress. The fetish belief in technological fixes and innovations as the answer to all problems takes deeper root as does the false idea that this must be the prime mover. This fetish belief is nurtured by that segment of capital that transforms innovation and technology into a big business with consultants on organisational form peddling recipes for better management, pharmaceutical companies creating remedies for diseases that do not exist, and computer experts insisting on automation systems that no one except a few experts can understand. Capitalist entrepreneurs and corporations adopt innovations not because they want to but because they are persuaded to or have to in order to acquire or retain their market share and thereby ensure their reproduction as capitalists.

One does not have to accept Marx's conceptual apparatus to see the cogency of his arguments concerning the origins of technological fetishism. The fetishism is not purely imaginary and has a very real basis. It appears as if productivity is the be-all and end-all of capitalist growth and stability and that the profit rate is crucially determined by it. When Alan Greenspan gives evidence in which the question of productivity gains is placed as central to the dynamics of US capitalism he is not engaging in fictitious ramblings. The danger, as we now see in the recent turmoil in capital markets, is in attributing to productivity gains a role which they simply cannot fulfil. Productivity gains have helped produce the current malaise of instability and volatility. Lags in productivity likewise produce serious problems for the spiral of endless accumulation.[17] It would be entirely wrong (and fetishistic), therefore, to look for a technological fix to the present dilemmas of economic instability. The answer almost certainly will have to be found in a transformation of social and political relations as well as in mental conceptions, production systems and all the other moments in the evolutionary process in combination with those technological and organisational changes that are appropriate for given social ends.

This does not mean that the overall thrust of technological evolution is arbitrary and directionless. The fetishistic belief in technological fixes supports the naturalistic view that technological progress is both inevitable and good, and that there is no way we can or even should try to collectively control, redirect, let alone limit it. But it is precisely in the character of fetish constructs to open up social action to mythical beliefs. While these beliefs may have a material grounding they quickly escape material constraints only to have, once applied, marked material consequences.

Consider, for example, control over the labour process which has always been central to valorisation. The fantasy that the worker can be made over into a mere appendage of the circulation of capital takes root in this process. Many industrial innovators have had this as their primary goal. A French industrialist renowned for his innovations in the machine tools industry openly proclaimed that his three goals were increasing precision, increasing productivity and the disempowerment of the worker.[18] The factory system, Taylorism, automation, robotisation and the ultimate displacement of living labour altogether through artificial intelligence (AI) respond to this desire. Robots do not (except in science fiction accounts) complain, answer back, sue, get sick, go slow, lose concentration, go on strike, demand more wages, worry about work conditions, want tea breaks or simply fail to show up.[19] The fetish fantasy of total control over the labourer and the ultimate displacement of the labourer via technology has its roots in the imperative to increase productivity by whatever means possible.

In the labour market, technologically induced unemployment weakens the bargaining power of labour. De-skilling and homogenisation of labour processes eliminate the monopoly powers that derive from non-replicable labour skills. John Stuart Mill considered it 'questionable if all the mechanical inventions yet made have lightened the day's toil of any human being'. That this was so was obvious, Marx argued, because the purpose of machinery is to extract more profit from labour and not to lighten the load of labour.[20] Occasionally it is recognised that this fantasy of total control over labour power via machine technology is seriously wanting, so capitalists then turn to organisational forms of cooperation, collaboration, responsible autonomy, quality circles, flexible specialisation and the like. Capital can take over any organisational form labourers themselves might propose and shape it to their own purpose which is the production of surplus value. The dream becomes a nightmare. Frankenstein is unleashed, HAL the computer in *2001: a Space Odyssey* assumes a volition of his own, the replicants in *Blade Runner* seek power and perpetuation in their own right. The dark powers of anti-value emerge from the shadows to challenge labour controls.

If living labour is the source of value and profit then replacing it with dead labour or robotic labour makes no sense either politically or economically. This, in Marx's view, was one of the central contradictions of capitalism. It undermined the capacity of capitalism to keep on a balanced growth path. But it also produces the unintended consequences that Marx spells out in the *Grundrisse*:

> To the degree that large industry develops, the creation of real wealth comes to depend less on labour time and on the amount of labour employed than on the power of the agencies set in motion during labour time, whose powerful effectiveness is itself in turn out of all proportion to the direct labour time spent on

their production, but depends rather on the general state of science and the progress of technology, or the application of science to production. (The development of this science, especially natural science, is itself in turn related to the development of material production) ... (The worker) inserts the process of nature, transformed into an industrial process, as a means between himself and inorganic nature, mastering it. He steps to the side of the production process instead of being its chief actor. In this transformation, it is neither the direct human labour he himself performs, nor the time during which he works, but rather the appropriation of his own general productive power, his understanding of nature and his mastery over it by virtue of his presence as a social body – it is, in a word, the development of the social individual which appears as the great foundation-stone of production and of wealth. The theft of alien labour time on which the present wealth is based, appears a miserable foundation in face of this new one, created by large scale industry itself. As soon as labour in the direct form has ceased to be the well-spring of wealth, labour time ceases and must cease to be its measure, and hence exchange value (must cease to be the measure) of use value. The surplus labour of the mass has ceased to be the condition for the development of general wealth, just as the non-labour of the few, for the development of the general powers of the human head. With that, production based on exchange value breaks down ... Capital itself is the moving contradiction, (in) that it presses to reduce labour time to a minimum, while it posits labour time, on the other side, as the sole measure and source of wealth ... On the one side, then, it calls to life all the powers of science and of nature, as of social combination and social intercourse, in order to make the creation of wealth independent (relatively) of the labour time employed on it. On the other side, it wants to use labour time as the measuring rod for the giant social forces thereby created, and to confine them within the limits required to maintain the already created value as value ...[21]

This has been highlighted as a central contradiction in the evolution of capital and one that has far-reaching consequences.

Once technology became a business it did what every business tries to do which is to extend its reach, build new markets and attract investment of interest-bearing capital to sustain and enhance its position as a thriving sphere of value and surplus value creation within the overall division of labour. When Marx was writing, this business was in its incipient, formative stages. But he clearly recognised that the machine tool and mechanical engineering industries (with the steam engine its prime exhibit) were destined to play a powerful role within the technology sector through the creation of generic technologies. But Marx, concentrated as he was in Volume 1 of *Capital* on the valorisation process, did not probe very deeply into the new technologies and organisational forms evolving around realisation and consumption, around social reproduction (including the reproduction of labour power). The technologies now at work in an average household in the United States are far beyond anything that Marx could have imagined. Nor did Marx investigate in any detail the complicated arenas of distribution (though he did acknowledge the importance of forms of industrial organisation such as the joint stock company and innovations in the world of banking and finance along with the flourishing sphere of anti-value creation within the credit system). Marx had very little to say about the rapid transformations occurring in the field of physical infrastructures though, of course, the canals, steamships, railways, telegraphs and gas lighting along with improved water supplies and sewage disposal all rated a mention. The technologies of state administration, public health and education, and military innovation barely register. The last of these has long been a major centre of innovation with respect to the design of new products and new modes of organisation, softwares and hardwares. Militarised modes of surveillance and control, of policing and regulating have become widespread. Technology as a business has had absolutely no inhibitions at going where Marx failed to venture. It has colonised all of these areas with gusto.

The impression we are left with from reading Marx is of capital circulating with the technological mix constantly changing, often in very disruptive ways, at the point of production while the rest of the circulation process through realisation, distribution and reinvestment remains untouched. The truth, of course, is that the technologies of circulation have also been dramatically changing. The question this poses is to what degree do Marx's insights and prescient commentaries stand up to contemporary scrutiny given his obvious blind spots.

No one, I think, would claim that technological shifts in the sphere of valorisation are irrelevant. To the degree that Marx shows through his study of it that capital must be technologically dynamic no matter what, then this makes a universal statement about capital's nature that carries over from Marx's time to ours. Technological and organisational change is endogenous and innate rather than exogenous and accidental (as it is often presented in other accounts).

Marx recognises several cognate facts. First, innovations in one sphere have proliferating externality effects everywhere else such that there is a consequent diffusion of technological and organisational impulses throughout the totality of any capitalist system. Secondly, when technology becomes an independent business, it no longer responds primarily to needs, but it creates innovations that have to find and define new markets. It has to create new wants, needs and desires not only on the part of producers (through productive consumption) but also, as we see all around us on a daily basis, on the part of final consumers. This business thrives upon and actively promotes the fetish belief in technological fixes for all problems.

Thirdly, the way Marx situates these technological shifts in relation to mental conceptions, social relations, the relation to nature, daily life, the materiality of commodity production and institutional arrangements of the state and civil society, stands firm as a mode of thinking that is desperately in need of further articulation. It is from this perspective – which seems to me to be a brilliant way to organise our own critical thinking – that it is possible to attack all those single bullet theories of social change including the one that is all too often hung around Marx's neck.

Finally, Marx's dark hints of the erroneous thinking and politics that derive from technological fetishism demand attention. The idea, for example, that the construction of smart cities managed through the mining of vast data sets can be the answer to all urban ills such that poverty, inequalities, class and racial discriminations and the extraction of wealth through evictions and other forms of accumulation by dispossession will all disappear is plainly ludicrous. It is counter-productive if not counter-revolutionary. It creates a fetish fog – a vast distraction – between political activism and the urban realities, pleasures and travails of daily life that need to be addressed.

The belief in the inevitability of technological and organisational progress has long been with us. In recent times it has taken some severe knocks and increasingly, if contemporary popular culture is to be believed, challenged by dystopian imaginaries. Marx shows us a way to get out of that utopian/dystopian binary and look for practical technological paths that address the crying need for new social relations, new mental conceptions, new relations to nature and all the other transformations that will be required to exit from the current morass. The tendency to fetishise technology is a barrier that needs to be removed and on this point Marx is as good a critic as anyone. Yet it is also the case that the range of technological mixes and possibilities with which we are now surrounded is greater than it has ever been in human history. On this point, the basic Marxist insight stands: the problem for emancipatory politics is to liberate the immense productive forces from their social and political constraints, in short from their domination by capital and a particularly noxious form of an imperially minded and increasingly authoritarian state apparatus. This task could not be clearer.

7
The Space and Time of Value

'Where science comes in,' wrote Marx to Louis Kugelmann shortly after the publication of the first volume of *Capital*, 'is to show how the law of value asserts itself.'[1] It is typical of Marx's approach to first derive and specify a law by a process of abstraction from material circumstances (such as acts of market exchange) and then explore all the possible counter-tendencies that might negate the law. To do things the other way round, he wrote, 'one would have to provide the science before the science'. Consider, then, how the law of value – so far explored abstractly and schematically as value in motion – 'asserts itself' in space and time.

If capital is defined as 'value in motion' then something has to be said about the time–space configuration of the world in which this motion occurs. Motion cannot occur in a vacuum. We need to shift from a visualisation of value in motion that is ungrounded anywhere to seeing it as it creates geographies of cities and transport networks; forms agrarian landscapes for the production of foodstuffs and raw materials; encompasses flows of people, goods, information; creates territorial configurations of land values and labour skills; organises spaces of labour, structures of governance and administration. We also need to take account of the significance of accumulated working class traditions and know-how in particular places and times, of skills and social relations (not only of class), all the while acknowledging how the political and social struggles of people living in particular places leave behind memories and hopes of alternative unalienated ways of living and being.

Marx recognised early on that it was inherent in the very nature of capital to create the world market but that in doing so it would have to produce a new kind of space. This theme is articulated at some length in the *Communist Manifesto*. The merchant capitalists undermined the static powers of feudal landed property. They used their superior command over space to assemble great wealth and power by buying cheap in one place and selling dear in another. With the rise of industrial capitalism, 'the need of a constantly expanding market for its products chases the bourgeoisie over the whole surface of the globe. It must nestle everywhere, settle everywhere, establish connexions everywhere.' This gives

> a cosmopolitan character to production and consumption in every country ... All old established national industries have been destroyed or are daily being destroyed. They are dislodged by new industries, whose introduction becomes a life and death question for all civilised nations, by industries that no longer work up indigenous raw materials, but raw material drawn from the remotest zones; industries whose products are consumed, not only at home, but in every quarter of the globe. In place of the old wants, satisfied by the productions of the country, we find new wants, requiring for their satisfaction the products of distant lands and climes. In place of the old local and national seclusion and self-sufficiency, we have intercourse in every direction, universal inter-dependence of nations.

Revolutions in the means of transport and communications draw all nations together while 'the cheap prices of its commodities are the heavy artillery with which it batters down all Chinese walls ... It compels all nations, on pain of extinction, to adopt the bourgeois mode of production ... In one word, it creates a world after its own image.'

This is an astonishingly prescient evocation of the processes that we have in recent times come to call globalisation. But this is not all.

> The bourgeoisie has subjected the country to the rule of the towns. It has created enormous cities ... (it) keeps more and

more doing away with the scattered state of the population, of the means of production, and of property. It has agglomerated population, centralised means of production while independent, or but loosely connected provinces with separate interests, laws and governments and systems of taxation, become lumped together in one nation, with one government and one code of laws, one national class interest, one frontier and one customs tariff.[2]

The processes that led to the creation of the unification of Germany and Italy in the late nineteenth century and the European Union, the World Trade Organisation (WTO) and the power of the International Monetary Fund (IMF) in the twentieth were already identifiable.

Similar sentiments are expressed in the *Grundrisse*:

A precondition of production based on capital is therefore the production of an ever-widening sphere of circulation ... The tendency to create the world market is directly given in the concept of capital itself. Every limit appears as a barrier to be overcome ... The production of relative surplus value ... requires the production of new consumption ... Firstly: quantitative expansion of existing consumption; secondly: creating new needs by propagating existing ones in a wide circle; thirdly: production of new needs and discovery and creation of new use values ... Capital drives beyond national barriers and prejudices as much as beyond nature worship, as well as all traditional, confined, complacent, encrusted satisfactions of present needs, and reproductions of old ways of life. It is destructive towards all of this, and constantly revolutionises it, tearing down all the barriers which hem in the development of the forces of production, the expansion of needs, the all-sided development of production, and the exploitation and exchange of natural and mental forces.[3]

The law of value internalises this imperative to form the world market and to reshape the geographies of production and consumption in capital's own image. 'It is only foreign trade, the development of the market to the world market, which causes money to develop to world money and abstract labour into social labour. Abstract wealth, value, money, hence abstract labour, develop in the measure that concrete labour becomes a totality of different modes of labour embracing the world market ... This is at once the pre-condition and the result of capitalist production.'[4]

For all this to happen, the physical barriers to movement had to be reduced. In Marx's time the coming of the steamships and railways, the building of ports, harbours, canals and roads, were all very much in evidence. The invention of the telegraph allowed the closing prices of wheat in Buenos Aires, Chicago and Danzig to be printed the following day as the Liverpool and London commodity exchanges opened. This took a vast investment in expensive and long-lived physical infrastructures that changed the face of the earth and facilitated the geographical flows of commodities and money capital. Since Marx's time, innovations and investments of this sort have taken pride of place in capital's technological history. 'While capital must on one side strive to tear down every spatial barrier to intercourse, i.e. to exchange, and conquer the whole earth for its market, it strives on the other side to annihilate this space with time ... The more developed the capital ...the more does it strive simultaneously for an even greater extension of the market and for the greater annihilation of space by time.'[5] Hence the utopian dream of capital to operate in a frictionless spatial world (now largely achieved with the mobility of cyber-money). This does not make the role of geographical differences irrelevant: it heightens their importance because money capital can now move costlessly to exploit even minor differences in production conditions to generate excess profits. Working populations all around the world are put in competition with each other. A world market of labour supply, forged by the hyper-mobility of money capital, is becoming an ever more prominent reality. Plainly, the reduction of physical barriers to international trade must be accompanied by the reduction of social, political and cultural barriers: hence the hegemony of free trade ideology and politics even in the face of public resistance.

The circulation and accumulation of capital occurs in a specific organisation of space and time even as it simultaneously defines and redefines the times and spaces within which it moves. Marx welcomed much of this as disruptive of traditional 'encrusted' ways of life, as a kind of middle passage between the ancient and the modern. He was decisively on the side of the modern and even had positive things to say about the civilising influence of capital on human life. But all that is solid did not so easily 'melt into air' as he suggested it would in the *Communist Manifesto* and populations did not submit so easily to the new disciplinary apparatus of space and time that capital mandated. Furthermore, no sooner had populations settled to the new conditions of capitalist industrialisation than yet another wave of disruption swept across the land, leaving behind a detritus of abandoned industrial landscapes and disposable and disgruntled populations. The deindustrialisation that destroyed whole communities and hollowed out a by-then traditional industrial working class from the 1980s onwards in much of North America and Europe tells a rather different story. Rootedness in place for many is a virtue. Defence in place against the disruptive powers that attach to endless capital accumulation becomes a major line of anti-capitalist struggle. The longing and the search for unalienated social relations and relations to nature cannot ignore the processes of place construction as one avenue for building a better daily life. The dialectical relation between space and place is central to understanding both the constructive and the destructive aspects of the motion of capital in space and time.

Aspects of this problem are embedded within capitalism's own dynamic. Once investments are embedded in the land in a particular place, then capital has to use them in that place if they are not to be devalued. The movement of capital is spatially constrained by investments dedicated to increasing its fluid movement over an ever-greater spatial range. The annihilation of space by time is an important phenomenon within the drive to reshape the relative space–times of the world market. But that imperative does not necessarily imply spatial dispersal because agglomeration in places can be just as effective. The search for economies of circulation time that limit the loss of value can be prosecuted in different ways. Industries economise on circulation costs and times through clustering together in space. Agglomeration economies and efficient configurations of transport and communication networks play key roles in reducing circulation times and retaining a greater surplus value for capital. Improvements in the means of transportation tend 'in the direction of the already existing market, that is to say, towards the great centres of production and population, toward ports of export, etc … These particularly great traffic facilities and the resultant acceleration of the capital turnover … give rise to quicker concentration of both the centres of production and the markets.'[6]

Capital, we can now say, creates a physical landscape and spatial relations appropriate to its needs and purposes (both in production and consumption) at one point in time, only to find that what it has created becomes antagonistic to its needs at a future point in time. Part of the dynamic of capitalist accumulation is the necessity to 'build whole landscapes and spatial relations only to tear them apart and build anew in the future.'[7]

For much of *Capital*, Marx puts this process to one side. In Volume 1 he writes 'in order to examine the object of our investigation in its integrity, free from all disturbing subsidiary circumstances, we must treat the whole world of trade as one nation, and assume that capital is established everywhere and has taken possession of every branch of industry.'[8] The problem of the creation of new wants, needs and desires on the world market is eliminated by the assumption that all commodities exchange at their value. Marx evidently wanted to study the temporal dynamics in isolation. So he assumes capital hermetically sealed in a closed space within which all commodities exchange at their value. Occasionally he breaks away from this constraint. He notes, for example, how the rise of the factory system led British capital to seek raw materials and new markets through imperial conquests (as in India) or colonial expansion (as in Australia). The result was the production of 'a new and international division of labour ... one suited to the requirements of the main industrial countries' such that 'one part of the globe' was converted 'into a chiefly agricultural field of production for supplying the other part, which remains a pre-eminently industrial field'.[9]

The last chapter of Volume 1, somewhat surprisingly, takes up the topic of colonisation. Marx was almost certainly provoked by a formulation in Hegel's *Philosophy of Right*. In that text, Hegel saw the inner (class) contradictions of capital producing intolerable and unsustainable differentiations in distributions of wealth between the classes. Marx adopts almost identical language in his statement of the general law of capitalist accumulation in Volume 1 of *Capital*. The parallels are almost certainly not fortuitous. Civil society, Hegel argued, would be driven by its 'inner dialectic' to 'push beyond its own limits and seek markets, and so its necessary means of subsistence, in other lands that are either deficient in the goods it has overproduced, or else generally backward in industry'. Colonies would permit a part of its population 'a return to life on the family basis in the new land' and simultaneously create 'a new demand and field for its industry'. Civil society would be forced, in short, to seek an outer transformation through geographical expansion because its 'inner dialectic' creates contradictions that admit of no internal resolution. Capital mandates a perpetual search for 'a spatial fix' to its internal contradictions.[10] Whether or not Hegel thought geographical expansion would stabilise matters is, however, not clear.

Marx's chapter on colonialism responds to Hegel's thesis in two ways. First, he takes up Wakefield's colonial proposals for the settlement of Australia (laid before the British Parliament). These specified that labourers should be barred from access to free land in the colonies. The barriers of private property in land and land rent were needed to ensure an adequate supply of exploitable wage labour for capital. Thus was the political economy of the Old World forced, Marx gleefully notes, to reveal in its approach to the New World the secret it had long sought to conceal: that capital is produced by denying labour access to the basic means of production (land in particular).[11] Secondly, the implication is that there can be no permanent 'outer' resolution or 'spatial fix' to the internal contradictions of capital. Pursuit of colonial and imperialist solutions merely ends up reproducing the internal contradictions of capital (particularly its class relations) on a grander geographical and ultimately world scale. Marx seems to have concluded that he should, therefore, concentrate in *Capital* on the internal contradictions of capital and pay no mind to any purported external solutions of the sort Hegel proposed.

In the same way that Marx refuses to integrate any study of feudal residuals into his theory of capital, so he refuses to attribute any significance to a spatial or external resolution to the internal contradictions of capital. Many years later, of course, Rosa Luxemburg in her critique of Marx's theoretical work (particularly as laid out in Volume 2 of *Capital*) vociferously denied that capital could ever survive without an external solution to its market imbalances and its resource constraints. Colonialism and imperialism were, in her view, necessary and central to capital's survival.[12]

Only in Volume 3, in the chapters dealing with merchant's capital and with banking, finance and a credit system that was deeply embroiled in the funding of long distance trade, does the spatial structure of the world market re-emerge as a variable feature of Marx's analysis. It is in the context of realisation and distribution through the circulation of merchant, money and interest-bearing capital, that Marx finds it impossible to maintain a boundary between the internal and external contradictions of capital. Holding on to the assumption of no problems of realisation allowed Marx to build a tightly organised theoretical understanding of capital circulation, but at the cost of limited realism with respect to processes creating the world market. There is nothing wrong with making such assumptions. But we are entitled to ask what happens when they are relaxed or abandoned.

The globalisation that Marx and Engels envisaged in the *Communist Manifesto* has been an eternity in the making and even now is far from complete. Over the last century and a half, vast amounts of capital have been absorbed in pursuit of a spatial fix to problems of realisation through the growth of both final and productive consumption across the world market. While it well may be that the final result is nothing more than the replication of the internal class contradictions of capital on a grander and grander scale (as witnessed by the proliferation of billionaires in China, India, Mexico, Russia, etc. over the last two decades), this process has been a long time in the coming and has been associated with disastrous geo-economic and geopolitical conflicts. The planet has been plunged into inter-imperialist world wars and all manner of conflicts within the territorialised structures of the state system. Nevertheless, through it all, it would be hard to deny the validity of Marx's proposition that 'the tendency to create the world market is directly given in the concept of capital itself'. It was left to the theorists of colonialism, imperialism and of uneven geographical development to seek to incorporate such processes into the general theory of capital accumulation.

Marx's writings on colonialism in general and on Ireland and India, along with slavery in the United States in particular, were voluminous and informative (as befits a correspondent to the *New York Herald Tribune*). He saw conflicts emerging along the frontiers of settler colonialism. 'There the capitalist regime everywhere comes into collision with the resistance of the producer, who, as owner of his own conditions of labour, employs that labour to enrich himself, instead of the capitalist. The contradiction of these two diametrically opposed economic systems, manifests itself here practically in a struggle between them. Where the capitalist has at his back the power of the mother country, he tries to clear out of the way by force, the modes of production and appropriation, based on the independent labour of the producer.'[13] That this is one of the key roles of the capitalist state was later explicitly confirmed by President Woodrow Wilson of the United States in the 1920s. 'Since trade ignores national boundaries, and the manufacturer insists on having the world as a market, the flag of his nation must follow him, and the doors of the nations which are closed against him must be battered down ...'[14]

In *Capital*, however, Marx unquestionably privileges the study of time over space. Value is socially necessary labour time on the world market, which contrasts with the multitude of concrete clock-times producing use values. While surplus value is one thing, the division of the working day into necessary and surplus labour time (and the length of the working day that enhances absolute surplus value) is a magnitude fought over daily as capital purloins as much extra labour time as it possibly can by all manner of subterfuges in and outside the workplace. That it is easier for capital to realise its objectives by imprisoning workers within that 'House of Terror' called the factory is purely incidental.

Two recent books by Massimilano Tomba and Stavros Tombazos along with an illuminating essay by Daniel Bensaid discuss in detail how the concept of time operates in Marx's works.[15] They concur that the temporality of Volume 1 of *Capital* is linear and progressive as befits a study of perpetual technological change and the endless accumulation of capital. Time in Volume 2 is cyclical as befits a study of the reproduction of capital from valorisation through realisation and distribution and back again to valorisation. The temporality of Volume 3 is said to be 'organic' but it is not entirely clear what that might mean except that it is something appropriate to understanding capital as a totality in the full flood of evolutionary change. If Volume 3 is regarded as a synthesis of the perspectives of the first two volumes, then its distinctive temporality should be that of a spiral. This is a geometrical figure that Marx more than once plays with in the *Grundrisse* to contrast with the circle of simple reproduction. 'By describing its circle, (capital) expands itself as the subject of the circle and thus describes a self-expanding circle, a spiral.'[16] It roughly fits with the combination of linear technological change (registered as an ever increasing productivity of labour) with the circular motion involved in perpetual accumulation that frames Marx's theory of the tendency of the rate of profit to fall. The transformation from a circle to a spiral is where a lot of capital's problems begin. Hence the potency of the phrase 'spiralling out of control'.

There are two basic ways to think about space and time in human affairs. In elaborating on them I venture into complicated territory that may be hard to follow. But I think it vital to try.[17]

Either: we presuppose some universal and fixed temporal and spatial frame and use it to locate, order and calibrate activity within that frame. This is what the clock-time and measured spaces of Descartes and Newton backed by Euclidean geometry provides. This is the favoured space and time of the capitalist state, of bureaucratic administration, the law and private property and capitalistic calculation. How this space and time came to dominate is a story well covered by economic and cultural historians. Within this frame private property rights and territorial sovereignties can be defined (with maps) along with social contracts (like an eight hour day or a thirty year mortgage). Movements of capital, labour, money and commodities can be coordinated so that everything is in the right place at the right time (as in just-in-time production systems). Without such a framework the liberal political and commercial order could not work. 'If all the watches in Berlin suddenly went wrong in different ways even as much as an hour,' wrote the sociologist Georg Simmel, 'its entire economic and commercial world would be derailed for some time.'[18]

Or: we accept that there are multiple ways in which time and space can be conceptualised and experienced, recognise that every process internalises its own spatio-temporality and patiently work through the conflicts, contradictions and confusions that arise as phenomena from different time–space worlds clashing in particular situations. An oak tree internalises a certain measure of space–time as it grows. Its measure is very different from that defined by growing corn. The time–space of bird migrations is quite different from the time–space of geological movement of tectonic plates or the rates of radioactive decay. The space–time of factory labour conflicts with that of family time, child-rearing and the reproduction of labour power. A universal ban on child labour has to confront different definitions in different societies of when childhood ends. Capitalist anthropology, Marx noted, determined that the age of childhood ended at age ten! The formation of a wage labour force requires workers to submit to time and spatial disciplinary regimes that are hard to inculcate except through coercion and violence. The optimum rate of exploitation of a natural resource such as oil looks very different from the perspective of geological time as opposed to an economic temporality defined by the discount rate. Any calculus based upon the latter is profoundly at odds with the conceptualisation of time and space needed to confront global warming. The diversity of cultural and religious constructions of time and space has been much studied and remarked upon. Apocalyptic visions that proclaim the end is nigh contrast with a progressive teleology that proclaims the inevitability of communism or arrival in some other promised land in our future. Indigenous cosmologies are radically different from scientific modernist accounts of the origins of the time–space of the universe. The conceptualisation of time and space in early Christianity until late feudalism was very different from that which arose with the emergence of capitalism. Even our contemporary scientific understandings appear unstable. Notions of space and time in physics have evolved from Newtonian through Einstein's relativity to the relational space–time implied in the quantum mechanics of Niels Bohr.

Within all this diversity, one conceptualisation of space and time – such as clock-time and cadastral Euclidean space – may come to dominate in daily economic life. If it did not then, as Simmel pointed out, nothing could be coordinated, planned or regulated. Something as simple as a bus, train or flight schedule could not be specified. The variety of local times in different spaces had to be reduced by international agreement to a system of time-zones in order to facilitate communication and exchange.[19] Capital circulation and accumulation have also shaped and reshaped definitions of space and time. The time–space of contemporary financial markets is completely different from that which existed in 1848. Capital, being the revolutionary force it patently is, has transformed the spatial and temporal frameworks of daily life, of economic calculation and of bureaucratic administration and financial transactions. Acceleration of turnover times, precarity of work over the course of a working life and reductions in the frictions of distance have altered lifestyles as well as the rhythms of capital accumulation. While moments may be the elements of profit, the intensity of labour rather than actual hours comes to define a different temporality entirely. Time future, in the form of the anti-value of credit, now dominates time present to an extent never seen before. How many are now involved in the laborious and often tedious work of redeeming debts contracted long ago?

Within all of this it is useful to distinguish between three different major conceptions of time and space. This is where matters get somewhat complicated.

1. Absolute space and time

A plot of land is leased for twenty-one years. The plot is clearly defined on a cadastral map protected by laws of private property. Its area is known so cost of the lease per square metre can be calculated. The lease begins on 1 January 2000 and ends on 31 December 2020. Unless there are specific covenants and restrictions, the lessee can do with that plot of land whatever he or she likes during twenty-one years of calendar time. This is what absolute space and absolute time are about. This is the time of a working day (measured in hours) of a labourer confined within the closed space of a factory over which capital has absolute legal control. The absolute conception of space and time dominates the opening of Volume 1 of *Capital*, particularly in the chapter on the working day and the production of absolute surplus value. What Marx calls 'concrete labour' occurs in absolute space and time. 'The desolate space and time of physics now constitute the formal conditions of any knowledge, whether of nature or the economy', writes Bensaid, 'crowning the victorious coalition of the absolute and the true against the apparent and the commonplace.'[20]

2. Relative space–time

Position in relative space–time affects what can be done with the absolute space of the plot of land over the time of its lease. The lessee wants to maximise revenues but cannot grow fresh fruits and vegetables because labour is scarce and the plot is too far away from the main urban market which can be reached only by horse and cart over a bumpy road. If, after ten years, a motorway is built close by, more workers come to live in the area and a refrigerator truck allows the lessee to switch from food grains to more profitable fresh fruits and vegetable production. The market can be reached in an hour when it used to take the best part of a day. But it takes eight years to bring a fruit tree into bearing so given the terms of the lease it would not be rational to plant fruit trees, unless, that is, the lease can be renegotiated or some other legal solution can be arrived at that matches the temporality of peach tree growth. All of this presupposes relative space–time. Relative surplus value in *Capital* exists in a framework of relative time. Its measure is no longer hours of labour but the changing productivity and intensity of labour even as it still presumes, in Marx's account, the absolute space of the factory as the spatial site of production. Only in the chapters dealing with national differences in the value of labour power (wages) do we encounter the possibility of relative spaces also. But in Volume 2, the question of differential transport costs and distances to markets and various inputs enters into the analysis.

3. Relational space–time
Relational space–time is harder to grasp because, like value, it is immaterial and impossible to touch and measure but nonetheless of critical objective importance.[21] The changing monetary value of my house when I upgrade it affects the monetary value of the houses around me. The spatial range of this effect declines rapidly over distance. This is how appraisers work assessing housing valuation for a mortgage application. A bank invests in a tranche of mortgage debt on housing. How is that investment valued on the bank's books? We can study each property in absolute space and time and assess the position of each house in relative space–time but at the end of the day the valuation is based on 'best practices of valuation' in a relational space–time constructed around the idea of highest and best use. How do we assess the value of housing mortgages on the books

of some financial institution when the most favoured method of valuation called 'marked to market' cannot be calculated because the market has collapsed (as it did in 2008)? The answer is an informed guess.[22] Relational values change in tandem with market sentiments, confidence, expectations and anticipations. If the Federal Reserve suddenly changes interest rates or as Britain withdraws from the European Union, then property values in many parts of the world will surely be affected. We cannot identify atoms of influence flowing around, but the objective effects are plain to see. The same thing applies in the field of political struggles. A protest occurs in Gezi Park in Turkey which is influenced by the Arab Spring and this has impacts in Brazil a few weeks later as huge demonstrations of political protest unfold against the deteriorating conditions of urban life. Contagion effects, borne along these days by waves of exhortations on social media, are everywhere in evidence. A wave of left wing governments come to power in Latin America and then the whole wave seems to recede some dozen years later.

This threefold categorisation of relations between time and space produces interesting concordances:

> *Absolute space and time* is the space and time of concrete labour, of the working day, the factory, and of absolute surplus value through struggles over the length of the working day. *Relative space–time* is the space and time of relative surplus value, or variable productivity and intensity of labouring of differential porosity of the working day and changing values of labour power. Relative location, ease of access and mode, cost and time of transportation become important. *Relational space–time* is registered as abstract labour develops 'in the measure that concrete labour becomes a totality of different modes of labour embracing the world market'. Abstract labour is the totality of concrete labours in relational space–time. At the more local level, externality effects over space play an important role in, for example, the valuation of uncultivated land.

Capital embraces these three forms of spatio-temporality simultaneously within the logic of capital as a whole. Bensaid puts it this way:

> The antinomies of capital (use value/exchange value, concrete labour/abstract labour) issue from the open fracture of the commodity in Volume One. The unity of use value and exchange value expresses a clash of temporalities. The time of general/abstract labour exists only through concrete particular labour. As the establishment of a relation between these two times, value emerges as an abstraction of social time. Reciprocally, time is established as a measure that must itself be measured. The determination of socially necessary labour time refers to the motion of capital as a whole.

For this reason 'the category of time is at the heart of (Marx's) critique of political economy'. But the different approaches to time coexist within Marx's reasoning. 'The mechanical time of production, the chemical time of circulation and the organic time of reproduction are thus coiled and slotted inside one another, like circles within circles, determining the enigmatic patterns of historical time, which is the time of politics.'[23]

While Volume 2 of *Capital* adopts a cyclical temporal framework, it does not probe very deeply into the space–time framework that the study of the circulation of capital demands. It holds technology and organisational form constant so the progressive dynamics that dominate Volume 1 disappear from the analysis. Marx puts most of his efforts into the analysis of simple reproduction (the circle form of a virtuous infinity) as opposed to the spiral form (the bad infinity) of perpetual capital accumulation. The assumptions allow Marx to look more closely at certain aspects of the differential motion of different forms of capital free of disruptions. His focus is on different turnover times – the relative times different capitals take to get from the money form through valorisation, realisation and distribution and back into the money form once more. Marx breaks the total circulation process down into production time and circulation time. The former is defined in terms of the production of value and the latter as its negation. He then examines the relationship between the working period – the actual hours that labour takes in production – as contrasted with the production time, which includes in many instances time when no labour is being applied. In agriculture, for example, the working period when labour is being applied can often be quite short while the production time for most crops will be a year. Wine and liquors take a lot of fermentation time when no labour is applied. Vintage wines mature in the barrel and then in the bottle. Does this count as socially necessary labour time? Marx says no even though the price of the wine rises as it matures. But wines typically trade at a monopoly price and are, hence, outside of the general laws of competition that dictate socially necessary labour times. How to coordinate relations between different turnover, production and circulation times poses a lot of problems for capital circulation as a whole. Building a house, constructing a cruise ship, producing a mobile phone, a hamburger or a concert performance entail completely different spatio-temporal frameworks within which capital and labour work.

This brings us to the thorny problem of how to understand the circulation of fixed capital. How does the value of the machine get transferred into the commodities produced when there is no material transfer? Some social accounting convention has to be devised. And social conventions are always controversial and subject to modification. More generally, how does value flow through fixed capital formation and use? How does it flow through the construction of the large and long-lasting physical infrastructures and built environments needed for the circulation and reproduction of capital? These issues could not be incorporated into the visualisation of capital with which we began. But they are important. Look at the New York skyline and consider the flows required to sustain it over time. The most crucial flow is that of the value coursing through all those buildings in the form of debt servicing (anti-value) and revenues (value generation or appropriation). Value flows, we earlier argued, are immaterial but objective. They are invisible to the naked eye. But go to Detroit or Havana to see what happens to built environments when value ceases to flow. The derelict urban landscape is there for all to see.

The investigation of fixed capital circulation is vital for two reasons. First, Marx's critics argue that fixed capital disrupts the value theory and undermines Marx's political economy. Marx recognised that the circulation of fixed capital 'contradict(s) Ricardo's doctrine of value'.[24] But Marx's value theory is different from Ricardo's and Marx's critics typically fail to notice this. The possibility nevertheless exists that Marx's theory may require modification to accommodate the peculiar problems of fixed capital formation and circulation. Secondly – and far more importantly in practice – recent crises of capital – most notably that which occurred in 2007–8 – have arisen in and around investments in the built environment. In what ways can Marx's analysis of fixed capital circulation and built environment formation lay a foundation for understanding why this might be so?[25]

Let us begin with the simplest form of fixed capital. An industrial capitalist buys a machine in order to increase the productivity of the labour employed. If the machine is state of the art, then the industrial capitalist gains extra surplus value by virtue of the superior productivity of the labour power employed. When everyone else buys the same machine, this ephemeral form of relative surplus value disappears. The value laid out in acquiring the machine has to be recuperated over its lifetime. How does this value circulate? The simplest way is to use straight-line depreciation. If the physical lifetime of the machine is ten years, then one tenth of the value of the machine passes into the value of the commodity produced during each year. At the end of the ten years, the producer should have enough money to buy a new machine and start the process all over again.

But new, cheaper and more efficient machines are coming onto the market all of the time, particularly once technological innovation becomes a business. Existing machines then face the threat of what Marx quaintly calls 'moral depreciation' and devaluation through competition from cheaper and more efficient machines. The replacement value does not correspond to the depreciated initial value. The lifetime of the machine is no longer a physical question because better new machines may force the early retirement of existing machines. This leads to three alternative ways of looking at the circulation of fixed capital. The first is the straight-line depreciation over an average physical lifetime already described. The second is varying replacement cost during the physical lifetime of the machine. The third is a perpetually changing valuation of the machine over a variable lifetime that depends upon its utility in securing relative surplus value in competition with other producers. The lifetime of the machine depends on its utility and economic viability. Marx accepts that the valuation of the machine is dependent upon its effectiveness in generating surplus value. The accounting fiction that accommodates such a schedule of depreciation is that of joint products. Marx noted this as a problem for his own value theory. Sheep produce wool, meat and milk and assigning a value to each commodity is not obvious. In the case of fixed capital the accounting fiction works like this: every year the capitalist produces commodities and at the end of the year also 'produces' the remaining physical machinery, the value of which can be realised in second-hand markets or redeployed for the next annual round of commodity production. This is incompatible with Ricardo's labour theory of value because the value of the machine depends entirely on its utility in value and surplus value production and has nothing to do with the labour originally embodied in it.

This last interpretation is the most interesting. It is easier to understand if the industrialist leases the machine on an annual basis. The industrialist chooses every year whether to renew the lease on the old machine or lease a new one. That decision will depend on the differential costs of leasing, the different contributions of the old and the new machines to productivity and a variety of other factors (e.g. servicing contracts on maintenance and repair). The annual lease agreement fixes the value of the machine for that year. The value may be completely different the next year. The relational value of the machine is perpetually shifting.

But there is something peculiar about this arrangement. The companies leasing the machines lend capital to producers in the fixed form of the machine rather than in the liquid form of money. In return they expect the equivalent of interest on the value of the machine plus some contribution to the payment of principle. This fact accords with the way fixed capital circulation is financed in general. If the producer lays out value to buy a machine, then over the lifetime of the machine's use the producer will have to save up each year enough money to be able to purchase a replacement machine. The capitalists either hoard the savings or put them in a financial institution to earn interest while they wait. Or, alternatively, they can borrow money (or a machine in the case of leasing) at the outset and pay off its value over its lifetime plus interest.

In both cases the circulation of interest-bearing capital enters into the picture as it also does in the case of the quite common practice of leasing rather than buying equipment. The circulation of interest-bearing capital and the circulation of value through fixed capital use become closely intertwined.

Unfortunately, Marx's assumptions in Volume 2 of *Capital* exclude consideration of both technological changes and the circulation of interest-bearing capital. This allowed him to evade any extended discussion of these issues when writing about fixed capital. His assumptions allowed him to look more carefully at the role of turnover times and the conditions that would have to be satisfied if demand and supply flows were to remain in equilibrium. But they prevent a full and proper consideration of the fixed capital circulation problem. The chapter on that topic in Volume 2 is, alas, not very helpful. The *Grundrisse* offers a much livelier and potentially fruitful if speculative mode of approach.

'Nature,' Marx writes, 'builds no machines, no locomotives, railways, electric telegraphs, self-acting mules, etc. These are the products of human industry; natural material transformed into organs of the human will over nature ... They are *organs of the human brain, created by the human hand;* the power of knowledge, objectified.'²⁶

These forces of production, together with the skill and knowledge they embody, must be appropriated by capitalists, shaped to the latter's requirements, and mobilised as a lever for further capital accumulation. 'The development of the (instruments) of labour into machinery is not ... accidental ... but is rather the historical reshaping of traditional inherited (instruments) of labour into a form adequate to capital. The accumulation of knowledge and of skill ... is thus absorbed into capital, as opposed to labour, and hence appears as an attribute of capital, and more specifically of *fixed capital*.'²⁷ So it is not only the machine that is fixed but the knowledge and the free gifts of human nature incorporated in it.

But for fixed capital circulation to be fully effective, a number of preconditions must exist:

The part of production which is oriented to the production of fixed capital does not produce direct objects of individual gratification ... *Hence, only when a certain degree of productivity has already been reached ... can an increasingly large part be applied to the production of means of production.* This requires that society be able to wait; that a large part of the wealth already created can be withdrawn from immediate consumption, and from production for immediate consumption, in order to employ this part for the labour which is *not immediately productive.*

This requires 'a certain level of productivity and of relative overabundance, and more specifically, a level directly related to the transformation of the circulating capital into fixed capital ... *Surplus population* (from this standpoint) as well as *surplus production,* is a condition for this.'²⁸

Capital tends, as we have seen, to produce surplus populations (an industrial reserve army) and surplus products (commodities facing problems of realisation). It thus systematically produces conditions conducive to fixed capital formation. The larger the scale of the fixed capital, the more surplus labour and surplus capital can be absorbed – 'thus more to build railways, canals, aqueducts, telegraphs, etc. than to build machinery'. [29] But for this to occur, capital must be assembled into concentrations of money power. Before the advent of the joint stock companies and the organisation of the financial sector into huge conglomerations of centralised money capital, large scale investments tended to be channelled through the state apparatus. In our own times consortia of private banks or public–private partnership are more favoured. Nevertheless, the inner connection between the institutions (such as pension funds) that organise the circulation of interest-bearing capital and fixed capital formation becomes stronger and more intricate over time.

This trend becomes even more obvious when we consider certain special kinds of fixed capital. An increasingly important part of it is that of 'an independent kind'. Physical infrastructures used in common (some of which have the character of public goods) are crucial as use values for capitalist forms of development. Many of these infrastructures (like houses, schools, hospitals and shopping malls) are used for purposes of consumption rather than production while others, such as railways and highways, can equally well be used for both. Marx briefly considers the relations between investments in fixed capital for production and investments into the consumption fund. Plainly, in our own times in the advanced capitalist world the latter investments are of great importance.

Marx also insists that we not confuse fixed with immoveable capital (such as a coal mine) even though the latter is in itself a very important category for consideration:

> Some of the means of labour … are held fast in their place once they enter into the production process as means of labour: machines, for example. Other means of labour, however, are produced at the start in static form, tied to the spot, such as improvements to the soil, factory buildings, blast furnaces, canals, railways, etc. … But the circumstance that some means of labour are fixed in location, with their roots in the soil, gives this part of

the fixed capital a particular role in the nation's economy. They cannot be sent abroad or circulate as commodities on the world market. It is quite possible for the property titles to this fixed capital to change: they can be bought and sold and in this respect circulate ideally. These property titles can even circulate in foreign markets, in the form of shares, for example. But a change in the persons who are owners of this kind of fixed capital does not change the relationship between the static and materially fixed part of the wealth of a country and the moveable part of it.[30]

We can trade shares to a company delivering water to a South African township on all the markets of the world, but the water system cannot be moved. Geographical fixity as opposed to geographical mobility becomes an important tension centred around fixed capital of an immoveable kind. The geographical fixity is in fact a produced space.

In all of this there is a deep and abiding contradiction. The 'dark matter' of anti-value purveyed through the circulation of interest-bearing capital demands its pound of flesh in future value production that must continuously rise to cover the compounding cost of interest payments. 'The greater the scale on which fixed capital develops ... the more does the continuity of the production process ... become an externally compelling condition for the mode of production founded on capital.'[31] When capitalists purchase or borrow fixed capital they are obliged to use it until its value is fully redeemed or face devaluation. Fixed capital 'engages the production of subsequent years', it 'anticipates further labour as a counter-value' and, therefore, exercises a coercive power over future uses. That coercive power applies in place. Fixed and immoveable capital embedded in the land has to be used *in situ* if its value is to be redeemed over the course of its lifetime. In this there is a paradox. A form of capital designed to provide the physical infrastructure in place to liberate the spatial mobility of capital in general ends up demanding that capital flow into that space which the fixed capital defines or the value of the latter will be devalued with serious consequences for the interest-bearing capital (e.g. the pension funds) that funded it. This is one of the potent ways that the crisis tendencies of capital come to a head.[32]

In Marx's view the demand for fixed capital of various kinds along with demands emanating from the need to create a consumption fund adequate to the needs of social reproduction and daily life, formed a crucial material basis for the growth and increasing sophistication of the institutions governing the flows of interest-bearing capital. 'The anticipation of the future fruits of labour is … not an invention of the credit system. It has its roots in the specific mode of realisation, mode of turnover, mode of reproduction of fixed capital.'[33] The other crucial basis lies in the growth and financing of long-distance trade. It is fascinating to note how considerations deriving from the space and time of value circulation converge upon the circulation of interest-bearing capital as a principal agent impelling the further accumulation of capital.

The contradiction involved in all this should, however, be readily apparent. On the one hand, fixed capital provides a powerful lever for accumulation. Fixed capital investment, particularly of an independent kind in the built environment, can provide temporary relief from problems of overaccumulation and relieve stress during phases of crisis when surpluses of capital and of labour exist side by side without otherwise profitable sources of employment. On the other hand, future production and consumption are increasingly imprisoned within fixed ways of doing things and increasingly committed to specific lines of production and particular spatial configurations way into the future. The future is mortgaged to the past. Capital loses its flexibility. The ability to adopt innovations is either checked, producing stagnation, or maintained but at the cost of devaluation of the fixed capital in use. Marx saw this clearly as yet another set of forces making for crises:

> The cycle of interconnected turnovers, embracing a number of years, in which capital is held fast by its fixed constituent part, furnishes a material basis for periodic crises. During this cycle

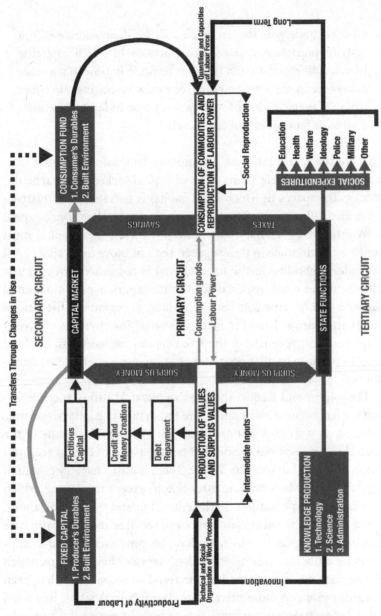

Figure 3 *The secondary and tertiary circuits of capital
in the production of physical and social infrastructures
for capitalist production and consumption*

business undergoes successive periods for depression, medium activity, precipitancy, crisis. True, periods in which capital is invested differ greatly and far from coincide in time. But a crisis always forms the starting point for new investments. Therefore from the point of view of society as a whole (it lays) a new material basis for the next turnover cycle.[34]

This contradiction takes on yet another dimension when we consider the immoveable forms of fixed capital locked into particular spaces. The spaces in which fixed capital is invested in infrastructures also differ greatly. Nor do they coincide in time. Once capital is invested in particular spaces and territories, then capital must continue to circulate in those spaces and not move into others until the value embodied in the fixed capital is redeemed through use. Either that, or whole regional economies experience devaluation of the sort that became common in industrial regions of the United States and Europe from the 1980s onwards. The rhythms of investment and disinvestment in the fixed capital embedded in the land vary to produce oscillating patterns of uneven geographical development in world capitalism.

Long-term and frequently massive physical infrastructure formation has become more and more important to capital over time. It forms, as it were, a secondary circuit of capital by virtue of the special way it responds to and dictates the paths of capital accumulation in general in space and time. There is also a tertiary circuit of capital, which Marx pays no attention to except in passing, which entails social expenditures on the education and training of labour, a large range of social expenditures and services such as health care and pension rights, to which we have become accustomed as supports for daily life. Traditionally these services have been provided by the state out of taxation but the trend in recent years has been towards more and more private provision. Nevertheless, like fixed capital of an independent kind, these expenditures on, for example, education entail long-term projects which may or may not contribute to rising productivity at a much later date. The flows of capital into the secondary and tertiary circuits of capital add another dimension entirely as to our understanding of what the capitalist laws of motion are all about (Figure 3, page 151). One thing is sure, however. Capital as value in motion cannot be understood without incorporating these secondary and tertiary circuits of capital, mediated not only through the market but also by state power, into our broad analysis of how capital works and reproduces in space and time. The visualisation of capital with which we began is confined to the circulation in a one-dimensional space. The other dimensions, here embraced as the secondary and tertiary circuits of capital over the long-term, supplement that understanding in crucial ways.

8
The Production of Value Regimes

The laws of motion of capital are enforced but not created, says Marx, by inter-capitalist competition. Throughout *Capital* Marx assumes (for the most part) a utopian condition of perfect competition. This assumption serves Marx well in his effort to show that the glorious utopia of the classical political economists – in which individual freedoms and private property coordinated through the market would redound to the benefit of all – would in practice produce a dystopian nightmare of increasing class inequalities, environmental degradations and economic crises galore. But it begs the question as to what happens when the enforcement mechanism of perfect competition goes AWOL or awry.

Marx tacitly assumes that perfect competition occurs in a space of zero transport costs and frictionless movement. But all spatial competition is monopolistic competition.[1] It is called that because firms have a monopoly over the particular space they occupy and only confront competition from a limited number of firms (if any) within a certain geographical range. Individual capitalists may be protected against competition from others by a combination of high transport costs and territorial barriers to trade (such as tariffs). The strength of this protectionist effect depends on the nature of the commodities, the tariff structure and the time and cost of transport. In Marx's time, heavy perishable items could not escape from local monopoly control, whereas the trade in gold, silver, diamonds, spices, silks, dyes and the like was not affected that much by transport costs though they may have been subject to tariffs. Producers of many basic and perishable goods (such as bread and beer) were protected against competition even from producers in neighbouring towns. Producers relying upon heavy raw materials inputs (like iron ore and coal in steel production) were protected against competition by locating close to their sources of raw materials. These are the kinds of conditions that location theory addresses.[2] Raw material orientation was a powerful force regulating the location of most heavy industries in nineteenth-century capitalism. Today, market orientation is probably more significant with some obvious exceptions. Mexican producers of refrigerators to this day have a locational advantage over their Asian competitors because of proximity to the US market.

The value of those commodities produced and marketed under conditions of local or regional monopoly cannot be determined on the world market in the same way as, say, the value of gold or diamonds or salt might be. Instead, the value would vary from place to place depending on changing transport times and costs and of tariff and other barriers to trade.

Marx recognised that the value of labour power varied from country to country, depending upon 'the price and the extent of the prime necessaries of life as naturally and historically developed, the cost of training the labourers, the part played by the labour of women and children, the productiveness of labour; its extensive and intensive magnitude'.[3] Geographical variations in the intensity of labour are particularly important. 'The more intense national labour ... produces in the same time more value which expresses itself in more money.' The law of value 'is here modified by national differences in wages' and by geographical variations in the length, intensity, productivity and porosity of the working day. Different productivities of labour according to natural differences (e.g. cheap food from fertile land in a favourable climate), the different definitions of wants, needs and desires according to natural and cultural situation and the dynamics of class struggles, mean that the equalisation of the rate of profit will not be accompanied by an equalisation of the rate of exploitation between countries.[4] In the event of trade between countries, 'the privileged country receives more labour in exchange for less, even though this difference, the excess is pocketed by a particular class, just as in the exchange between labour and capital in general'.[5] No prizes are given for guessing which class benefits. 'Here,' says Marx, 'the law of value undergoes essential modification ... the richer country exploits the poorer one, even where the latter gains by the exchange.'[6] This prevents any direct 'levelling out of values by labour time and even the levelling out of cost prices by a general rate of profit between different countries'.[7]

The social labour we do for others in one part of the world is different both qualitatively and quantitatively from that done in another. In the event of exchange between different regional value regimes the social labour in one region may end up subsidising and supporting the economy and lifestyle of another. High value producing regimes, such as those based on labour-intensive production (e.g. Mexico or Bangladesh), may be supporting high productivity capital-intensive regimes (e.g. the United States). Even more dramatically, the debt-bottling plants of New York and London that produce anti-value look for the redemption of that value in the factories of Bangladesh and Shenzhen and not in the backstreets of Manhattan or Soho.

The argument here has far-reaching implications. In Volume 1 of *Capital* Marx asks how it is that the equality presumed in competitive exchange relations can be rendered compatible with the inequality of surplus value production. The answer lies in the commodification of labour power and the exploitation of living labour in production. In Volume 3 of *Capital* Marx uncovers another surprising riddle. The equalisation of the rate of profit through competition forces commodities to be exchanged not at their value but at prices of production.[8] Capitalists receive surplus value according to the capital they advance and produce surplus value according to the labour power they employ. The redistribution of surplus value this produces in open trading situations within the capitalist class favours capital-intensive producers over labour-intensive producers.

The law of capitalist redistribution as laid out in Volume 3 of *Capital* evokes some interesting parallels. The Senate Committee investigating the 2007–8 crash asked Lloyd Blankfein, CEO of

Goldman Sachs, to define the bank's role. He replied that it was 'to do God's work'.[9] Presumably he was thinking of the biblical injunction from Matthew 25:29 'For unto every one that hath shall be given, and he shall have abundance: but from him that hath not shall be taken away even that which he hath.' This is what the equalisation of the rate of profit accomplishes. The consequences are potentially far-reaching, given Marx's (and Ricardo's) insistence that labour is the ultimate source of value. Trade between a capital-intensive value regime such as that of Germany and labour-intensive value regimes such as Bangladesh will transfer value and surplus value from the latter to the former. This will be accomplished 'silently' and 'naturally' through the market process. It requires no imperialist tactics of domination and extractivism, other than promotion of the practices of free trade, to make it work. This is the 'silent' way in which rich regions grow richer at the expense of the poor regions that get left further behind. For this reason many so-called developing countries look to protectionism, particularly of so-called 'infant industries'. This helps also explain why so many developing countries, beginning with Japan in the 1960s, prefer to organise and subsidise capital, rather than labour-intensive forms of capitalist development.[10] What is called 'moving up the value chain' towards higher value added production becomes a general ambition. When we add to such value transfers the ways in which the geography of value production and valorisation differ from that of realisation, then the fluid geography of value flows across and through the differentiating landscapes of capital circulation emerges as the material expression of what capital is about. Within these flows regional configurations emerge around which relatively stable and geographically fixed configurations of labour mobilisation, divisions of labour and investments in social and physical infrastructures and value production, realisation and distribution form at least for a while.

The case for postulating the existence of distinctive regional value regimes is bolstered by an examination of monetary arrangements. In Volume 1 of *Capital*, Marx notes a major disjunction between the global money commodities – gold and silver – and the many local fiat and paper moneys that exist to facilitate ease of exchange and which are 'an attribute proper to the state'.[11]

> When money leaves the domestic sphere of circulation it loses the local functions ... and falls back into its original form as precious metal in the shape of bullion. In world trade, commodities develop their value universally. Their independent value form thus confronts them here too as world money. It is in the world market that money first functions to its full extent as the commodity whose natural form is also the directly social form of realization of human labour in the abstract. Its mode of existence becomes adequate to its concept.

Thus 'the different national uniforms worn at home by gold and silver as coins' are 'taken off again when they appear on the world market.'[12] There is a 'separation between the internal or national spheres of commodity circulation and its universal sphere, the world market'. The 'true' value of commodities, Marx insists, lies on the world market and its most adequate money form of representation is gold.

If the disjunction between local and universal moneys is so obvious then why would we not imagine that the same might apply to value itself? The tacit assumption that value is singular and universal, rather than multiple and regionally disaggregated, is just that: an assumption. Marx's justification for it is that only on the world market can money acquire its universal material form – that of gold – which is outside of and beyond human manipulation. The global gold supply was and is relatively inelastic and most of it was and is already above ground in some form or another. The imperative to reduce transaction costs in exchange led to multiple localised moneys, which were mere symbols of value. But then so is gold itself a mere symbol. The difference is that these other non-metallic forms of money are vulnerable to arbitrary human manipulation. Even less reliable are 'moneys of account' and the many complicated systems of debt generation and credit moneys. Gold acted as the solid and reliable material pivot upon which all the other fictitious and otherwise uncontrollable forms of money turned.

Over time, however, gold became increasingly irrelevant to exchange even at the global level. The world monetary system abandoned the last vestiges of dependency on the gold standard after 1970 or so. Marx was adamant that this could never happen. But on this point he was clearly wrong and we have to consider the theoretical as well as the practical consequences of his error. Value even on the world market is now represented by money forms that have no material commodity base. These money forms are subject to human manipulation (such as quantitative easing among the central banks). The opportunity exists for currency regimes to emerge in competition with each other, vying for the power of representation of value on the world market. Any currency pushed to play the universal equivalent role, such as that now performed by the US dollar, is not only perpetually under challenge but inherently unstable.

Marx could easily have theorised this had he cared to. Value, as we've seen, arises in the course of the practices of market exchange. The exchanges that begin with barter postulate as many value forms as the concrete labour times embodied in the commodities produced. Imagine this process proliferating within a given territory such that a particular money form arises to represent the average of all labour times within that territory. A form of abstract labour or socially necessary labour time consolidates across all spaces of the territory. It is not hard to imagine this process operating in two closed territories next to each other, each of which will produce its own value regime.

It is in the nature of capital to 'burst its local bonds' and 'break through all the individual and local limitations of the direct exchange of products'.[13] Trade will begin between different territories with different value regimes represented by different currency systems. The drive inherent in capital to create the world market described in the *Communist Manifesto* and the *Grundrisse*, becomes in *Capital* the drive towards universal exchangeability.[14] This entails the creation of a universal equivalent which 'by social custom finally become(s) entwined with the specific natural form of the commodity gold'. But the completion of this process depends upon the removal of all barriers to trade, including that entailed in transport costs. While those costs have been much reduced in whole or in part (particularly with respect to the hyper-mobility of the money form) it is impossible to reduce the circulation costs to zero.

Marx clearly understood the contradictions embedded in any universal money form. In the case of gold the way these contradictions apply is obvious but it is not so easy in the case of the US dollar as a global reserve currency. In effect, the total productivity of concrete private labours producing use values within the US economy is considered the representative of abstract labour on the world stage, but the social convention to accept US manipulations of that standard is not assured. When the total productivity of labour in the United States falls below that in, say, Japan and West Germany (as happened in the 1980s) then why look to US dollars to represent values? There is no stable pillar for the universal equivalent. The evolution of different value regimes occurs in the context of unpredictable shifts in the relative values of the world's major currencies.

The production of regional value regimes has been a critical feature of capital's historical geography. These regimes were initially highly localised and loosely integrated through the exchange of a limited number of non-perishable, often high value and not easily reproduced commodities. The money commodities (gold and silver) performed the role of connector and coordinator, which explains Marx's interest in them as a central feature to his political economic theorising. As trading links proliferated and thickened over time, so convergence of the different value regimes has accelerated first at a regional level (as evidenced by the trading regimes of the European Union, North American Free Trade Agreement (NAFTA), MERCO-SUR and the like) as well as at a more global scale. As late as 1970, foreign cheeses and wines could not be found in local supermarkets in the United States and even beer was for the most part locally brewed. If I was drinking National Bohemian I was in Baltimore, if it was Iron City I was in Pittsburgh and Coors meant Denver. This has changed dramatically since 1970. Every local supermarket has food commodities from all over the world and I can drink beer from almost anywhere in most major cities.

Much of the history of capital since 1945 has been given over to the gradual elimination of barriers to trade by persistent falls in transport costs and by the gradual reduction of political barriers (e.g. tariffs and other forms of regulation). The geographical landscape for competitive production has been changing through free trade initiatives such as the General Agreement on Tariffs and Trade (GATT set up in 1947) and its more far-reaching successor, the World Trade Organisation (WTO set up in 1995), and a host of proposed agreements such as the proposed Trans-Pacific Partnership (TPP). Such indicators would seem to suggest that the differentials between regional value regimes are disappearing and that we are much closer now to a globally unified and singular value regime, and perhaps even a more secure world money system to represent it. The fact that China has still not been awarded Market Economy Status in the WTO tells us, however, that this process is incomplete. Furthermore, the rising tide of protests against free trade agreements suggests that a movement to disaggregate is actively engaged.

Consider, for example, the recent attempts to create trade agreements like the Transatlantic Trade and Investment Partnership (TTIP) (and its Pacific twin). In the case of the TPP, the agreement is specifically designed by the United States and Japan to constrain the ability of Chinese and European companies to build market share in Asia. The real character of the TPP becomes clear immediately the fundamental economic data for its twelve intended signatory countries are examined. The potential signatories are dominated by the G7 economies of the United States, Japan and Canada. These, together with Australia, constitute 90 per cent of the GDP of potential signatories. Participating developing economies – Mexico, Malaysia, Chile, Vietnam and Peru – make up only 8 per cent. The TTIP and TPP are really attempts by the United States to create a particular value regime, one that will stop the decline in its market share of global trade at others' expense, while counteracting weakening economic growth and profitability at home. In 1985 economies in the proposed TPP countries accounted for 54 per cent of world GDP; by 2014 this had dropped to 36 per cent. From 1984–2014 the US share of world GDP fell from 34 per cent to 23 per cent. In the same period the US share of world merchandise trade dropped from 15 per cent to 11 per cent. So the TPP is not some great free trade arrangement but an agreement by a group of advanced economies, with a fringe of developing countries, whose share in world GDP has been significantly declining, to keep others out, with the United States playing the role of dominant power at its centre. The benefits do not, of course, go to labour, since as Marx commented, any 'excess is pocketed, as in any exchange between capital and labour, by a certain class'. Similar effects flowed from the creation of the Eurozone as a supposedly coherent value regime armed with its own currency. But German capital has dominated and extracted maximum benefits while Greece, Italy, Portugal and Spain have been systematically drained of value. The abandonment of the Trans-Pacific accord by the United States has created an opening for China to step in and construct its own version of a value regime in the vacuum created by anticipated US withdrawal.

As spatial monopolistic competition has diminished, both materially and politically, other forms of monopoly have been re-emphasised. The large corporation possessed of great market power has been a major feature of capitalism since the latter half of the nineteenth century but the gradual breakdown of spatial barriers has meant a shift from national to global perspectives on corporate power particularly after 1970 or so. Monopolistic power in the United States in the 1960s meant the big three car companies in Detroit. Paul Baran and Paul Sweezy's classic work on *Monopoly Capital*, published in 1966, recognised the need for an alternative value theory but confined much of its analysis to the United States with international offshoots. During those years US labour (in fact all major national labour forces) was largely protected against foreign competition other than that made possible by immigration. Each large nation state was, in effect, constituted as a distinctive value regime with capital controls to secure sovereignty over its own economy. But this monopoly was challenged in the 1980s by fierce competition from, for example, foreign car companies (German, Italian, Japanese, then Korean and now Chinese) while US companies set up in China and elsewhere. Similar stories of the shift from national to global monopoly power can be told for agribusiness (Monsanto and Cargill), energy (the seven sisters oil companies), pharmaceuticals (Bayer, Pfizer) and telecommunications. Then there are the new upstart monopolists like Google, Amazon and Facebook along with a movement to enclose the world's knowledge commons in global systems of patents, licences and legal forms. The latter is what the Trade-Related Aspects of Intellectual Property Rights (TRIPS) agreement within the WTO framework supports and seeks to guarantee.

Competition, Marx pointed out in *The Poverty of Philosophy*, inevitably results in monopoly since only the fittest firms survive in the Darwinian world that capitalist competition creates. Marx takes this process a step further in *Capital* when he depicts what he calls 'the laws of centralisation of capital', much facilitated by the organisation of the credit system, that go well beyond the simple concentration and increase in size of firms consequent upon the accumulation process.[15] The importance of economies of scale in enhancing productivity cannot be overemphasised. This is the competitive advantage that capital seeks in its reckless pursuit of centralisation and increase of scale. The accumulation of market power by the corporate sharks allows them to swallow up the small fish through mergers and acquisitions.[16] The unification of the world's stock markets in the 1980s has also permitted this process to go global.

The wave of technological and organisation innovations that have occurred since the mid 1980s have radically restructured regional value regimes. Transport costs and even more importantly coordination times have fallen away as tariffs and other border barriers have either been diminished or selectively removed. Speed up in production and circulation has been the fetish quest of the times. The creation of global production chains permits cross-border production combinations in which, for example, US firms provide design, organisational and marketing skills combined with low-cost labour in Mexico in much the same way as German firms do in Poland.[17] Some benefit accrues to Mexico and Poland but most value is captured by corporations in the United States or Germany even as labour in the United States and Germany faces far fiercer competition from foreign workers and benefits not at all from the reorganisation (except, perhaps, in the form of cheaper consumer goods). But the organisation is regional in the sense that the cross-border relation is mostly with proximate states such that organisations like NAFTA and the Eurozone become an institutional form of expression in absolute space seeking to frame the relative space–times of the moving global value chains. Most so-called global cross-border trade is in fact regional (e.g. China's trade into East and Southeast Asia or Britain's trade into Europe). It is in this way that the evolution of technology as a business becomes an active agent in the definition and reshaping of perpetually evolving regional value regimes.

This brings us to an all too brief consideration of the part played by what we have hitherto designated as the 'free gifts' of nature and of human nature in the geographical configuration of value regimes. These free gifts are use values which can be appropriated by capital without cost (or with minimal cost) and which can thereby contribute to surplus value production. These free gifts are not evenly distributed over the earth's surface. High concentrations of so-called natural resources along with concentrations of populations with cultural characteristics, skills, institutional arrangements and aptitudes amenable to incorporation into the dynamics of capital valorisation, realisation and distribution create a world of differential geographical advantages for capital accumulation to proceed. The mosaic of regional value regimes has all along been supported by the proliferation, preservation and in some cases active creation of local cultural traditions, habits and preferences to which local populations subscribe and adhere even without invoking the often overwhelming power of nationalist sentiments. It is here that capital's definition of value confronts and in some respects bleeds into more traditional ideals of value as articulated through ethics, religion, culture or ethnic heritage.

The free gifts of nature and human nature are not constant. They depend on the capitalist evaluation of the potential use values on offer. Natural resources are not natural but economic, technical, social and cultural appraisals of elements available in nature. For a time, access to water power was important but the advent of the steam engine liberated capital from such locational constraints. Uranium was an irrelevant resource until the invention of nuclear power. Rare earth metals were irrelevant until new technologies made them critical resources. The labour skills honed to perfection in industrialised regions before the 1970s were subsequently rendered redundant by technological shifts that incorporated the skills into machine technology and automation. Cultural aptitudes are important to the evolution of certain kinds of consumerism that underpin the feverish pursuit of signs of distinction, class and good taste in certain markets of the world. The production of wants, needs and desires, as we earlier pointed out, is a crucial aspect of capital's history without which it would long ago have disappeared. The nature and the human nature that offer all sorts of free gifts to capital accumulation are neither given 'by nature' nor by some unchanging 'human nature'. Nor are they evenly distributed across the world. They are produced and ever-changing, and capital itself plays a very significant role in their production. The result is not global homogeneity but regional diversification. The value of labour power, for example, 'differs according to climate and level of social development; it depends not only on physical needs but also on historically developed social needs, which become second nature'.[18]

Fixed capital investments in the land that were long ago amortised become part of this 'second nature' while cultural evolution has not been immune to the influences of capital accumulation. The spirit of entrepreneurialism is created not given and it is unevenly distributed just as are the investments that produce a second nature. To point to the importance of all this in the formation of distinctive value regimes is not to resort to either physical or cultural determinism but to open up, but not close, a discussion on the dialectical integration of capital accumulation with the perpetual evolution of the contextual geographical conditions of nature and human nature in which this process occurs.

Not all of the gifts are benign – droughts, floods, hurricanes, earthquakes and volcanic eruptions along with revolutions, religious and cultural wars, nationalist rivalries and anti-immigrant movements are among the most conspicuous of the many untoward or unintended consequences that configure the complex relations between capital accumulation and the evolution of nature and human nature. More insidiously, the power of past investments to impose geographical inertia cannot be ignored. Capital may prefer greenfield sites to avoid entrapment in older networks of power and sclerotic infrastructures. In the early stages of the industrial revolution, for example, industrial capital avoided the merchant capitalist cities like Norwich and Bristol and set up in small rural villages with names like Birmingham and Manchester to avoid the power of organised labour in the guilds as well as the conservative powers of the merchant capitalists who dominated then-existing city governments. Even more emphatically in today's world, the increase of unproductive labour and the proliferation of regulations exercises a negative drag on prospects for capitalist development. The rise of urban and regional entrepreneurialism on the part of state apparatuses attempts to counteract this problem by local subsidies, promises of infrastructural investments and a promised 'light touch' when it comes to environmental and social regulation. Meanwhile, the rising power of the institutions of anti-value creation and the work of coordinating the flows of interest-bearing capital rest on the availability of sophisticated communications and an easy regulative environment if they are to flourish without constraint.[19] The tension between positive and negative natural and human environments for different forms of capital accumulation is everywhere in evidence.

Marx encountered some of these questions in his analysis of differential rents. Such rents arise in the first instance as free gifts of nature. Superior natural fertility and/or location yields a higher profit rate to firms blessed with such advantages. The advantages are relatively permanent (since no competitor can move on to their privileged site for production given the monopoly that always attaches to the land[20]) though in the case of location, position in relative space can change dramatically with transport investments. The excess profits can and usually are taxed away by landowners as ground rent. This has the effect of equalising the rate of profit between firms in a world of geographically uneven use value endowments. This was what justified, in Marx's view, the continued appropriation of rent – predominantly a feudal institution – under capitalism.

The conditions that allow for the appropriation of differential rents can also be actively produced. Fixed capital investments of an independent kind embedded in the land lead to the second form of differential rent. Competitive advantages that did not exist before can be produced and created in and on the land as privileged use values for capital to use as free gifts deriving from 'second nature'.

Long-term investments in what I call the secondary and tertiary circuits of capital through which the physical and social infrastructures for capital accumulation are produced furnish a basic mechanism by ways of which capital constructs the necessary physical and social conditions appropriate to its own needs at a particular historical time and place.[21] The mobilisation of capital flows to construct these infrastructures is a complicated affair and frequently requires not only a sophisticated credit system but also state organisation, financing and other forms of intervention. In the process a wholly different form of temporal circulation is generated and superimposed upon the visualisation of capital as value in motion with which we began (see Figure 3, page 151).

The structures that result can be long-lasting and influential in the formation and sustenance of value regimes. Baron Haussmann's boulevards (and his sewage and water works and the parks like Bois de Boulogne) last to this day, as do the works of Robert Moses across the New York metropolitan region in the immediate post-1945 period in New York. The investments in higher education that were paralleled by the enhancement of the research universities in the

United States conferred competitive advantage on the United States for two generations at least, and shaped its value regime in very distinctive ways. A flood of investment of a similar sort in recent years into higher education in China (largely modelled on the success of Singapore) may well do the same for them long into the future.

Investments in social and physical infrastructures create geographical concentrations of relative advantage to which capital is inevitably drawn. The free gifts of nature and human nature need to be produced before they can be gifted to capital. Poor regions grow poorer and rich regions typically grow ever richer unless some crisis occurs which breaks the circular and cumulative causation process at work behind the uneven development of distinctive geographical value regimes.[21] Long-lasting advantages persist well beyond the date at which the value of the fixed capital or the consumption fund is redeemed. Earlier investments in higher education in the United States made it possible to counter the deindustrialisation that afflicted manufacturing from the 1970s onwards. Internet and high tech firms like Google, Microsoft, Amazon and the like quickly established themselves as global monopolists, though, as usual, the benefits flow to capital and not to labour.

The relations between different value regimes were crisis prone even in Marx's day. 'The crisis may first break out in England, the country which advances most of the credit and takes the least, because the balance of payments ... which must be settled immediately, is unfavourable even though the general balance of trade is favourable. The crash in England, initiated and accompanied by a gold drain, settles England's balance of payments ... Now comes the turn of some other country.' The costs of devaluation are then forced back upon the initiating region by 'first shipping away precious metals; then selling consigned commodities at low prices; exporting commodities to dispose of them or obtain money advances on them at home; increasing the rate of interest, recalling credit, depreciating securities, disposing of foreign securities, and finally bankruptcy, which settles a mass of claims.'.[22] Britain, faced with the problem of overaccumulation in the nineteenth century, solved its problem by lending money to Argentina to build the railways that used British-made surplus equipment. There is much that is all too recognisable in this sort of sequence. But the tacit assumption of Marx's account is that the world needs to be studied and understood in terms of fluctuating power relations between different value regimes in the global economy.

The big difference between Marx's day and now is that the appearance of such crises is not primarily marked by a gold drain (though that does occur) nor can it be settled by shipping away precious metals even as the balance of payments between countries is a crucial source of global instabilities. It is usually settled by a loan from the IMF at the cost of severe austerity measures imposed upon the population. Any diminution in the volumes of world trade or instabilities in the balances of trade crises, are even more important now than they ever were. Declining volumes of world trade are widely accepted now as clear harbingers of global crises, unless the institutions at what I call 'the state–finance nexus' of capital (now constituted by the US Federal Reserve and the US Treasury backed by the IMF and then by the other main central banks) manage the dollar balances in world trade effectively. Without the gold standard, we now live in a world where human manipulation and management are all there is that stands between us and a catastrophe in global financial and commodity markets. This is not a plea to bring back the gold standard. That would be equally if not more disastrous.

The case for thinking of regional value regimes that intersect and relate to each other dynamically over time appears irrefutable. That the value regimes have been converging more and more particularly in their labour market practices over the last forty years or so is likewise undeniable. We are closer to a global labour market now than ever before in human history. That there are signs of an increasing homogenisation of wants, needs and desires among middle class populations everywhere is also undeniable. But there is still a considerable way to go before there is total homogenisation of the multiple value regimes that currently exist. But, as so often happens with Marxist style propositions, it is not hard to spot counteracting forces of disintegration, dispersal and realisation such that the tension between universal and particular remains permanently with us to be internalised within the law of value itself.

There is and never can be any single system of values. It is impossible to escape the obvious historical materialist practices by which the motion of capital across the world stage utilises and constructs geographical differences in how the social labour done for others is conceptualised, utilised and measured. Geographical differentiations and uneven geographical developments are major features that need to be negotiated. The universality of world money encounters in the course of its spatial movement radically different opportunities for valorisation as well as substantially different conditions for realisation not only because of variation in wants, needs and desires but also because of differentiation in the ability to pay. While competition (even of a monopolistic sort) may work to smooth out some of these differences, in other instances it actively creates geographical differences most conspicuously through differential investments in the fixed capital and consumption fund of the built environment which are the source of differential land and property rents on the world stage.[23] This leads to sharpening competition between local, regional and power block economies on the world stage. The active construction of alternative spaces across the global economy becomes one of the prime, if generally neglected, features of what the law of motion of capital is about.

The definition and identification of regional value regimes is no easy matter. The absolute spaces and times of individual states or groups of states such as the European Union or NAFTA certainly have a role to play as the recent intricate politics of attempts at geopolitical engineering of the world economy indicate. The absolute boundaries of NAFTA may work well to combine US know-how with Mexican low-cost labour but that does not in any way preclude the use of Chinese parts and African raw materials in the making of a product in Mexico to be marketed in the United States. The increasing complexity of global value chains superimposes a relative space–time dimension on almost all activity and such movements do not stop, even if they have to pause, at borders. As in the case of value in general, however, the immaterial but objective aspects captured by relational space–time can be decisive in the configuration of regional value regimes, even as hegemonic constellations of political-economic power are centralised at certain key nodal points within the complex networks and flows of material goods, information, knowledge and reputational influence. Regional value regimes can be nested at different scales. They are identifiable within states. The so-called sun-belt of the United States is very different from the rust-belt, and Catalonia is not Andalusia any more than Hamburg is the same as Bavaria. Regional value regimes are unstable and floating configurations of influence and power that exist and have powerful manifestations even as they have no clear material definition.

We began this exploration of the space and time within which the laws of motion of value assert themselves with the more than plausible assertion that it is within the nature of capital itself to conquer and construct the world market. We now see after traversing the contradictory terrain over which those laws must work that it is also in the nature of capital to shatter the uniformity, homogeneity and supra-sensible rationality of the world market into so many potentially dangerous and incompatible shards of heterogeneity, difference and uneven geographical development, irrespective of all the irrational human failings that spatter the collective history of humanity with blood and gore. That all of this morphs into questions of geopolitical struggles between power-blocs on the world stage is a matter of great consequence. The geopolitical history of capitalism has been a rather ugly affair (and continues to be threateningly so).[24] Considerations that flow from the creation of distinctive value regimes in space and time have a subtle role to play in that historical geography. But for some reason or other, neither Marx nor subsequent thinkers working in the Marxist tradition have gone much deeper into this aspect of value theory than variations on the early twentieth-century theoretical debates on capitalist imperialism and the role of colonialism and neocolonialism in the origins and reproduction of the capitalist world system.[25]

9
The Madness of Economic Reason

When commodities that are the bearers of value are finally consumed they drop out of circulation. They thereby 'cease to be a moment of the economic process'. But this disappearance is contingent on the prior conversion of value from the commodity into the money form, and money has the capacity to remain in circulation in perpetuity. 'In the case of money,' writes Marx, 'it becomes *madness*; madness, however, as a moment of economics and as a determinant of the practical life of peoples.'[1] Daily life is held hostage to the madness of money. But wherein lies this madness?

From the standpoint of commodities, exchange value is 'only of passing interest' since the immediate aim of commodity production is to satisfy social needs. Money in a world of exchange simply facilitates the exchanges. But in the world of capital and surplus value production money takes on a quite different character. Value here 'preserves itself through increase; and it preserves itself precisely only by constantly driving beyond its quantitative barrier ... Thus, growing wealthy is an end in itself. The goal determining activity of capital can only be that of growing wealthier, i.e. of magnification, of increasing itself.' Money, insofar as it works as a measure of wealth, must likewise engage in 'the constant drive to go beyond its quantitative limit; an endless process. Its own animation consists exclusively in that; it preserves itself as a self-validated exchange value distinct from use value only by constantly multiplying itself.' This is what distinguishes money under capitalism from all of its multifarious pre-capitalist forms. 'Money as a sum of money is measured by its quantity. This measuredness contradicts its character, which must be oriented towards the measureless.'[2] It can never be contained or constrained.

This is what Hegel refers to as 'bad infinity'. This is the form of infinity that has no ending and which, like God's wisdom, surpasses all human understanding. The number sequence is its paradigmatic form. For every number there is always a larger one which goes beyond. The world's money supply, absent the constraint of any material gold base, is a bad infinity. It is simply a set of numbers. Contemporary capitalism is locked into the bad infinity of endless accumulation and compound growth. In Marx's interpretation, Wayne Martin suggests, 'capitalism is essentially oriented to an incompleteable infinitude, an orientation grounded in the ontology of capital itself'.[3] Money can accommodate to the infinite need for the expansion of value simply by having the central banks add zeros to the money supply, which is what they do through quantitative easing. This is bad infinity, the spiral that gets out of control, run riot. We used to speak in terms of millions, then it became billions and trillions and soon, doubtless, we will speak in terms of quadrillions of dollars in circulation, a number which surpasses any real understanding.

Hegel's virtuous infinity is the circle, the Möbius strip or the Escher staircase in which motion can continue for ever but where everything is calculable and knowable in advance. In the first two volumes of *Capital*, Marx devotes lengthy chapters to simple reproduction. It is almost as if he wishes to explore the virtuous cyclical forms of reproduction that might be possible in a non-capitalist world of zero accumulation. The trouble starts with the production of surplus value and the necessity of its perpetual expansion, which entails the shift from a cyclical virtuous infinity to a spiral of endless accumulation. It is this shift that forces the perpetual pursuit of an 'incompleteable infinitude' on the part of capital. Use values, though clearly limited by material constraints, are not, as we shall see, immune to this madness. There are 'attempts to raise consumption to an imaginary boundlessness' while much else 'appears as limitless waste' in which the accelerating degradation of the environmental commons features so prominently.[4]

In the third volume of *Capital* Marx uncovers another dimension to this madness. Interest-bearing capital is judged 'the mother of every insane form'.[5] In this case, money reverts to its role as a commodity but one whose use value is that it can be lent out in infinite quantities to others to produce surplus value. Its exchange value is interest. Money, the representation of value, itself acquires a money value. Interest is an 'irrational expression right from the start'. The upshot is an 'absurd contradiction' in which the 'inner tendency of capital appears as a compulsion exercised over it by alien capital'.[6] Anti-value takes over. When the circulation of interest-bearing capital (the power of the stock and bondholders) becomes the prime force for keeping value in motion, then 'the fetish character of capital and the representation of this capital fetish is now complete'.[7] The madness of economic reason gets disguised by fetish forms in which money appears to have the magical power of making more money without cease. I place my money in a savings account and the money increases at a compound rate without me doing anything.

It is, however, 'damned difficult,' Marx argues, 'for Messrs the economists to make the theoretical transition from the self-preservation of value in capital to its multiplication'.[8] Our understanding of the world is held hostage to the insanity of a bourgeois economic reason that not only justifies but promotes accumulation without limit while pretending to a virtuous infinity of harmonious growth and continuous and attainable improvements in social well-being. The economists have never confronted the 'bad infinity' of endless compound growth that can only culminate in devaluation and destruction. Instead, they laud the virtues of a bourgeoisie who have triumphantly 'subjugated historical progress to the service of wealth'.[9] They steadfastly evade the question of whether crises are inherent in such a system. Crises, they say, are due to acts of God or nature or to human errors and miscalculations (particularly those attributable to misguided state interventions). Any or all of these can derail the supposedly immaculate machine of endless free market capitalism. But the machine in itself, the economists hold, is the epitome of perfection. When confronted with a crisis, the economists can only claim 'that if production were carried on according

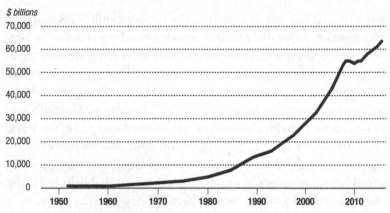

Figure 4 *Growth of public, corporate and private debt
in the USA (Federal Reserve Bank of St Louis)*

to the textbooks, crises would never occur'. 'Every reason which they (the economists) put forward against crisis is an exorcised contradiction, and therefore a real contradiction. The desire to convince oneself of the non-existence of contradictions, is at the same time the expression of a pious wish that the contradictions, which are really present, should not exist.'[10] Contemporary economic science is contradiction-free.

It is in this context that Marx decided to dedicate so much of his intellectual effort and working life to the *critique* of political economy and the madness of economic reason. In the process, he uncovers deeper and deeper irrationalities and 'insane forms' in the systemic thought and political programme that is supposed to guide us to a utopianism of everyday life. The contradictory laws of motion that he identifies solely advantage a capitalist class and its acolytes, while reducing whole populations to exploitation of their living labour in production, to paltry possibilities in their daily life and debt servitude in their social relations.

The madness of bourgeois economic reason, Marx discovers, is further magnified by the growing antagonisms between value and its monetary representations. As money is necessarily cut free from any material base (such as that of the money commodities of gold and silver) so its idealist constructions (as numbers of dollars, euros, yen, etc.), and even more importantly its increasing appearance as forms of credit money, become vulnerable to the vagaries of human judgments, open to excesses and manipulations by whoever holds the reins of power. 'From its servile role ... as mere medium of circulation, (money) suddenly changes into the lord and god of the world of commodities' that can be 'tangibly brought into the possession of a particular individual.' Money is an individualised claim upon the social labour of others in exactly the same way that debt is a claim over the future labour of those others. Money gives its possessor 'a power over society, over the whole world of gratifications, labours, etc.'[11] The gap between the proliferation of such claims and the value base upon which such claims might be based has widened enormously since Marx's day. If everyone in the world went to the banks to demand cash equal to their deposits then it would take several months if not years to print the notes required. Two trillion dollars a day change hands on foreign exchange markets.

But this is only the tip of an iceberg of phenomena within the financial world. The flows of credit moneys, of that form of anti-value which capital itself creates, have increased enormously since the 1970s (Figure 4, page 175).[12] In the first instance these flows lubricate activities within the field of distribution itself. The latter more and more appears as a black hole into which a mass of value disappears in the name of debt redemption, without any security that it will ever re-emerge. Inter-bank lending is at an all-time high as are the interchanges between financial institutions and the central banks. Banks have long lent to governments against the security of the state's power to tax. The power of the state to tax is reciprocally used to bail out banks in trouble. The escalating national debts of the leading states have not the faintest hope of ever being legally retired. But significant flows of tax revenues into debt redemption become normalised within the field of distribution as a whole. Much of the effective demand derived from state expenditures, on the other hand, is fictitious capital (anti-value) generated within the

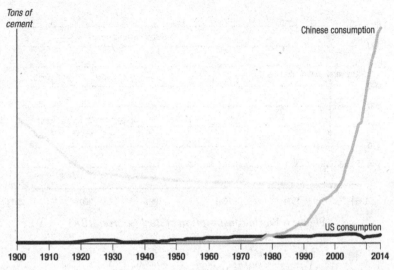

Figure 5 *Chinese consumption of cement (redrawn
from original in* National Geographic*)*

credit system and lent to the state. The claims to future value production endlessly expand. Consumer credit (some of it of a predatory sort) is made available to everyone (including workers and students) and typically escalates as it circulates. The fantasy of 'an imaginary boundlessness' in consumption is avidly pursued. Credit flows to land and property owners. It fuels speculation in rents and other asset values that then have the power to magically increase without limit. Merchants and industrialists borrow even in the face of the potent power of anti-value that may destroy them at some future date. Merchants, land and property owners, states and anyone else who saves (including more privileged sectors of the working classes) deposit surplus funds in financial institutions in the expectation (sometimes deceived) of a rate of return.

Marx recognised the importance of fictitious capital formation and asset speculation while highlighting the madness of their economic reason. He understood full well that these inter-distributional relations constitute acute 'moments of economics' affecting

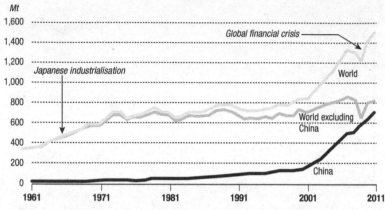

Figure 6 *World consumption of steel (source: RBA)*

'the practical life of peoples'. But, as everyone knows, this is a notoriously opaque and mystified arena of capitalist activities that eludes any easy summary or even superficial description.

But this 'limitlessness' cannot be confined to the world of credit moneys. It has implications for the worlds of use values and value production. 'Capital is the endless and limitless drive to go beyond its limiting barrier ... Capital as such creates a specific surplus value because it cannot create an infinite one all at once; but it is the constant movement to create more of the same. The quantitative boundary of the surplus value appears to it as a mere natural barrier, as a necessity which it constantly tries to violate and beyond which it constantly seeks to go.'[13]

To study capitalist economic history is to study this madness in action. Consider the following astonishing but all too concrete fact. Between 1900 and 1999, the United States consumed 4,500 million tons of cement. Between 2011 and 2013, China consumed 6,500 million tons of cement. In two years, the Chinese consumed nearly 45 per cent more cement than the United States had consumed in the whole of the preceding century (Figure 5, page 177).[14] Those of us who live in the United States have seen plenty of cement used over our lifetimes. But what has happened in China is extraordinary. The

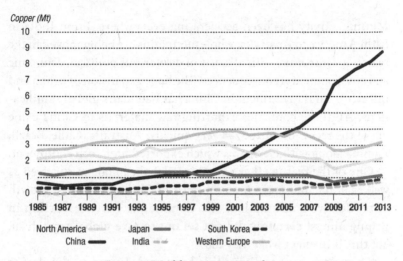

Figure 7 *World consumption of copper*

increase in the scale of spreading cement around is unprecedented. It provokes worrying questions. What might the environmental, political and social consequences be? There seems to be more than a touch of madness about it. Is this the 'imaginary boundlessness' of which Marx speaks?

Cement is used in construction. This means a massive invest-ment in the creation of built environments, in urbanisation and the construction of other physical infrastructures (transport systems, dams, container terminals and airports). It is not only cement that is used. There has been an enormous expansion of steel production and use. In recent years, more than half of the world's steel output and use has taken place in China (Figure 6, page 178). A lot of iron ore is required to make that steel. It comes from faraway places like Brazil and Australia. Many other materials, like copper, sand and minerals of all sorts, have been consumed at unprecedented rates. In the last few years, China has been consuming at least half (and in some instances 60 or 70 per cent) of the world's key mineral resources (Figure 7).

Raw-material prices have, until recently, tended to soar as a result.

Mining activity has been accelerating everywhere. From India to Latin America to Australia, whole mountains are being moved in the search for minerals, with all sorts of deleterious political, economic and environmental consequences. The huge expansion of urban and infrastructural investment in China has had many global ramifications. All those countries exporting raw materials to China came out of the recession of 2007–8 very quickly: Australia, Chile, Brazil, Zambia along with Germany, which exported high tech equipment.

One of the reasons that a troubled global capitalism survived as well as it did after 2007–8 was because of China's sustained growth of productive consumption. The Communist Party leadership in Beijing almost certainly did not set out to save global capitalism, but this is in effect what they did.

To explain how and why this happened, I need to dig deeper into the recent geo-economic history of the different regional value regimes. A financial crisis occurred in the United States in 2007–8. Because it originated in the United States it was defined as a global crisis. Earlier crises occurred in Southeast Asia in 1997–8 or in Turkey and Argentina in 2001–2; but they were considered regional crises within particular value regimes. The United States still has one of the largest and most influential economies in the world and major disruptions within it are bound to spill over to affect other regional value regimes. There is also some evidence that US institutions and policy makers actively sought to disperse the negative effects of the financial crisis around the world (through the control of international institutions such as the IMF and through the mechanism provided by the dollar as the global reserve currency) in the hope of diluting its effects at home. Crises always tend to move around but they do so more rapidly with some effective support from agencies of state power and the politicians.

The crisis of 2007–8 was at first instance quite localised. It originated particularly in the southern and southwestern United States, and arose largely out of intense speculation in housing and property markets fuelled by easy credit and 'sub-prime' lending. Speculative money poured into US property markets (as it did in Ireland and Spain, among other places) after the stock market crashed in 2001. The world was awash with surplus liquidity during those years and interest-bearing capital had few opportunities for investment. Much of it was absorbed in property markets and raw material extraction forcing prices up and up. When the speculative housing bubble burst, there was a huge foreclosure crisis on housing loans in the United States as well as in Ireland, Spain and some other countries.

People who have been foreclosed upon and who are unemployed don't go out and buy things. The consumer market in the United States tanked. China was a primary supplier of goods to that consumer market. Export industries in China tanked in turn. This was one link whereby a localised crisis went global. The other link was through the financial system. Financial institutions had structured mortgage debt on housing so as to be able to pass it on to others as an investment yielding good returns that were supposedly 'as safe as houses'. But many of the mortgages were not secured by an ability to pay. Anyone who had been gulled into investing in the new financial instruments lost money. The banks that held a serious part of the debt were threatened with failure and tightened credit, including credit to already cautious consumers everywhere. The weakness in the US consumer goods market spread and deepened. The downward spiral threatened to engulf the whole world in depression.

In 2008, China faced a 30 per cent contraction in exports. Factories in southern China were closing down. Chinese statistics are notoriously unreliable, but by some accounts, between 20 and 30 million jobs were lost. The Chinese government has always been nervous about potential social unrest. Twenty or thirty million unemployed workers posed a signal danger, which the Chinese government needed to address if it was to maintain its legitimacy and its power.

By 2010, a joint report from the International Monetary Fund and the International Labour Organisation tallied up estimates of the global net job loss from the crisis.[15] The United States had the

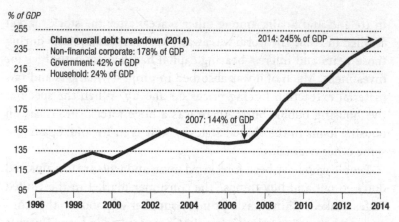

Figure 8 *Rising debt (state, corporate and household) in China (Morgan Stanley)*

largest net loss of 7.5 million jobs, while China's net job loss was only about 3 million. Somehow, China had managed to absorb at least 17 million people and possibly many more back into the labour market in the space of about one year. This is an astounding and totally unprecedented performance.

How did China absorb such vast amounts of surplus labour so fast? It seems the central government told everybody to take on as many infrastructure and mega-projects as possible. The banks were told to lend to developers without restraint. In the United States, when the Federal Reserve and the US Treasury gave money to the banks to lend in 2008, the banks used the money to retire their bad debts (de-leveraging it is called) and even bought back their own stock. In the United States, the government does not have power over the banks. The Chinese banking system does not work that way. In China, if bankers are told by the central government to lend, they lend. And they evidently did, incidentally making a lot of people ultra-wealthy in the process. Suddenly China became a world populated by billionaires, second only to the United States.

The mass construction effort in China was debt-financed.

The country's debt quadrupled between 2007 and 2015. By 2016 the formal debt stood at 250 per cent of GDP. The debt had to be extended to both production and consumption. Household debt has risen dramatically (otherwise who would buy all those new housing units?).[16] Easy credit pushed property prices upwards. Speculation in housing values became rife. In the summer of 2016 housing prices nationally were rising at 7.5 per cent a year while in the ten top metropolitan areas in China the increase was 20 per cent.[17] Meanwhile, local, state and municipal governments borrowed up to the hilt. Rumours surfaced in 2014 of a mass of toxic debts hidden within a shadow banking system and in the bowels of municipal finance.[18] Fears of some sort of financial crash in the offing periodically erupt in the financial press. China's debt is not, however, denominated in dollars but in its own currency. So there is no prospect of outside intervention from, for example, the IMF or foreign bondholders (as was the case for hapless Greece). The central government has large foreign exchange reserves which could be used, as they had been in previous periods of financial difficulty, to recapitalise financial institutions.

China in effect unleashed the power of anti-value to force value production upwards to absorb as much surplus labour as possible. China was not the only country to do this. The IMF reports a huge increase in global levels of debt finance since 2007–8 (Figure 8, page 182). Global non-financial sector debt now stands at $152 trillion, the highest levels in history (225 per cent of global GDP).[19] The United States is one of the few countries where some reduction in net debts occurred after 2008, mainly by way of austerity politics at all levels of government and continuing problems of housing finance. This resulted in stagnant effective demand which held back the recovery from the crisis.

The unprecedented pace of global debt creation since the 1970s suggests a global economy that is increasingly growing by the deployment of the smoke and mirrors of anti-value creation within the world's multiple regional monetary systems. A lot of the debt is probably toxic, covered by the creation of even more debt (as happens in Ponzi schemes). It is not clear where the value will come from to redeem the ever-escalating debt.

China absorbed a massive amount of labour by launching a huge programme of investment in productive consumption in the built environment. A quarter of GDP came from the production of housing alone and another quarter or more from infrastructural investments in highways, water systems, rail networks, airports and the like. Whole new cities were built (several of them 'ghost cities' that have yet to be populated[20]). The space economy of the nation is better integrated with highways and high-speed rail networks, connecting southern and northern markets in a much stronger way, developing the interior so that it was much better linked to the coast. While clearly the central government had wanted to do something like this for some time (plans were laid for the high-speed rail network during the 1990s), it mobilised everything it could during this period to absorb the surplus and potentially restive labour force. In 2007 there were zero miles of high-speed rail in China. By 2015 there were nearly 12,000 miles linking all the major cities. This, by any standard, was a phenomenal performance.

There was, however, nothing new about the manner of China's response to its economic difficulties. Consider the case of the United States after World War II. The US economy needed to absorb the huge increase in productive capacity created during the war and create well-paying jobs for a large number of returning veterans. Policy makers knew that if veterans returning to civilian life were faced with unemployment on the scale of the 1930s, then there would surely be serious political and economic unrest. The reproduction of capitalism was at stake.

The first front was to repress all oppositional left wing thinking through the anti-communist movement known as McCarthyism. The second front was to confront the economic problem of surplus capital and surplus labour supply. This was done in part through US imperialism, the Cold War and an expansion of militarism (the rise of the famous 'military industrial complex' that President Eisenhower unsuccessfully tried to thwart). These initiatives were supplemented by a massive wave of investments into physical and social infrastructures (such as higher education). The interstate highway system pulled together the West Coast and the South, and spatially integrated the US economy in new ways. Los Angeles was an ordinary-sized city in 1945, but by 1970 it had become a megalopolis. Metropolitan areas were totally re-engineered with transport, highways and cars, and above all with sprawling suburbs. The figure of Robert Moses, the genius planner who reconfigured the whole design of the metropolitan region of New York, bestrode the world of both ideas and practice of urbanisation and modernist metropolitan re-engineering.[21] The development of a whole new suburban lifestyle (acclaimed in popular TV sitcoms like *The Brady Bunch* and *I Love Lucy* which celebrated a certain kind of 'daily life of peoples') along with all sorts of propaganda for the 'American Dream' of individualised homeownership stood at the centre of a huge campaign to construct new wants, needs and desires, a totally new lifestyle, in the population at large. Well-paid jobs were required to support the effective demand. Labour and capital came to an uneasy compromise at the urging of the state apparatus in which a white working class made economic gains, even as minorities were left out. The 1950s and 1960s were, in many respects, the golden years of capital accumulation in the United States: high rates of growth, a satisfactory situation for a white working class, even as a powerful civil rights movement and uprisings in central cities showed that all was not well for the impoverished and marginalised African-American and immigrant populations. But the overaccumulation problem was solved for fifteen or more years by these means. As the Chair of the San Francisco Federal Reserve was reported to have said, the United States 'gets out of crises by building houses and filling them with things'.[22] But, as later became obvious in the foreclosure wave of 2007–8, this is how capital gets into crises as well.

A similar example of using urbanisation to solve economic and political problems had occurred much earlier in Second Empire Paris.[23] The economic crisis of 1848 prompted working class and bourgeois revolutions in that city. Both failed and Louis Napoleon (nephew of Bonaparte) was elected President on the promise of making France great again. He took absolute power in a coup d'état in December 1851 and declared himself Emperor in 1852. He immediately set up a network of spies and secret police to inform upon and control all opposition. But he also knew that he would not last long unless he put labour and capital back to work. A fan of the utopian theories of Saint-Simon, he initiated public works projects funded by associated capital and brought Haussmann to Paris to oversee the rebuilding of the city. Capital and labour were soon fully and profitably employed, creating the new boulevards, parks, department stores, fresh piped potable water and sewers and the like. Daily life was transformed into the bourgeois consumerism of the city of light, the cafés and the music halls and urban spectacles (fashion displays upon the boulevards) flourished. We still see the consequences of this effort at urban transformation today when we walk Haussmann's boulevards, sit in the corner cafés and drink the tap water in central Paris.

But the scale and speed of these changes were nowhere near that wrought by Robert Moses in the United States after 1945 and dwarf into insignificance when compared to the scale and the speed of the transformations in China in recent times.

In all these instances there was a common underlying problem. New credit institutions and methods of financing had to be created to sustain the building efforts. Anti-value had to be created to force the production of value. A new kind of credit-driven banking became more prominent in Paris in the 1850s. But at a certain point, debt creation and scepticism as to the value that stood behind the debt came to the fore. Paris's debt crisis of 1867 (fifteen years after Louis Bonaparte's coup) engulfed not only the speculative financial institutions but also the finances of the city. Haussmann was forced to resign (much as Moses did in New York a century later). Unemployment and unrest ensued. Louis Bonaparte sought to save himself with a nationalist strategy that led into the Franco-Prussian War of 1870–1. He lost the war and fled to England. In the wake of the war and the German siege of Paris the inhabitants of Paris made their own revolution – the Commune of 1871 – one of the greatest urban uprisings in human history. The people took back 'their' city from the bourgeoisie and the capitalists who had in their view plundered and despoiled it. The wants, needs and desires of working people and a radicalised bourgeoisie offended by the conspicuous consumption of the Second Empire surged to the fore. They sought to create a different kind of society and a different kind of city.[24] But the upper classes, expelled from the city, rallied rural sentiments and ruthlessly destroyed the Commune in a blood bath in which some 30,000 communards were killed.

Solving the overaccumulation problem through rapid urbanisation comes at a certain cost. In the United States, new mortgage finance and other institutions had been put in place in the 1930s, but even greater levels of state intervention occurred after 1945 (such as the GI bill that gave returning veterans privileged access to housing and higher education). The system worked well for a time, but stresses were evident as early as 1967. Around then, Moses was forced out of power. The whole process came to a crashing halt with the rising political discontents of the '68 generation and a civil rights movement that fostered inner-city uprisings. First wave feminists saw the suburbs as hostile territory and the '68 generation, inspired by Jane Jacobs's critique of Moses's sterile modernist planning style, was in open revolt against the conventional lifestyle of the suburbs and arid attempts at corporate urban renewal. The wants, needs and desires of the '68 generation were radically different, demanding of a different kind of urbanisation and lifestyle. To top it all, the property market collapsed shortly thereafter, culminating in the technical bankruptcy of New York City in 1973–5 (the city had one of the largest public budgets in the capitalist world at that time).[25] This initiated a period of serious recession and capitalist restructuring in the United States that also affected the United Kingdom, Europe and the rest of North America, eventually extending globally in a wave of neoliberal restructuring of capitalism in general.[26] The restructuring entailed the accelerating growth of indebtedness and the circulation of interest-bearing capital as the prime energy source for endless capital accumulation. It also ushered in the rise of a new kind of urban and suburban lifestyle more in tune to the libertarian demands of the '68 generation.

After 2008, the Chinese in effect copied (probably without knowing it) what Louis Bonaparte did in Paris after 1848 and the United States had done after World War II (even to include major investments in higher education). But they did it much faster and at a much larger scale, as the data on cement construction show. This change of scale and speed is consistent with Marx's portrait of the drive of capital to reproduce itself by way of accelerating expansion of use as well as exchange values.

It was not only China that sought to emulate this history of existing crises by construction projects and filling them with things. Turkey, for example, went through the same kind of expansion in its urbanisation: a new airport for Istanbul, a third bridge over the Bosphorus, the urbanisation of the northern part of the city to create a city of some 45 million people. Every city in Turkey witnessed a building boom. As a result, Turkey was hardly affected by the crash of 2008 (although it too saw its export industries suffer). Turkey had the second highest growth rate after China in the post-2008 period. As so often happens, this led to an urban revolt (faint echoes of the Paris Commune) focused on Gezi Park in Istanbul in 2013. Spectacular urbanisation in the Gulf States also absorbed a lot of surplus capital, though in this case it was imported immigrant labour that was involved. In major urban centres in North America and Europe, property markets quickly revived after 2009 but mainly for high-end housing projects for the affluent. New York City and London soon were experiencing property revivals in high-end construction in the midst of a chronic absence of any investment in affordable housing for the less well off.

Step back a moment and think about what is happening. There is something insane about the spectacular urbanisation ('limitless waste and boundless consumption') of the Gulf States in a region of the world desperate for mass improvements in the well-being of the common people. The same has to be said about the investment in high-end condos for the rich and the ultra-rich in New York City where there is a crisis of affordable housing and 60,000 homeless people on the streets. The seething slums of Mumbai are punctuated by palatial buildings for the newly minted billionaires. Many of these high-end buildings are not lived in. Walk the streets of New York and see how many lights are on at night in those spectacular condos for the affluent soaring high into the night sky. The buildings are simply investment vehicles not only for the ultra-rich but for anyone who has some spare cash to save.

When China relaxed its foreign exchange controls in 2016, a flock of Chinese buyers appeared in New York City, Vancouver, San Francisco and elsewhere, looking for a place to park their money rather than a place to live. When Irish entrepreneurs were flush with money before 2007 they also bought into Manhattan real estate. The Russians, the Saudis, the Australians are doing the same. And it's not only the billionaires who are doing it. Upper-middle-class people are pursuing a property and land grab wherever they can. Workers' pension funds invest in predatory real estate equity schemes because that is where the rate of return is highest. It can happen that these funds connive at the eviction of tenants who have investments in the pension funds that provide the financing.[27]

Capital is building cities for people and institutions to invest in, not cities for the common people to live in. How sane is this?

As the construction boom in China receded, surplus productive capacity in cement and steel production became a problem. The global demand for raw materials slackened and the terms of trade for raw material producers turned unfavourable. In 2013, Brazil was flush with money. By 2016 it was in deep recession. Since 2014 most of Latin America has seen deepening economic distress, because the Chinese market is not so vigorous any more. Even Germany, which exports high tech machine tools and equipment to China, felt the draught.

Capital continues to move around in search of a 'spatial fix' to its overaccumulation problems but at an accelerating rate. This is what economic imperialism was traditionally about. Surplus capital and labour from Britain in the nineteenth century came to the United States or went to Australia, South Africa and Argentina. Britain lent funds to those countries to build their railways and infrastructures using surplus steel and rolling stock produced in Britain. The improved productivity of the recipient economy redeemed the debt in time. This is how foreign aid is typically structured to this day. Dynamic capitalist economies were produced in new locations (as in the case of the United States vis-à-vis Britain and more recently through US investments in China). Imperial strategies of protecting market share and curbing competition from the new spaces, as Britain did in the case of India, were less successful. They failed to produce compounding global growth and in the 1930s helped produce a depression.

Seeking spatial fixes to solve overaccumulation problems continues to be a common capitalist practice. The Japanese took to exporting surplus capital from the late 1960s on; South Korea followed suit in the late 1970s; and Taiwan in the early 1980s. Flows of surplus capital from these territories went all over the world but were particularly important in building productive capacity in China.[28]

Now it is China's turn to export. Overcapacity exists in steel production. How is it to be managed? The state seeks to reduce capacity through plant closures. But this is difficult given fierce local resistance to job losses. The Chinese are proposing another bout of investment in urban infrastructures. They plan to create a city of some 130 million people – equivalent to the population of the United Kingdom and France combined. It will be centred on Beijing. Investments will be focused on high-speed transport and communications.[29] What is being proposed is the rationalisation of three major urban regions: one centred in Beijing, the second in Shanghai and the third in Guangdong Province. Several multimillion cities already exist in each of these regions. The plan seems to be to seek a higher order rationalisation of space relations between them as a way to mop up surplus cement and steel production capacity for the next few years.

China is also exporting as much steel as it can at low cost. Higher cost steel plants elsewhere (in Britain, for example) are being forced to close. China is being challenged before the WTO for dumping subsidised steel in the world market. It will almost certainly be obliged to stop this trade if it wants 'Market Economy Status' in the WTO. But Chinese corporations are also lending money on relatively easy terms to countries to build railways, highways and physical infrastructures in, for example, East Africa using Chinese steel as well as surplus Chinese labour, even though there is plenty of local surplus labour available. The same is happening in Latin America. Proposals exist to build a competitor to the Panama Canal through Nicaragua, and transcontinental rail lines running from the Pacific to the Atlantic coasts. It will then be possible to get from the port of Lima to São Paulo in about a day and a half overland. Several proposals of this kind were laid out some time ago in Latin America but nobody took them seriously until the Chinese came along and said they had plenty of cement and steel and that they would lend the money to purchase these materials and build the infrastructures. While the cost of shipping will remain much lower it is also slower and 'time is money' in the sphere of circulation these days. China is also rebuilding the Silk Road route from Inner China to Istanbul (and into Europe) via Tehran. A fast, high-capacity rail network is planned through Central Asia into Europe (under the heading of 'One Belt, One Road').[30] This project, with its offshoot through Pakistan to the Arabian Sea port of Gwadar, will absorb plenty of surplus capital and mop up some of the surplus steel capacity. Central Asian cities along the Silk Road route are already experiencing building booms and rapid expansions of trade with China and the easier access to the Gulf States through Pakistan (avoiding the tedious sea journey through the congested and militarily vulnerable Straits of Malacca) almost certainly means a considerable expansion of accessible Chinese trade outlets into that region.

The relative spaces of the global economy are being revolutionised (yet again!) not because it is a good idea or desperately wanted and needed in itself, but because this is the best way to stave off depression and devaluation. The absorption of surplus capital is the aim. Marx understood this all too well. 'Next in urgency, perhaps, to the desire to acquire money, is the wish to part with it again for some species of investment that shall yield either interest or profit; for money itself, as money, yields neither ... Enterprises which entail a large capital and create an opening from time to time for the excess of unemployed capital ... are absolutely necessary ... so as to take care of the periodic accumulations of the superfluous wealth of society, which is unable to find room in the usual fields of application.'[31] The result in this particular case is a wholly new material base of space relations for the reconstruction of the world's divergent value regimes.

Capital is not the only agent involved in this spatial restructuring. Mass migratory movements are bringing labour forces together into competitive configurations. This has also happened before but it is now, like the case of Chinese cement, at an unprecedented scale. It is not only the volume of migratory movement that counts. The labour forces of the world have been brought into a competitive relation with each other by declining transport and communications costs, organisational technologies and changing speed (rather than costs) of movement as well as through the development of complex commodity chains. Time–space compression in both capital and labour force relations produces a range of political stresses and responses varying from anti-immigrant movements, the rekindling of nationalist fervours or, on the more positive side, the willing embrace of multiculturalism as a harbinger of a different human future.

The stresses from all these rapid changes are everywhere in evidence and affected populations know it, feel it and sometimes act out upon it. On the night of 20 June 2013, for example, more than a million people throughout the cities of Brazil took to the streets in a massive protest movement. The largest protest, of more than 100,000 people, occurred in Rio de Janeiro. Typically, it was met with significant police violence. Sporadic protests had been occurring for more than a year in various Brazilian cities. Led by a 'Free Pass' youth movement that had long been agitating for free public transportation for students, the earlier protests were largely ignored. But by early June 2013, fare increases for public transportation sparked more widespread protests. Many other groups, including the black block anarchists, sprang to the defence of the 'Free Pass' protestors and others when the latter came under police attack. By 13 June the movement had morphed into a general protest against police repressions, the failure of public services to match social needs and the deteriorated qualities of urban life. The huge expenditures of public resources to host mega-events such as the World Cup and the Olympic Games to the detriment of the public interest but to the great benefit, it was widely understood, of corrupt construction and urban development interests, added to the discontents.[32]

The protests in Brazil came less than a month after thousands of people turned out on the streets of Turkey's major cities, as anger over the redevelopment of the all-too-rare green space of Gezi Park in Istanbul as a shopping centre, spread into a broader protest against the increasingly autocratic style of the government and the violence of the police response. Long simmering discontents over the pace and style of urban transformation, including the wholesale evictions of populations from high value land in inner city locations, added fuel to the protests. The deteriorating qualities of urban life in Istanbul and other cities for all but the most affluent classes was clearly an important issue.[33]

The protests in Turkey and Brazil, led Bill Keller of the *New York Times* to write an op-ed piece entitled 'The Revolt of the Rising Class'. The uprisings were 'not born in desperation,' he wrote. Both Brazil and Turkey had experienced remarkable economic growth in a period of global crisis. They were 'the latest in a series of revolts arising from the middle class – the urban, educated haves who are in some ways the principal beneficiaries of the regimes they now reject' but who also had something to lose by taking to the streets in protest. 'By the time the movements reached critical mass, they were about something bigger and more inchoate, dignity, the perquisites of citizenship, the obligations of power.'[34] The revolts signified 'a new alienation, a new yearning' that needed to be addressed. In both Turkey and Brazil political power has chosen the path of reaction and repression (violently so in Turkey) rather than accommodation in response.

So what is this 'new alienation' all about and what does it signify? There have been abundant signs of it everywhere, from the anti-globalisation protests that first came to public prominence in Seattle in 1999, through the various movements in Europe (the Indignados in Spain and the Athens protests in Syntagma Square), the uprisings that were dubbed 'the Arab Spring' that began in Tunisia and spread via Egypt and Syria to the Ukraine, followed by the various 'Occupy' movements in New York and London and autonomy movements from Scotland to Catalonia and Hong Kong to more recent right wing manifestations in Brazil up until the election of far-right governments in Hungary, Poland and the United States along with the secessionist Brexit vote in Britain – all of these suggest a deepening climate of dissent, discontent and even despair. The madness of economic reason with all of its impacts via austerity and free market economics seems to be producing a parallel madness – in this case anger – in the political sphere as well.

In *Seventeen Contradictions and the End of Capitalism*, I had suggested there were three contradictions that posed a clear and present danger to the survival of capitalism in the present era.[35] The first was the deteriorating state of our relation to nature (everything from global warming to habitat and species destruction, water scarcities and environmental degradations). The second was compound growth for ever that had reached that inflexion point on the exponential growth curve that was rapidly proving harder and harder to perpetuate in the face of increasing paucity of profitable investment opportunities. It was also putting intense pressure on that one form of capital that can increase without limit, particularly the credit forms of money that seemed to be spiralling out of control. The third was what I called universal alienation. Marx does not use this concept much in *Capital* but it echoes right throughout his earlier writings from the *Economic and Philosophic Manuscripts of 1844* to culminate as a dominant motif in the *Grundrisse*. The labour theory of value in *Capital* describes alienated labour without calling it that, perhaps because Marx felt the Hegelianism of the term would not appeal to his target audiences (the British and French working classes). Dropping the term does not, however, abolish its content.[36]

Value in Marx is socially necessary alienated labour. Since capital is value in motion, then the circulation of capital entails the circulation of alienated forms. To what degree do these alienations underpin the evident political manifestations of discontent and despair?

The alienation inherent in valorisation is well known and long-standing. The labourer who creates value is separated (alienated) from access to the means of production, from command over the labour process, the product and the surplus value. Capital makes it appear as if many of the inherent powers (and free gifts) of labour and of nature belong to and originate with it because it is capital that gives them meaning. Even the mind and bodily functions of the labourer along with all the natural forces freely deployed in production appear as contingent powers of capital because it is capital that mobilises them. The alienation of the relation to nature and to human nature is a precondition, therefore, for the assertion of capital's productivity and powers. In addition, the productivity of labour is driven by technologies chosen by capital to confirm not only its control over the labourer but to undermine the dignity and putative powers of labour both in production and in the market place. Meaningless jobs, contingent employment and unemployment and ever lower rates of remuneration are the fate of labour unless resistance is effectively mobilised to counteract them. In many parts of the world there is no question that the alienation of labour has been intensifying and deepening through technological changes, the suppression of the organised power of the working class movements and the mobilisation of global competition through the reorganisation of the world's territorial value regimes. Unemployment and, just as important, underemployment and loss of meaning have been a by-product of the strong currents of technological and organisational change. Contemporary utopian accounts of how the new technological configurations based in artificial intelligence are bringing us to the brink of a brave new world of emancipatory consumerism and disposable time for all, ignore entirely the dehumanising alienation of the residual and disposable labour processes that result. The collective traumatic and dissolving effects of manufacturing plant closures on the social ties that had previously bound people together in a given place and time cannot be glossed over. Marx, for his part, thought there was an important distinction to be drawn between workers who were objectified and exploited by capital but felt they were needed (thereby retaining same pride and dignity) on the one hand and those who were alienated, dispossessed and felt themselves to be disposable on the other.[37] The trend in employment conditions attendant upon mechanisation and automation was towards labour of the latter sort. The loss of dignity and respect is felt almost as hard as the loss of a job.

But there are other dimensions to this problem. Workers are hired individually and compete for job opportunities. They have to sell themselves to capital as bearers of labour power by advertising their qualities while diminishing and even denigrating the qualities of their competitors. Competition between workers frustrates cooperation and hinders the building of class solidarities. It introduces all manner of fragmentations. Workers become estranged from each other. This becomes even more invidious when infused with racism, gender discriminations, sexual, ethnic or religious hostilities in the labour market (divisions which capital has a history of avidly encouraging). Heightened competition (under conditions of widespread unemployment and the closer spatial integration of the world's labour forces) is everywhere intensifying these splits and tensions within the labour force with predictable political results, particularly in situations where previous social solidarities have been dissolved through deindustrialisation. These were, for example, the sentiments that Donald Trump so successfully exploited in his presidential campaign of 2016 in the United States.

Alienation upon realisation takes quite different as well as multiple and often double-edged forms. The state of wants, needs and desires always lies at the root of demand. Marx considered, without irony, that the creation of new wants and needs was part of the civilising mission of capital.[38] That opinion is hard to dispute when we consider, for example, all those use values that can now be mobilised in the cause of extending average life expectancy from thirty-five years or so in the early years of capitalism to seventy years or more in many areas of the world today. Capital produces a cornucopia of use values from which it is in principle possible for people to create unalienated social relations and ways of being in nature and with each other. The potentiality is there. The world is dotted with heterotopic spaces in which groups strive to construct unalienated ways of living and being in the midst of a sea of alienation. The alienations experienced in production stand to be recuperated through a compensatory consumption of use values that improve the qualities of daily life.[39] On the other hand, the wants, needs and desires of the military-industrial complex, the gun lobby or the car producers have formed and continue to form potent sources of aggregate demand engineered through corporate influence over the state apparatus and through imposed lifestyle choices. Their contributions to social well-being are dubious at best. A city like São Paulo has as its economic base a car industry that produces vehicles that spend hours stationary in traffic jams as they clog the city streets spewing pollutants and isolating individuals from each other. How sane an economy is that?

What to do about cars is one of the critical questions of our time, which no one much wants to talk about (except in terms of better management of flows through smart city technologies). Yet the warning signs are everywhere. In the early winter of 2016, all Chinese cities north of the Yangtze experienced killer smogs that closed airports and snarled traffic for many days. Similar events occurred in New Delhi, Tehran and extended even to Paris and (less intensely) to London. Life expectancy has been declining north of the Yangtze over the last two decades and deteriorating air quality is suspected as the prime reason. Some of the worst industrial polluters, it should be remarked, are steel and cement along with coal-fired power stations.

The relation between realisation and the history of consumerism overlaps with the historical evolution of distinctive lifestyles. The building of the suburbs and gated communities in the United States may have saved global capitalism from return to depression conditions, but it also corralled housing choices in ways that attach not only to material requirements (e.g. a car and private property in housing) but also is accompanied by political and ideological justifications of a way of life (designated as 'The American Dream') that limits and imprisons rather than liberates the horizons of personal fulfilment. The rise of 'compensatory consumerism' for the working classes is supplemented by conspicuous consumption of 'hedonistic goods' within all classes that add up to nothing more than conspicuous waste. The endless pursuit of satisfactions of wants, needs and desires that can never be fulfilled, necessarily parallels endless compounding growth in production. While it would be wrong to consider the reconfiguration of all new wants, needs and desires as 'alienated' it is not hard to see how alienations flourish and have in many places and among certain marginalised classes been intensifying in the kind of consumerist society that capital necessarily constructs. The gap between the promise and the realisation has been widening.

If the circulation of capital is under immense competitive pressure to accelerate, then this requires speed-up in consumption. I still use my grandparents' knives and forks. If capital produced only items of this sort it would long ago have fallen into permanent crisis. Capital evolves a whole range of tactics, from planned obsolescence to mobilising advertising pressures and fashion as tools of persuasion, all in the cause of accelerating turnover time in consumption. Consider the case of a Netflix original. The fact that I consume it does not prevent it being consumed by others and the consumption time is that of an hour or so, compared to my knives and forks that have lasted more than 100 years. The value entailed in the production and transmission through intricate communication infrastructures is recuperated by literally millions of users paying their Netflix subscriptions. Hardly surprisingly, capital has cultivated a 'society of spectacle' in order to assure a form of market growth of ephemeral products for instantaneous consumption.[40] The social consequences of this are far-reaching and double-edged. Rapid transformations in lifestyles, technologies and social expectations multiply social insecurities and increase social tensions across generations as well as between diversifying social groups. Everybody seems intent on consulting their mobile phones or their tablets rather than talking with each other. The rootedness of cultural meanings becomes less secure, open to casual reconstructions in accord with contemporary fantasies. Identities float in a sea of transitory and ephemeral attachments. People and products that correspond to this are needed if capital is to meet the requirement of endless compound growth. This is what 'rational consumption' looks like from the standpoint of endless capital accumulation.

The conditions and location of the realisation and appropriation of value are very different from those of production. The Netflix original may be made in Los Angeles but the realisation takes place in media markets all over a country or even the world. My computer is produced in Shenzhen by Foxconn and its value is realised by Apple in the United States. The former earns a very low rate of profit while the latter takes the bulk of the value and surplus value for itself. This is how transfers of value are engineered from one space to another.[41] The fairness of this is being very much called into question.

Opportunistic forms of capital also intervene at the moment of realisation to appropriate far more value than is warranted. When hedge funds take over pharmaceutical companies or buy up large swathes of foreclosed housing and then turn around and make them available to needy consumers at exorbitant prices, then realisation becomes a moment for the systematic organisation of accumulation by dispossession.[42] If you ask people what the major forms of exploitation experienced in the United States are today, they mention credit-card fees. They mention landlords and rents and property speculators. They mention what telephone companies do to their telephone bills by adding all these weird charges that say you were roaming someplace where you weren't. They mention health insurance companies, local taxes, transport costs and so on. There is an immense amount of racketeering (sometimes akin to robbery) that goes on at the point of realisation. The politics of struggles over realisation are apparent everywhere. The discontents are legion.

The politics involved in the extraction of wealth at the moment of realisation are different from those generated around production. Such struggles are difficult to theorise and organise. It is not capital versus labour but capital versus everybody else, between buyers and sellers rather than between labour and capital. Middle-class populations are buyers and get involved in struggles (sometimes of the not-in-my-backyard sort) against racketeering merchants. Do working class populations seek them out as allies against the property speculators? The politics are just as robust and torment ridden as those of valorisation even though they have a different structure and reflect different forms of alienation. Revolutionary movements, like the Paris Commune of 1871 or the '68 movement, were, it turns out, often as much indebted to a radicalised and alienated bourgeoisie barred from realising their dreams and ambitions as they were to the working classes. But cross-class organising can be difficult as well as often frustrating. The increasing prominence of accumulation by dispossession (with the massive losses in the recent foreclosure crisis in the forefront) deepens despair and discontent in many segments of the population.[43]

While a lot of wealth is extracted by capital from realisation, even more is sucked out from distribution. The most blatant form of redistribution has to highlight the declining share of labour in the national product in much of the world and the failure of labour in recent times in particular to receive any benefits from rising productivity. Labour has suffered instead from the unemployment and the rapid deteriorations of qualities of work through technological change. The shift from productive to unproductive labour accompanied by excessive bureaucratisation within both the state and corporations has not helped. Increasing inequality in incomes and wealth almost everywhere throughout the capitalist world (with some rare exceptions) adds to the mix of forces making for deep political discontents.[44]

The politics and the mechanisms of other redistributions are, however, very different and the consequent alienations that arise are so complex as to require a whole book to deal with them. The different factions of capital – merchants, financiers, property owners and industrial capitalists – sometimes cooperate and complement each other. But they also compete and are not averse to stealing from and exercising power over each other. Usurious practices should have disappeared according to Marx but capitalist financiers – who typically exhibit the 'nicely mixed character of swindler and prophet'[45] – rule the roost for financial transactions and channel the circulation of interest-bearing capital in ways that are often far from beneficial except to themselves. Tactics of predatory lending are, for example, widespread. This lending is not intended to promote the production of value but to entangle producers in such a web of debt obligations as eventually they have no option except to surrender their property rights to the lender. Such tactics were well known in Marx's time and frequently referred to in Volume 3 of *Capital*. Financial institutions engaging in predatory lending towards the working classes have in recent years successfully raided the housing asset values of vulnerable populations. Predatory lending to states often leads to structural adjustments imposed by the IMF, which diminish the well-being of whole populations in order to redeem accumulated debts (as is the problem for Greece).[46] The punitive treatment of Argentina after court judgments (rendered in Manhattan because the debts were dollar denominated) in favour of the demands of 'vulture capitalists' meant the transfer of wealth into the pockets of hedge funds. Governments in many parts of the world are also notorious for their corruption – Brazil, China and Italy are frequently mentioned in the financial press.

Marx's own writings on this in Volume 3 of *Capital* reflect both the confusions of the subject matter and his own confusions as to how to integrate the peculiar circulation of interest-bearing capital into his overall conception of capital as value in motion. I tried to reconstruct his views and synthesise these writings in *A Companion to Marx's Capital, Volume 2*.[47] Since I cannot possibly repeat this reconstruction here, I will confine myself to citing a lengthy passage in which Marx describes a typical sequence of events in the financial sphere. I invite readers to compare it to the broad outlines of what happened in the financial crisis of 2007–8 (substituting 'mortgages' for 'bills of exchange:

> In a system of production where the entire interconnection of the reproduction process rests on credit, a crisis must evidently break out if credit is suddenly withdrawn and only cash payment is accepted ... At first glance, therefore, the entire crisis presents itself as simply a credit and monetary crisis, and in fact all it does involve is simply the convertibility of bills of exchange [mortgages] into money. The majority of these bills [mortgages] represent actual purchases and sales, the ultimate basis of the entire crisis being the expansion of these far beyond the social need. On top of this, however, a tremendous number of these bills [mortgages] represent purely fraudulent deals, which now come to light and explode, as well as unsuccessful speculations conducted with the borrowed capital, and finally commodity capitals [houses] that are either devalued or unsaleable ... It is clear that this whole artificial system of forced expansion of the reproduction process cannot be cured by now allowing one bank, e.g. the Bank of England [the Federal Reserve], to give all the swindlers the capital they lack in paper money and to buy all the depreciated commodities [houses] at their old nominal values. Moreover, everything here appears upside down, since in this paper world the real price and its elements are nowhere to be seen ... This distortion is particularly evident in centres such as London, where the monetary business of an entire country is concentrated, here the whole process becomes incomprehensible.[48]

This brings us to consider the power and importance of that aspect of distribution that functions as a clearing house for the conversion of idle money into the circulation of interest-bearing capital. It is here that the madness of economic reason takes over through the creation of anti-value and the promotion of debt peonage. In a world that is awash in surplus liquidity (as the IMF frequently refers to it in its reports) then these moneys have to be mobilised, centralised and lent out on the security and certainty of future surplus value production. The conversion of surplus money into a form of anti-capital that demands its pound of future flesh is carried out within financial institutions. The lender retains the property right to the money throughout and expects a return of that money value within a certain time-frame plus the surplus that is interest and the capital gain that may also be achieved as stock market valuations of company assets increase.

The overall management of this conversion operation (or metamorphosis as Marx would prefer to call it) from money into anti-value is largely located in what I have elsewhere called 'the state finance nexus'.[49] In the United States (as well as in most Western democracies) this is constituted by close collaborations between a treasury department (which always has a special status within the state apparatus) and a central bank which is the apex of the private banking system. A structure of this kind first came into being with the foundation of the Bank of England in 1694. Wealthy merchants were granted a monopoly by bank charter from William and Mary with extensive powers in return for providing credit and finance to a state that had been left bankrupt by the profligacy of the Stuart kings. The balance of power between state and finance has shifted over time. Ever since Bill Clinton in the early years of his presidency conceded that his economic programme depended on the consent of the bondholders, the key office of the Secretary of the Treasury in the United States has mainly been held by someone from Goldman Sachs.

This state–finance nexus is not subject to democratic or popular control. It has for its mandate the regulation and control of the private banking system for the benefit of capital as a whole. Finance, Marx suggests, is about how 'the common capital of the class' shall be managed.[50] The state–finance nexus, when taken as a whole, is analogous to the central nervous system embodied within any organic totality. It sanctions and guarantees leveraging practices which convert idle moneys in deposits into anti-capital. The role of anti-capital, as we earlier saw, is to foreclose upon the future of as many economic agents as possible and to condemn all and sundry – consumers as well as producers, merchants, landlords and even the financiers themselves – to a state of debt peonage.

Capital 'as a special kind of commodity' has always 'had a special kind of alienation peculiar to it'.[51] 'The entire immense extension of the credit system, and credit as a whole, is exploited by the bankers as their private capital. These fellows have their capital and revenue permanently in the money form or in the form of direct claims to money. The accumulation of wealth by this class may proceed in a very different way from that of actual accumulation, but it proves in any case that they put away a good proportion of the latter.'[52] The problem is that finance typically 'gives rise to monopoly in certain spheres and hence provokes state intervention. It reproduces a new financial aristocracy, a new kind of parasite in the guise of company promoters, speculators and merely nominal directors; an entire system of swindling and cheating with respect to the promotion of companies, issue of shares and share dealings.'[53] Furthermore, 'if surplus value is conceived in the irrational form of interest, the limit is only quantitative' and the consequences of this, Marx adds, 'beggars all fantasy'.[54] Bad infinity raises its ugly head. The bonuses the Wall Streeters gave themselves during the years of collapse 'beggared all fantasy'. This was what outraged the Occupy movement that suddenly appeared in 2011 in Wall Street's Zuccotti Park.

The disciplining effect of debt encumbrance is vital to the reproduction of the contemporary form of capital. Debt means we are no longer 'free to choose', as Milton Friedman in his paean to capitalism supposes. Capital does not forgive us our debts, as the Bible asks, but insists we redeem them through future value production. The future is already foretold and foreclosed (ask any student who has $100,000 in student loans to pay). Debt imprisons within certain structures of future value production. Debt peonage is capital's favoured means to impose its particular form of slavery. This becomes doubly dangerous when the power of the bondholders subverts and seeks to imprison the sovereignty of the state. It is for this reason that the only mode of capital's survival is through the coherence and fusion achieved through the state–finance nexus. With this, the alienation of whole populations from any real influence and power is complete. Neither state nor capital can offer any relief to deprivations and disempowerments. Athens is traditionally celebrated as the cradle of democracy. Today it is merely the cradle of debt peonage, the full and complete demolition of any democracy whatsoever.

The corrupting and alienating power of money – which, when it takes the form of interest acts like 'love possessed' – is part of the problem. It was not only Marx who recognised the alienations involved. Even Keynes, a deep defender of the bourgeois order but on occasion a trenchant critic, weighed in on the matter:

> When the accumulation of wealth is no longer of high social importance, there will be great changes in the code of morals. We shall be able to rid ourselves of many of the pseudo-moral principles which have hag-ridden us for two hundred years, by which we have exalted some of the most distasteful of human qualities into the position of the highest virtues. We shall be able to afford to dare to assess the money motive at its true value. The love of money as a possession – as distinguished from the love of money as a means to the enjoyments and realities of life – will be recognised for what it is, a somewhat disgusting morbidity, one of those semicriminal, semi-pathological propensities which one hands over with a shudder to the specialists in mental disease. All kinds of social customs and economic practices, affecting the distribution of wealth and of economic rewards and penalties, which we now maintain at all costs, however distasteful and unjust they may be in themselves, because they are tremendously useful in promoting accumulation of capital, we shall then be free, at last, to discard.[55]

That human wealth, which should have all manner of social meanings, is increasingly imprisoned in the unique metric of money power is in itself problematic. 'When the limited bourgeois form is stripped away,' writes Marx,

> what is wealth other than the universality of individual needs, capacities, pleasures, productive forces etc., the absolute working out of ... creative potentialities? ... Where he does not reproduce himself in one specificity, but produces his totality? Strives not to remain something he has become, but is in the absolute movement of becoming. In bourgeois economics – and in the epoch of production to which it corresponds – this complete working out of the human content appears as a complete emptying-out, this universal objectification as total alienation, and the tearing down of all limited one-sided aims as sacrifice of the human end in itself to an entirely external end.[56]

This is what 'beggars all fantasy'. This is the insane and deeply troubling world in which we live.

Coda

The philosopher Jacques Derrida coined the phrase 'the madness of economic reason' in his commentary on Marcel Mauss's account of the 'potlatch' ceremonies of British Columbian indigenous communities. These periodic ceremonies entailed competition between households to give away or destroy possessions in order to acquire prestige, honour and status. Early Western accounts of the ceremonies interpreted them in terms of economic concepts of a market economy. From that standpoint as well as from that of Enlightenment reason, the sacrifice of personal and household wealth painstakingly accumulated over many years appeared irrational. Mauss found that language misleading. He replaced the concepts of 'debt' and 'repayment' with that of 'presents made' and 'repaid'. Hence the concept of an alternative non-market gift economy, which some still find attractive to this day. Derrida seems to have celebrated it as an adequate replacement for state managed social welfare. But what also impressed Mauss and by extension Derrida so mightily was the frenzied madness of destruction with which the potlatch so often culminated. 'It is not even a question of giving and returning,' Mauss wrote, 'but of destroying, so as not to want even to appear to desire repayment. Whole boxes of olachen (candle-fish) oil or whale oil are burnt as are houses and thousands of blankets. The most valuable copper objects are broken and thrown into the water, in order to crush and to "flatten" one's rival.' This is what Mauss considered truly mad. 'There is always a moment,' comments Derrida, 'when this madness begins to burn up the word or the meaning gift itself and to disseminate without return its ashes …'[1]

It is not my intention here to suggest that capital sometimes gives in to some primordial instinct to tear down whatever it has built, much as some children seem to delight in stomping on the castles laboriously built by other children on the sand. For it was Marx's point to show how what seemed like (or was presented as) an act of fate or of the gods in the history of capitalism was in fact a product of capital itself. But he needed an alternative conceptual apparatus to show this. For example, the capitalist mode of production must recognise, Marx wrote, that 'a devaluation of credit money ... would destroy all the existing relationships'. The banks, as we now all too well know, must be rescued no matter what. 'The value of commodities is thus sacrificed in order to ensure the fantastic and autonomous existence of this value in money. In any event, a money value is only guaranteed as long as money itself is guaranteed.' Inflation, as we also know, must be kept under control at all costs. 'This is why many millions' worth of commodities have to be sacrificed for a few millions in money. This is unavoidable in capitalist production and forms one of its particular charms.' Use values are sacrificed and destroyed no matter what the social need.[2] How insane is that?

Capital, we have argued, is value in motion. Within the circulation process of capital, blockages periodically appear. Capital then remains 'congealed in one of its phases of reproduction because it cannot complete its metamorphoses'. In the crisis that ensues,

> everyone has goods to sell and cannot sell, even though they have to sell in order to pay ... Capital already invested is in fact massively unemployed, since the reproduction process is stagnant. Factories stand idle, raw materials pile up, finished products flood the market as commodities. Nothing could be more wrong, therefore, than to ascribe such a situation to a lack of productive capital. It is precisely then that there is a surplus of productive capital, partly in relation to the normal though temporarily contracted scale of reproduction and partly in relation to the crippled consumption.[3]

This is the madness which we have lived through time and time again over the last forty years. Surplus capital and an ever increasing mass of surplus and disposable labour sit side by side without there being any way to put them together to produce the use values so desperately needed, even as a third of the children in the United States, still the richest country in the world, live in poverty and often in toxic environments, suffer from hunger and lead poisoning even as they are denied access to elementary social services and educational opportunities by an enforced politics of austerity. What can be madder than that?

What Marx in *Capital* as well as in his other political-economic writings does is to suggest a way to cut through all the confusions of the daily workings of a capitalist mode of production and get to its essence – its inner laws of motion – through the formulation of abstractions woven into some simple (and in the end not-so-simple) theory of endless capital accumulation.

Where the real science begins is when we take these concepts, abstractions and theoretical formulations back up to the surface of daily life and show how they can illuminate the whys and wherefores of the daily struggles which people in general, but workers in particular, face in their struggles for survival. This is what the concept of capital is designed to do and this is what Marx hoped *Capital* as a book would help us accomplish. What I hope this exposition of Marx's thought has done, is to suggest that Marx's way was not a unique highway to be followed but an open door through which we could progress to ever higher understandings of the underlying problems that inform our current reality. If that reality with all of its confusing and seemingly insane contemporary political expressions is to be understood, then some investigation of how capital works is surely foundational. If today's politics look insane (as they seem to me to be), then surely the madness of economic reason has something to do with it. Indeed, it sometimes seems as if we are in a vicious and violent political world in search of a subject to torture and to blame. To be sure, capital is not the only possible subject for any thorough and complete reckoning of current ills. But to pretend it has nothing to do with our current ailments and that we do not need a cogent, as opposed to a fetishistic and apologetic representation of how it works, how it circulates and accumulates among us, is an offence against humanity that human history, if it manages to survive that long, will judge severely.

Notes and references

Works by Marx

Capital: A Critique of Political Economy, Volume 1, London: New Left Review, 1976.

Capital: A Critique of Political Economy, Volume 2, London: New Left Review, 1978.

Capital: A Critique of Political Economy, Volume 3, London: New Left Review, 1981.

A Contribution to the Critique of Political Economy, London: Lawrence and Wishart, 1970.

The Economic and Philosophic Manuscripts of 1844, New York: International Publishers, 1964.

Grundrisse, London: Penguin Books, 1973.

The Poverty of Philosophy: New York, International Publishers, 1963.

Results of the Immediate Process of Production (Appendix to *Capital, Volume 1*) in *Capital, Volume 1*, London: New Left Review, 1976.

Theories of Surplus Value, Part 1, London: Lawrence and Wishart, 1969.

Theories of Surplus Value, Part 2, London: Lawrence and Wishart, 1969.

Theories of Surplus Value, Part 3, London: Lawrence and Wishart, 1972.

Value: Studies by Marx (ed. A. Dragstedt), London: New Park Publications, 1976.

Wage Labour and Capital, Peking: Foreign Languages Press, 1978.

Wages, Price and Profit, Peking: Foreign Languages Press, 1965.

Works by Marx and Engels

Manifesto of the Communist Party, Moscow: Progress Publishers, 1952.

Selected Correspondence, Moscow: Progress Publishers, 1955.

Other Sources
Tucker, R., *The Marx-Engels Reader* (2nd edn), New York: Norton, 1978.

Prologue
1 Sperber, J., *Karl Marx: A Nineteenth Century Life*, New York: Liveright Publishing, 2013; Stedman Jones, G., *Karl Marx: Greatness and Illusion*. Cambridge, MA: Belknap Press, 2016.

Chapter 1
1 Much of the pre-history of the labour theory of value has been covered in Meek, R., *Studies in the Labour Theory of Value*, London: Lawrence and Wishart, 1973. A comprehensive survey of the state of contemporary thinking in the 1970s, when value theory was much debated, can be found in the eleven contributions assembled in Steedman, I. (ed.), *The Value Controversy*, London: Verso/New Left Books, 1981. I have drawn from the following texts: Elson, D. (ed.), *Value: The Representation of Labour in Capitalism*, London: CSE Books, 1979; Heinrich, M., *An Introduction to the Three Volumes of Karl Marx's Capital*, New York: Monthly Review Press, 2004; Henderson, G., *Value in Marx: The Persistence of Value in a More-Than-Capitalist World*, Minneapolis: University of Minnesota Press, 2013; Larsen, N., Nilges, M., Robinson, J., and Brown, N., *Marxism and the Critique of Value* (eds), Chicago: MCM Press, 2014; Ollman, B., *Alienation*, London: Cambridge University Press, 1971; Rosdolsky, R., *The Making of Marx's Capital*, London: Pluto Press, 1977; Rubin, I., *Essays on Marx's Theory of Value*, Montreal: Black Rose Books, 1973.
2 *Grundrisse*, p. 309.
3 *Grundrisse*, pp. 1, 149.
4 *Grundrisse*, pp. 251–4.
5 Fraser, N., 'Behind Marx's Hidden Abode: For an Expanded Conception of Capitalism', *New Left Review*, 86 (2014).

Chapter 2

1 *Capital, Volume 1*, chapter 2.
2 *Capital, Volume 1*, p. 799.
3 *Capital, Volume 2*, p. 109.
4 *Capital, Volume 2*, p. 469.
5 *Capital, Volume 2*, pp. 199, 225, 261, 357, 396.
6 *Capital, Volume 2*, p. 391.
7 *Selected Correspondence*, p. 206.
8 *Capital, Volume 3*, p. 267.
9 *Capital, Volume 3*, p. 311.
10 *Capital, Volume 3*, p. 490.
11 *Capital, Volume 3*, p. 516.
12 *Capital, Volume 3*, chapter 29.
13 *Capital, Volume 3*, p. 57.
14 Graeber, D., *Debt: Updated and Expanded –The First 5,000 Years*, Brooklyn: Melville Books, 2014.
15 *Capital, Volume 3*, p. 501.
16 For the importance of fictitious capital see Harvey, D., *A Companion to Marx's Capital, Volume 2*, London: Verso, pp. 240–66; Durand, C., *Fictitious Capital: How Finance is Appropriating our Future*, London: Verso, 2017.
17 *Grundrisse*, p. 278.
18 *Grundrisse*, pp. 99–100
19 *Capital, Volume 1*, p. 92.
20 For a systematic discussion of the various plans that Marx set out, see Rosdolsky, R., *The Making of Marx's Capital*, London: Pluto Press, 1977.
21 *Theories of Surplus Value, Part 3*, p. 120.

Chapter 3

1 *Capital Volume 1*, pp. 128, 138–9.
2 *Grundrisse*, pp. 149, 236.
3 *Grundrisse*, p. 776.
4 *Grundrisse*, p. 535.
5 *Capital, Volume 1*, pp. 169–72.
6 *The Poverty of Philosophy; Grundrisse*, pp. 115–238.

7   Hudis, P., *Marx' Concept of the Alternative to Capitalism*, Chicago, Haymarket, 2012, p. 107.
8   Harvey, D., *Paris: Capital of Modernity*, New York: Routledge, 2003, chapter 8.
9   *Capital, Volume 1*, pp. 91–2.
10 Nelson, A., *Marx's Concept of Money*, New York: Routledge, 2014; Greco, T., Jr, *The End of Money and the Future of Civilisation*, White River Junction, VT: Chelsea Green Publishing, 2009.
11 Piore, M., and Sable, C., *The Second Industrial Divide: Possibilities for Prosperity*, New York: Basic Books, 1986; Harvey, D., *The Condition of Postmodernity*: Oxford, Blackwell, 1989.
12 Bauwens, M., 'Towards the Democratisation of the Means of Monetisation,' mimeo, Brussels, 21 October 2013; Huws, U., *Labor in the Digital Economy*, New York: Monthly Review Press, 2014.
13 *Grundrisse*, p. 134.
14 *Grundrisse*, pp. 145–6.
15 *Grundrisse*, p. 776.
16 *Grundrisse*, pp. 122–3.
17 Nelson, A., *Life Without Money: Building Fair and Sustainable Economies*, London: Pluto Press, 2011.
18 *Capital, Volume 1*, p. 148.
19 *Capital, Volume 1*, p. 150.
20 *Capital, Volume 1*, p. 151.
21 *Capital, Volume 1*, pp. 229–30.
22 *Grundrisse*, p. 146.
23 *Grundrisse*, p. 146.
24 *Capital, Volume 1*, chapter 3.
25 *Capital, Volume 1*, pp. 221–2.
26 *Grundrisse*, p. 210.
27 *Capital, Volume 1*, p. 196.
28 *Capital, Volume 1*, p. 197.
29 *Capital, Volume 1*, p. 236.
30 Bourdieu, P., *Distinction: A Social Critique of the Judgment of Taste*, Cambridge, MA: Harvard University Press, 1984; Arvidsson, A., and Peitersen, N., *The Ethical Economy: Rebuilding Value After the Crisis*, New York: Columbia University Press, 2013.

31 *Capital, Volume* 3, p. 727.
32 *Capital, Volume* 3, p. 708.
33 *Capital, Volume* 3, p. 649.
34 *Capital, Volume* 3, pp. 706–8.
35 *Capital, Volume* 3, p. 528.
36 *Capital, Volume* 3, p. 569.
37 *Capital, Volume* 3, p. 516.
38 *Capital, Volume* 3, chapter 23.
39 *Capital, Volume* 3, p. 569.
40 *Capital, Volume* 3, p. 570.
41 *Capital, Volume* 3, pp. 570–71.

Chapter 4

1   *Capital, Volume* 1, p. 131.
2   *Grundrisse*, p. 543.
3   *Capital, Volume* 1, p. 202.
4   *Capital, Volume* 1, p. 103; Moseley, F., and Smith, T. (eds), *Marx's Capital and Hegel's Logic: A Reexamination*, Chicago: Haymarket Press, 2015.
5   *Grundrisse*, p. 441.
6   *Grundrisse*, p. 621.
7   *Grundrisse*, pp. 403, 447, 542, 621. See also Harvey, D., *The Limits to Capital*, Oxford: Basil Blackwell, 1982, pp .85–9.
8   *Theories of Surplus Value, Part 2*, p. 514.
9   *Grundrisse*, p. 621.
10 *Capital, Volume* 1, p. 201; *Grundrisse*, p. 527.
11 *Capital, Volume* 2, p. 396; 'The Immediate Results of Production' in *Capital, Volume* 1, p. 1033.
12 Tronti, M., 'Our Operaismo', *New Left Review*, 73 (2012); Negri, A., *Marx Beyond Marx: Lessons on the Grundrisse*, New York: Autonomedia, 1991.
13 Marx, K., 'The Civil War in France' in Tucker, R., *The Marx-Engels Reader* (2nd edn), New York: Norton, 1978, p. 636.
14 *Capital, Volume* 3, p. 991.

15 Cf. Henderson, G., *Value in Marx: The Persistence of Value in a More-Than-Capitalist World*, Minneapolis: University of Minnesota Press, 2013.

16 *Capital, Volume 2*, chapter 8.

17 *Grundrisse*, p. 535.

18 *Capital, Volume 1*, p. 254.

19 *Capital, Volume 1*, p. 233.

20 Roy, A., *Poverty Capital: Microfinance and the Making of Development*, New York: Routledge, 2011.

21 Blackburn, R., *Banking on Death: Or Investing in Life*, London: Verso, 2004.

22 *Capital, Volume 1*, pp. 208–9.

23 *Capital, Volume 3*, p. 599.

24 *Capital, Volume 3*, chapter 24.

25 *Capital, Volume 3*, pp. 572–3.

26 Wade, R., and Veneroso, F., 'The Asian Crisis: The High Debt Model versus the Wall Street-Treasury-IMF Complex', *New Left Review*, 228 (1998): 3–232.

27 *Theories of Surplus Value, Part 2*, pp. 495–6.

28 *Grundrisse*, p. 531; *Capital, Volume 3*, p. 199.

29 *Capital, Volume 2*, chapter 6.

30 *Capital, Volume 1*, p. 344.

31 Hudis, P., *Marx's Concept of the Alternative to Capitalism*, Chicago: Haymarket, 2012.

32 On time in Marx, see Bensaid, D., *Marx for Our Times*, London: Verso, 2002; Tombazos, S., *Time in Marx: The Categories of Time in Marx's Capital*, Chicago: Haymarket, 2014.

33 *Grundrisse*, p. 708.

34 *Capital, Volume 1*, p. 644.

35 Himmelweit, S., and Mohun, S., 'Domestic Labour and Capital,' *Cambridge Journal of Economics*, 1 (1977): 15–311.

36 Harvey, D., *The Enigma of Capital*, London: Profile Books, 2010, chapter 5.

37 *Capital, Volume 3*, p. 357.

38 Hudson, M., 'The Road to Debt Deflation, Debt Peonage, and Neofeudalism', Working Paper No. 709, Annandale-on-Hudson,

NY: Levy Economics Institute of Bard College, February 2012; Hudson, M., *Killing the Host: How Financial Parasites and Debt Destroy the Global Economy*, ISLET-verlag, 2015.

Chapter 5

1 *Capital, Volume 1*, p. 751.
2 Smith, N., *Uneven Development: Nature, Capital and the Production of Space*, Oxford: Wiley, 1990.
3 *Capital, Volume 1*, p. 718.
4 *Capital, Volume 1*, p. 451.
5 Bauwens, M., 'Towards the Democratisation of the Means of Monetisation', mimeo, Brussels, 21 October 2013.
6 Moulier Boutang, Y., *Cognitive Capitalism*, Cambridge: Polity, 2011; Vercellone, C., 'From Formal Subsumption to General Intellect: Elements for a Marxist Reading of the Thesis of Cognitive Capitalism', *Historical Materialism*, 15 (2007): 13–36.
7 *Grundrisse*, pp. 685–95.
8 *Capital, Volume 1*, p. 284.
9 'Results of the Immediate Process of Production', in *Capital, Volume 1*, p. 1044.
10 Arvidsson, A., and Peitersen, N., *The Ethical Economy: Rebuilding Value After the Crisis*, New York: Columbia University Press, 2013.
11 Huws, U., *Labor in the Digital Economy*, New York: Monthly Review Press, 2014.
12 *Grundrisse*, pp. 690–706.
13 *Grundrisse*, p. 765.
14 Larsen, N., Nilges, M., Robinson, J. and Brown, N. (eds), *Marxism and the Critique of Value*, Chicago: M-C-M, 2014.
15 Harvey, D., 'Crisis Theory and the Falling Rate of Profit', in Subasat, T. (ed.), *The Great Meltdown of 2008: Systemic, Conjunctural or Policy Created?* Cheltenham: Edgar Elgar, 2016.
16 Harvey, D., 'The Art of Rent', in *Rebel Cities: From the Right to the City to the Urban Revolution*, London: Verso, 2012.
17 'Results of the Immediate Process of Production', in *Capital, Volume 1*, pp. 1019–49.

18 Mason, P. *PostCapitalism: A Guide to Our Future*, London: Penguin, 2016.
19 Ford, M. , *The Lights in the Tunnel: Automation, Accelerating Technology and the Economy of the Future*, United States of America: Acculent™ Pubishing, 2009.
20 Moseley, F., *Money and Totality: A Macro-Monetary Interpretation of Marx's Logic in Capital and the End of the 'Transformation Problem'*, Leiden: Brill, 2015.

Chapter 6

1   *Capital, Volume 1*, chapter 12.
2   *Capital, Volume 1*, pp. 393–7.
3   *Capital, Volume 1*, p.562
4   *Capital, Volume 1*, pp. 493–4.
5   Subasat, T. (ed.), *The Great Meltdown of 2008: Systemic, Conjunctural or Policy Created?* Cheltenham: Edgar Elgar, 2016; Larsen, N., Nilges, M., Robinson, J., and Brown, N. (eds), *Marxism and the Critique of Value*, Chicago: MCM Press, 2014.
6   Harvey, D., *A Brief History of Neoliberalism*, Oxford: Oxford University Press, 2003.
7   'Results of the Immediate Process of Production', in *Capital, Volume 1*, pp. 1019–49.
8   Harvey, D., 'Crisis Theory and the Falling Rate of Profit', in Subasat, T. (ed.), *The Great Meltdown of 2008: Systemic, Conjunctural or Policy-Created?* Cheltenham: Edgar Elgar, 2016; *Capital, Volume 1*, pp. 616–17.
9   *Capital, Volume 1*, p. 508.
10 *Capital, Volume 1*, pp. 512–13.
11 *Capital, Volume 1*, pp. 481–2.
12 *Capital, Volume 1*, pp. 620–21.
13 *Capital, Volume 1*, p 618.
14 *Capital, Volume 1*, p. 505.
15 *Capital, Volume 1*, p. 506.
16 *Grundrisse*, p. 704.

17 Gordon, R., *The Rise and Fall of American Growth: The U.S. Standard of Living since the Civil War*, Princeton: Princeton University Press, 2016.

18 Poulet, D., *Le Sublime*, Paris: 1980.

19 Brynjolfsson, E., and McAfee, A., *The Second Machine Age: Work, Progress, and Prosperity in a Time of Brilliant Technologies*, New York: Norton, 2014.

20 *Capital, Volume 1*, p. 492.

21 *Grundrisse,*

Chapter 7

1   *Selected Correspondence*, p. 208.

2   *Communist Manifesto.*

3   *Grundrisse*, p. 407,

4   *Theories of Surplus Value, Part 2*, p. 253.

5   *Grundrisse*, p. 539.

6   *Capital, Volume 2*, p. 328.

7   Harvey, D., 'The Geography of Capitalist Accumulation: A Reconstruction of the Marxian Theory', in Harvey, D., *Spaces of Capital: Towards a Critical Geography*, New *Capital, Volume 1*, p. 727.

8   *Capital, Volume 1*, pp. 579–80.

9   Capital, Volume 1, pp. 579–80.

10 Harvey, D., 'The Spatial Fix: Hegel, von Thünen and Marx', in Harvey, D., *Spaces of Capital: Towards a Critical Geography*, New York: Routledge, 2001.

11 *Capital, Volume 1*, chapter 33.

12 Luxemburg, R., *The Accumulation of Capital*, New York: Routledge, 1951.

13 *Capital, Volume 1*, pp. 931–2.

14 Cited in Chomsky, N., *On Power and Ideology*, Boston: South End Press, 1990, p. 14.

15 Tomba, M., *Marx's Temporalities*, Chicago, Haymarket Books, 2014; Tombazos, S., *Time in Marx: The Categories of Time in Marx's Capital*, Chicago: Haymarket, 2014; Bensaid, D., *Marx for*

Our Times: Adventures and Misadventures of a Critique, London: Verso, 2009.

16 *Grundrisse*, p. 746.

17 In what follows I rely heavily on the essay 'Space as a Key Word' in Harvey, D., *Spaces of Global Capitalism: A Theory of Uneven Geographical Development*, London: Verso, 2006.

18 Simmel, G., 'The Metropolis and Mental Life', in Levine, D. (ed.), *On Individuality and Social Forms*, Chicago: Chicago University Press, 1971.

19 Kern, S., *The Culture of Time and Space, 1880–1918*, London: Weidenfeld and Nicolson, 1983.

20 Bensaid, D., *Marx for Our Times: Adventures and Misadventures of a Critique*, London: Verso, 2009, p. 73.

21 Whitehead, A., 'La Théorie Relationiste de l'Espace', *Revue de Métaphysique et de Morale*, 23 (1916): 423–54.

22 McDonald, O., *Lehman Brothers: A Crisis of Value*, Manchester: Manchester University Press, 2016.

23 Bensaid, D., *Marx for Our Times: Adventures and Misadventures of a Critique*, London: Verso, 2009, p. 77.

24 *Capital, Volume 2*, p. 301.

25 I rely on the much more detailed account in Harvey, D., *The Limits to Capital*, Oxford: Basil Blackwell, 1982, chapter 8.

26 *Grundrisse*, p.706.

27 *Grundrisse*, p. 694.

28 *Grundrisse*, p. 707.

29 *Grundrisse*, p. 707.

30 *Capital, Volume 2*, p. 242.

31 *Grundrisse*, p. 731.

32 *Capital, Volume 2*, p. 186.

33 *Grundrisse*, p. 731.

34 *Capital, Volume 2*, p. 264.

Chapter 8

1 Darnell, A. (ed.), *The Collected Economics Articles of Harold Hotelling*, New York: Springer Verlag, 1990.

2   Haggett, P., *Locational Analysis in Human Geography*, London: Edward Arnold, 1965.

3   *Capital, Volume 1*, p. 701.

4   The details of Marx's scattered comments on this topic are brought together in Harvey, D., 'The Geography of Capitalist Accumulation: A Reconstruction of the Marxian Theory', published as chapter 12 in Harvey, D., *Spaces of Capital: Towards a Critical Geography*, New York: Routledge, 2001.

5   *Capital, Volume 3*, pp. 345–6.

6   *Theories of Surplus Value, Part 3*, p. 106.

7   *Theories of Surplus Value, Part 2*, pp. 201, 474–5.

8   *Capital, Volume 3*, chapter 9.

9   Dealbook, 'Blankfein Says He's Just Doing "God's Work"', *New York Times*, 9 November 2009.

10 Johnson, C., *MITI and the Japanese Miracle*, Stanford: Stanford University Press, 1982.

11 *Capital, Volume 1*, p. 222.

12 *Capital, Volume 1*, pp. 240–41.

13 *Capital, Volume 1*, pp. 183, 207.

14 *Capital, Volume 1*, p. 162.

15 *Capital, Volume 1*, pp. 775–8.

16 *Capital, Volume 3*, p. 571.

17 Baldwin, R., *The Great Convergence: Information Technology and the New Globalisation*, Cambridge, MA: Belknap, 2016.

18 *Capital, Volume 3*, p. 999.

19 Harvey, D., 'From Managerialism to Entrepreneurialism: The Transformation in Urban Governance in Late-Capitalism,' *Geografiska Annaler, Series B, Human Geography*, 71 (1) (1989): 3–17.

20 *Capital, Volume 3*, p. 1001.

21 Harvey, D., *The Limits to Capital*, Oxford: Basil Blackwell, 1982, chapters 12 and 13.

22 Myrdal, G., *Economic Theory and Underdeveloped Regions*, London: Methuen, 1965.

23 *Capital, Volume 3*, 623–4.

24 Wood, E., *The Origin of Capitalism: A Longer View*, London: Verso, 2002; Harvey, D., *The New Imperialism*, Oxford: Oxford University Press, 2003. See the discussion and debate on these two books in *Historical Materialism*, 14(4) (2006).

25 The works of Samir Amin, Giovanni Arrighi and Peter Gowan have opened a way to go beyond the arid formalism of Wallerstinian world system theory and the dead end of the state debate of the 1970s and its aftermath to probe more deeply into a value theoretic perspective on geopolitical relations. See in particular Amin, S., *The Law of World Wide Value*, New York: Monthly Review Press, 2010; Amin, S., *Three Essays on Value Theory*, New York, Monthly Review Press, 2013; Arrighi, G., *The Long Twentieth Century: Money, Power and the Origins of Our Times*, London: Verso, 1994; Arrighi, G., and Silver, B., *Chaos and Governance in the Modern World System*, Minneapolis: University of Minnesota Press, 1999; Gowan, P., *The Global Gamble: Washington's Faustian Bid for World Dominance*, London: Verso, 1999.

Chapter 9

1 *Grundrisse*, p. 269.
2 *Grundrisse*, pp. 270–71.
3 Martin, W., 'In Defense of Bad Infinity: A Fichtean Response to Hegel's Differenzschrift,' mimeo, Department of Philosophy, University of Essex; Arthur, C. *The New Dialectic and Marx's Capital*, Leiden: Brill, 2004, pp. 137–52.
4 *Grundrisse*, p. 270.
5 *Capital*, Volume 3, p. 595.
6 *Grundrisse*, p. 413.
7 *Capital*, Volume 3, pp. 476, 516.
8 *Grundrisse*, pp. 270–71.
9 *Grundrisse*, p. 590.
10 *Theories of Surplus Value, Part 2*, pp. 468, 549. Most economists recognise market imperfections that arise from externality effects and from imperfect information (and even study them as 'market failures'). Those with Keynesian inclinations recognise a

state role for proper aggregate demand and supply management mainly directed at dampening business cycles in the hope of eliminating crises and depressions. But their aim is to correct for imperfections and to define optimal policies for state involvements which will restore the concept of harmonious equilibrium to its rightful theoretical place. None of them, even those like Paul Krugman, Joseph Stiglitz and Jeffrey Sachs, who lay claim to progressive political positions, have any conception of the internal contradictions of capital or the dangers of the 'bad infinity' of endless compound growth.

11 *Grundrisse*, p. 221.

12 Federal Reserve Bank of St Louis, *Economic Reports*.

13 *Grundrisse*, pp. 334–5.

14 'Towering Above', *National Geographic*, 229(1) 2016'

15 International Monetary Fund/International Labour Organisation, 'The Challenges of Growth, Employment and Social Cohesion' discussion paper, Joint ILO-IMF Conference in Cooperation with the Prime Minister of Norway, 2010; available at http://www. osloconference2010.org/discussionpaper.pdf

16 Agence Presse Français, 'China's Property Frenzy and Surging Debt Raises Red Flag for the Economy', *Guardian*, 27 November 2016.

17 Reuters, 'China's Property Boom Continues as Prices Rise at Record Rate', *Fortune*, 21 October 2016.

18 Shen Hong, 'China's Plan for Local Debt Amounts to a Bailout', *Wall Street Journal*, 23 June 2015.

19 International Monetary Fund, 'Debt: Use It Wisely', *Fiscal Monitor*, World Economic and Financial Surveys, October 2016.

20 Shepard, W., *Ghost Cities of China*, London: Zed Books, 2015.

21 Robert Caro, *The Power Broker: Robert Moses and the Fall of New York*, New York: Vintage, 1975.

22 Appelbaum, B., 'A Recovery that Repeats its Painful Precedents', *New York Times*, 28 July 2011.

23 Harvey, D., *Paris: Capital of Modernity*, New York, Routledge, 2003.

24 Marx, K., 'The Civil War in France', in Tucker, R., *The Marx-Engels Reader* (2nd edn), New York: Norton, 1978.

25 Tabb, W., *The Long Default: New York City and the Urban Fiscal Crisis*, New York: Monthly Review Press, 1982.

26 Harvey, D., *A Brief History of Neoliberalism*, Oxford: Oxford University Press, 2005.

27 Goldstein, M., Abrams, R., and Protess, B., 'How Housing's New Players Spiraled into Banks' Old Mistakes', *New York Times*, 26 June 2016.

28 Harvey, D., *The New Imperialism*, Oxford: Oxford University Press, 2003.

29 Ridge, M., 'Three New "Engines of Growth" to Watch in China', *Financial Times*, 18 September 2014.

30 Clover, C., and Hornby, L., 'China's Great Game: Road to a New Empire', *Financial Times*, 12 October 2015.

31 *Capital, Volume 3*, p. 595.

32 Carvalho, B., Cavalcanti, M., and Venuturupalli, V. (eds), *Occupy All Streets: Olympic Urbanism and Contested Futures in Rio de Janeiro*, New York: Terraform, 2016.

33 Ozturkmen, A., 'The Park, the Penguin and the Gas: Performance in Progress of Gezi Events', *The Drama Review*, Guest editor Carol Martin, 2014.

34 Keller, B., 'The Revolt of the Rising Classes', *New York Times*, 30 June 2013.

35 Harvey, D., *Seventeen Contradictions and the End of Capitalism*, London: Profile Books, 2013.

36 Ollman, B., *Alienation*, London: Cambridge University Press, 1971.

37 *Grundrisse*, pp. 831–2.

38 *Grundrisse*, p. 287.

39 Gorz, A., *Critique of Economic Reason*, London: Verso, 1989; on the limits to compensatory consumerism for workers see *Grundrisse*, pp. 204–7.

40 Debord, G., *The Society of the Spectacle*, Montreal: Black and Red Books, 2000.

41 Hadjimichalis, C., *Uneven Development and Regionalism: State, Territory and Class in Southern Europe*, London: Croom Helm, 1987.

42 Harvey, D., *The New Imperialism*, Oxford: Oxford University Press, 2003, chapter 4.

43 Sassen, S., *Expulsions: Brutality and Complexity in the Global Economy*, Cambridge, MA, Belknap Press, 2014.

44 Piketty, T., *Capital in the Twenty First Century*, Cambridge, MA, Belknap Press, 2014.

45 *Capital, Volume 3*, p. 573.

46 Lapavitsas, C. with Flassbeck, H., *Against the Troika: Crisis and Austerity in the Eurozone*, London: Verso, 2015.

47 Harvey, D., *A Companion to Marx's Capital, Volume 2*, London: Verso, 2013.

48 *Capital, Volume 3*, 621–2.

49 Harvey, D., *Seventeen Contradictions and the End of Capitalism*, London: Profile Books, 2013, pp. 44–7.

50 *Capital, Volume 3*, p. 490.

51 *Capital, Volume 3*, p. 470.

52 *Capital, Volume 3*, p. 609.

53 *Capital, Volume 3*, p. 569.

54 *Capital, Volume 3*, p. 523.

55 Keynes, J. M., *Essays in Persuasion*, New York: Classic House Books edn, 2009, p. 199.

56 *Grundrisse*, p. 488.

Coda

1 Derrida, J., 'The Madness of Economic Reason', in Derrida, J., *Given Time: I. Counterfeit Money*, Chicago: Chicago University Press, 1992; Mauss, M., *The Gift: The Form and Reason for Exchange in Archaic Societies*, London: Routledge, 1990.

2 *Capital, Volume 3*, p. 649.

3 *Capital, Volume 3*, p. 614.

Acknowledgements

I wish to acknowledge the gift of a free education and of adequate grants that took me through my university education free of charge up until the completion of my doctorate in Cambridge in 1961. I also wish to acknowledge the privilege of being part of the City University of New York which, in spite of many difficulties, still maintains its mission as a public university to serve the public interest in higher education for all.

I wish to express my appreciation of John Davey, my long-term friend and publisher, who suggested I write this book. Alas, he did not live to see it through to final publication. My good friend and colleague Miguel Robles-Duran helped me with the design of Figures 2 and 3 and drew the final versions.

Index